Student Supplement: Study Outlines, Solutions to Odd-Numbered Problems, and Ready Notes

for use with

Accounting:
What The Numbers Mean

Fourth Edition

David H. Marshall
Millikin University - Emeritus

Wayne W. McManus
International College of the Cayman Islands

Prepared by
Wayne W. McManus
International College of the Cayman Islands

**Irwin
McGraw-Hill**

Boston   Burr Ridge, IL   Dubuque, IA   Madison, WI   New York   San Francisco   St. Louis
Bangkok   Bogotá   Caracas   Lisbon   London   Madrid
Mexico City   Milan   New Delhi   Seoul   Singapore   Sydney   Taipei   Toronto

Irwin/McGraw-Hill

A Division of The McGraw·Hill Companies

Student Supplement: Study Outlines, Solutions to Odd-Numbered Problems, and Ready Notes for use with ACCOUNTING: What The Numbers Mean

3 4 5 6 7 8 9 0 COU/COU 9 3 2 1 0 9

ISBN 0-256-26855-X

http://www.mhhe.com

NOTE TO THE STUDENT:

Your textbook is the principal resource that will contribute to your success in the course for which it was purchased. Other resources include your instructor, your classmates, your study efforts, and the supplements that accompany the text. These supplements are:

- **Student Supplement: *Study Outlines, Solutions to Odd-Numbered Problems, and Ready Notes*.** (Shrink-wrapped with text.) This volume is designed to accelerate your learning efforts and to improve your performance in the course. The *Study Outlines* are reduced-size copies of the Teaching Acetates (transparency masters) that your instructor may use to highlight the Key Ideas, Key Points, Key Relationships, and Key Terminology of each chapter. The *Study Outlines* eliminate the need to copy information from the transparencies, and provide space for you to make your own class notes. You may find it is worthwhile to review the information contained in these outlines even if your instructor does not use the teaching acetates on a regular basis. The *Solutions to Odd-Numbered Problems* provide full solutions (not just check figures) for all odd-numbered problems in the text. Even-numbered problems are usually similar to the preceding odd-numbered problem. Having the full solution of the preceding problem available as a model provides additional examples beyond those in the text, reinforces learning, minimizes frustration, and facilitates your study efforts. The *Ready Notes* are reduced-size copies of the Ready Shows (PowerPoint® slides) that some instructors may use when making classroom presentations; as with the *Study Outlines*, space is provided for your note taking.

- **Study Guide and Working Papers.** The *Study Guide* contains chapter outlines, review questions (matching, true-false, and multiple choice) with explanatory answers, and short exercises with solutions. *Working Papers* are set up for each problem in the text to facilitate your approach to the correct solution and to eliminate "busy work." Student reviews of this supplement from the first three editions of the text have been highly favorable and quite encouraging. You can order a copy of the *Study Guide and Working Papers* volume through your bookstore, or by calling Irwin/McGraw-Hill at **1-800-338-3987**. When placing your order, ask for **ISBN# 0256268541**.

The appendix of the text is a copy of Intel Corporation's 1996 Annual Report. For investor information, including the most recent annual report, 10-K and 10-Q reports, or other financial literature (all of which are provided without cost), contact Intel's transfer agent and registrar:

Harris Trust & Saving Bank
311 West Monroe, P.O. Box A3504, Chicago, IL 60690-3504
Call **1-800-298-0146** for annual report ordering.

You are encouraged to visit Intel's World Wide Web site at: ***http://www.intel.com***. Specific information of interest to investors can be found at: ***http://www.intc.com***. The Web site for this text, ***http://www.mhhe.com/business/accounting/marshall***, also provides links to Intel and other real-world examples used in the problem materials.

Contents

STUDY OUTLINES

SOLUTIONS TO
ODD-NUMBERED PROBLEMS

ACCOUNTING IS THE PROCESS OF:

• IDENTIFYING, • MEASURING, and • COMMUNICATING	}	ECONOMIC INFORMATION ABOUT AN ENTITY FOR MAKING	}	• DECISIONS and • INFORMED JUDGMENTS

USERS OF ACCOUNTING INFORMATION

• MANAGEMENT

• INVESTORS

• CREDITORS

• EMPLOYEES

• GOVERNMENTAL AGENCIES

1

CLASSIFICATIONS OF ACCOUNTING

- FINANCIAL ACCOUNTING

- MANAGERIAL ACCOUNTING / COST ACCOUNTING

- AUDITING - PUBLIC / INTERNAL

- GOVERNMENTAL ACCOUNTING

- INCOME TAX ACCOUNTING

PROFESSIONAL DEGREES

- CPA - CERTIFIED PUBLIC ACCOUNTANT

- CMA - CERTIFIED MANAGEMENT ACCOUNTANT

- CIA - CERTIFIED INTERNAL AUDITOR

FINANCIAL ACCOUNTING STANDARD SETTING

FASB (FINANCIAL ACCOUNTING STANDARDS BOARD)

- *STATEMENTS OF FINANCIAL ACCOUNTING STANDARDS*
  OVER 130 ISSUED. DEAL WITH SPECIFIC ACCOUNTING
  AND FINANCIAL REPORTING ISSUES.

- *STATEMENTS OF FINANCIAL ACCOUNTING CONCEPTS*
  6 ISSUED. AN ATTEMPT TO PROVIDE A COMMON
  FOUNDATION TO SUPPORT FINANCIAL ACCOUNTING
  STANDARDS.

- **KEY OBJECTIVES OF FINANCIAL REPORTING (SFAC #1)**

  - RELATE TO EXTERNAL FINANCIAL REPORTING.

  - TO SUPPORT BUSINESS AND ECONOMIC DECISIONS.

  - TO PROVIDE INFORMATION ABOUT CASH FLOWS.

  - PRIMARY FOCUS IS ON EARNINGS BASED ON
    ACCRUAL ACCOUNTING.

  - NOT TO MEASURE DIRECTLY THE VALUE OF A
    BUSINESS ENTERPRISE.

  - INFORMATION REPORTED SUBJECT TO EVALUATION
    BY INDIVIDUAL FINANCIAL STATEMENT USERS.

  - ACCOUNTING STANDARDS ARE STILL EVOLVING.

INTERNATIONAL ACCOUNTING STANDARDS

- IASC (INTERNATIONAL ACCOUNTING STANDARDS COMMITTEE).

- STANDARDS DIFFER SIGNIFICANTLY AMONG COUNTRIES.

- INDIVIDUAL COUNTRY STANDARDS REFLECT LOCAL MARKET NEEDS AND COUNTRY REGULATION AND TAXATION PRACTICES.

ETHICS AND THE ACCOUNTING PROFESSION

- AICPA CODE OF PROFESSIONAL CONDUCT

- IMA STANDARDS OF ETHICAL CONDUCT FOR MANAGEMENT ACCOUNTANTS

KEY ELEMENTS OF ETHICAL BEHAVIOR

- INTEGRITY

- OBJECTIVITY

- INDEPENDENCE

- COMPETENCE

TRANSACTIONS TO FINANCIAL STATEMENTS

TRANSACTIONS →	PROCEDURES FOR SORTING, CLASSIFYING AND PRESENTING (BOOKKEEPING) SELECTION OF ALTERNATIVE METHODS OF REFLECTING THE EFFECTS OF TRANSACTIONS (ACCOUNTING)	→ FINANCIAL STATEMENTS

TRANSACTIONS
ECONOMIC INTERCHANGES BETWEEN ENTITIES.

EXAMPLES:

FINANCIAL STATEMENTS
- **BALANCE SHEET**
  FINANCIAL POSITION AT A POINT IN TIME

- **INCOME STATEMENT**
  EARNINGS FOR A PERIOD OF TIME

- **STATEMENT OF CASH FLOWS**
  SUMMARY OF CASH FLOWS FOR A PERIOD OF TIME

- **STATEMENT OF CHANGES IN OWNERS' EQUITY**
  INVESTMENTS BY OWNERS, EARNINGS OF THE FIRM, AND DISTRIBUTIONS TO OWNERS FOR A PERIOD OF TIME

6

FINANCIAL STATEMENTS

BALANCE SHEET (AT A POINT IN TIME)

Exhibit 2-1   Balance Sheet

MAIN STREET STORE, INC.
Balance Sheet
August 31, 1999

Assets		*Liabilities and Owners' Equity*	
Current assets:		Current liabilities:	
Cash	$ 34,000	Short-term debt	$ 20,000
Accounts receivable	80,000	Accounts payable.	35,000
Merchandise			
inventory	170,000	Other accrued liabilities	12,000
Total current assets	$284,000	Total current	
Plant and equipment:		liabilities	$ 67,000
Equipment	40,000	Long-term debt	50,000
Less: Accumulated		Total liabilities	$117,000
depreciation	(4,000)	Owners' equity	203,000
		Total liabilities and	
Total assets	$320,000	owners' equity	$320,000

KEY RELATIONSHIP

ASSETS = LIABILITIES + OWNERS' EQUITY

KEY TERMINOLOGY

- ASSETS
- CURRENT ASSETS
- ACCUMULATED DEPRECIATION
- LIABILITIES
- CURRENT LIABILITIES
- OWNERS' EQUITY

FINANCIAL STATEMENTS

INCOME STATEMENT (FOR A PERIOD OF TIME)

Exhibit 2-2   Balance Sheet

MAIN STREET STORE, INC.
Income Statement
For the Year Ended August 31, 1999

Net sales	$1,200,000
Cost of goods sold	850,000
Gross profit	$ 350,000
Selling, general, and administrative expenses	311,000
Income from operations	39,000
Interest expense	9,000
Income before taxes	$ 30,000
Income taxes	12,000
Net income	$ 18,000
Net income per share of common stock outstanding	$ 1.80

KEY RELATIONSHIP

REVENUES - EXPENSES = NET INCOME

KEY TERMINOLOGY

- REVENUES (SALES)
- GROSS PROFIT
- EARNINGS BEFORE TAXES
- NET INCOME PER SHARE
  OF COMMON STOCK

- COST OF GOODS SOLD
- OPERATING INCOME
- NET INCOME

FINANCIAL STATEMENTS

STATEMENT OF CHANGES IN OWNERS' EQUITY
(FOR A PERIOD OF TIME)

Exhibit 2-3   Statement of Changes in Owners' Equity

MAIN STREET STORE, INC.
Statement of Changes in Owners' Equity
For the Year Ended August 31, 1999

Paid-In Capital:

Beginning balance	$ -0-
Common stock, par value, $10; 50,000 shares authorized, 10,000 shares issued and outstanding .	100,000
Additional paid-in capital	90,000
Balance, August 31, 1999......................................	$ 190,000

Retained Earnings:

Beginning balance	$ -0-
Net income for the year...	18,000
Less: Cash dividends of $.50 per share	(5,000)
Balance, August 31, 1999	$ 13,000
Total owners' equity	$203,000

TWO PRINCIPAL COMPONENTS

- PAID-IN CAPITAL CHANGES
- RETAINED EARNINGS CHANGES

KEY RELATIONSHIP

```
   RETAINED EARNINGS BEGINNING BALANCE
 + NET INCOME FOR THE PERIOD
 - DIVIDENDS
 = RETAINED EARNINGS ENDING BALANCE
```

KEY TERMINOLOGY

- PAID-IN CAPITAL   • DIVIDENDS

FINANCIAL STATEMENTS

STATEMENT OF CASH FLOWS (FOR A PERIOD OF TIME)

Exhibit 2-4   Statement of Cash Flows

MAIN STREET STORE, INC.
Statement of Cash Flows
For the Year Ended August 31, 1999

Cash Flows from Operating Activities:

Net income	$ 18,000
Add (deduct) items not affecting cash:	
Depreciation expense	4,000
Increase in accounts receivable	(80,000)
Increase in merchandise inventory	(170,000)
Increase in current liabilities.....................................	67,000
Net cash used by operating activities	$(161,000)

Cash Flows from Investing Activities:

Cash paid for equipment	$ (40,000)

Cash Flows from Financing Activities:

Cash received from issue of long-term debt	$ 50,000
Cash received from sale of common stock	190,000
Payment of cash dividend on common stock	(5,000)
Net cash provided by financing activities	$ 235,000
et increase in cash for the year	$ 34,000

KE   MINOLOGY

- CA   OWS FROM OPERATING ACTIVITIES

- CASH   WS FROM INVESTING ACTIVITIES

- CASH F   'S FROM FINANCING ACTIVITIES

- CHANGE   ASH FOR THE YEAR

10

FINANCIAL STATEMENT RELATIONSHIPS

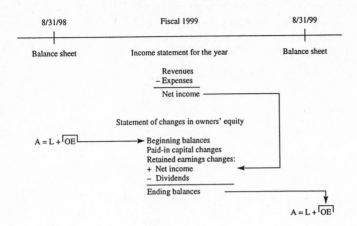

KEY IDEAS

- TRANSACTIONS AFFECTING THE INCOME STATEMENT ALSO AFFECT THE BALANCE SHEET.

- FOR THE BALANCE SHEET TO BALANCE, INCOME STATEMENT TRANSACTIONS MUST BE REFLECTED IN THE RETAINED EARNINGS PART OF OWNERS' EQUITY.

- THE STATEMENT OF CASH FLOWS EXPLAINS WHY THE CASH AMOUNT CHANGED DURING THE PERIOD.

11

A MODEL OF THE RELATIONSHIP BETWEEN THE BALANCE SHEET AND INCOME STATEMENT

BALANCE SHEET

INCOME STATEMENT

ASSETS = LIABILITIES + OWNERS' EQUITY ← NET INCOME = REVENUES – EXPENSES

KEY IDEAS

- THE ARROW FROM NET INCOME IN THE INCOME STATEMENT TO OWNERS' EQUITY IN THE BALANCE SHEET INDICATES THAT NET INCOME AFFECTS RETAINED EARNINGS, WHICH IS PART OF OWNERS' EQUITY.

- THE EFFECT OF TRANSACTIONS ON THE FINANCIAL STATEMENTS CAN BE ILLUSTRATED BY ENTERING THE TRANSACTION AMOUNTS IN THE APPROPRIATE COLUMNS.

- THE BALANCE SHEET MUST BE IN BALANCE (A = L + OE) AFTER EVERY TRANSACTION.

ACCOUNTING CONCEPTS AND PRINCIPLES

- ACCOUNTING ENTITY

- ASSETS = LIABILITIES + OWNERS' EQUITY
  (ACCOUNTING EQUATION)

- GOING CONCERN
  (CONTINUITY)

TRANSACTIONS →	PROCEDURES FOR SORTING, CLASSIFYING AND PRESENTING (BOOKKEEPING) SELECTION OF ALTERNATIVE METHODS OF REFLECTING THE EFFECTS OF TRANSACTIONS (ACCOUNTING)	→ FINANCIAL STATEMENTS

- UNIT OF MEASUREMENT

- COST PRINCIPLE

- OBJECTIVITY

- ACCOUNTING PERIOD

- MATCHING REVENUE AND EXPENSE

- REVENUE RECOGNIZED AT TIME OF SALE

- ACCRUAL CONCEPT

- CONSISTENCY

- FULL DISCLOSURE

- MATERIALITY

- CONSERVATISM

KEY CLARIFICATION

- MATCHING OF REVENUE AND EXPENSE MEANS THAT ALL EXPENSES INCURRED IN GENERATING REVENUES FOR THE PERIOD ARE SUBTRACTED FROM THOSE REVENUES TO DETERMINE NET INCOME. MATCHING DOES <u>NOT</u> MEAN THAT REVENUES EQUAL EXPENSES.

MEASUREMENTS AND TREND ANALYSIS

- PAT'S GPA LAST SEMESTER: **2.8**

  <u>JUDGMENT</u>: SO WHAT? HOW WELL HAS PAT PERFORMED?

- PAT'S GPA FOR THE LAST FOUR SEMESTERS: **1.9, 2.3, 2.6, 2.8**

  <u>JUDGMENT</u>: PAT'S PERFORMANCE HAS BEEN IMPROVING.

- GPA FOR ALL STUDENTS FOR LAST FOUR SEMESTERS: **2.85, 2.76, 2.70, 2.65**

  <u>JUDGMENT</u>: PAT'S PERFORMANCE HAS IMPROVED WHILE THE PERFORMANCE OF ALL STUDENTS HAS DECLINED.

<u>KEY POINTS</u>

- THE TREND OF DATA IS FREQUENTLY MORE SIGNIFICANT THAN THE DATA ITSELF.

- COMPARISON OF INDIVIDUAL AND GROUP TRENDS IS IMPORTANT WHEN MAKING JUDGMENTS.

RETURN ON EQUITY (ROE)

$$\text{RETURN ON EQUITY} = \frac{\text{NET INCOME}}{\text{AVERAGE OWNERS' EQUITY}}$$

KEY POINT

- AS IN ROI, NET INCOME IS <u>FOR THE YEAR</u>, THEREFORE IT IS RELATED TO THE AVERAGE OF THE OWNERS' EQUITY AT THE BEGINNING AND END OF THE YEAR.

KEY IDEAS

- ROI RELATES NET INCOME TO AVERAGE TOTAL ASSETS, AND EXPRESSES A RATE OF RETURN ON THE ASSETS USED BY THE FIRM.

- ROE RELATES NET INCOME TO AVERAGE OWNERS' EQUITY, AND EXPRESSES A RATE OF RETURN ON THAT PORTION OF THE ASSETS PROVIDED BY THE OWNERS OF THE FIRM.

WORKING CAPITAL AND MEASURES OF LIQUIDITY

WORKING CAPITAL

```
      CURRENT ASSETS
  -   CURRENT LIABILITIES
  =   WORKING CAPITAL
```

KEY DEFINITIONS

- CURRENT ASSETS: CASH AND ASSETS LIKELY TO BE CONVERTED TO CASH WITHIN A YEAR.

- CURRENT LIABILITIES: OBLIGATIONS THAT MUST BE PAID WITHIN A YEAR.

KEY IDEA

- A MEASURE OF THE FIRM'S ABILITY TO PAY ITS CURRENT OBLIGATIONS.

CURRENT RATIO

$$\frac{\text{CURRENT ASSETS}}{\text{CURRENT LIABILITIES}} = \text{CURRENT RATIO}$$

KEY IDEA

- THE CURRENT RATIO IS USUALLY A MORE USEFUL MEASUREMENT THAN THE AMOUNT OF WORKING CAPITAL BECAUSE IT IS A RATIO MEASUREMENT.

WORKING CAPITAL AND MEASURES OF LIQUIDITY

ACID-TEST RATIO (sometimes called QUICK RATIO)

$$\frac{\text{CASH (INCLUDING TEMPORARY CASH INVESTMENTS) + ACCOUNTS RECEIVABLE}}{\text{CURRENT LIABILITIES}}$$

KEY IDEAS

- BY FOCUSING ON CASH AND ACCOUNTS RECEIVABLE, THE ACID-TEST RATIO PROVIDES A MORE SHORT-TERM MEASURE OF LIQUIDITY THAN THE CURRENT RATIO.

- THE ACID-TEST RATIO EXCLUDES INVENTORY, PREPAID EXPENSES, AND OTHER CURRENT ASSETS FROM THE NUMERATOR.

VERTICAL GRAPH SCALES

ARITHMETIC SCALE

<u>KEY FEATURE</u>

• VERTICAL SCALE DISTANCES ARE EQUAL.

<u>KEY IDEA</u>

• A CONSTANT RATE OF GROWTH PLOTS AS AN
  INCREASINGLY STEEP LINE OVER TIME.

LOGARITHMIC SCALE

<u>KEY FEATURE</u>

• VERTICAL SCALE DISTANCES ARE INCREASINGLY NARROW
  AND COMPRESSED.

<u>KEY IDEA</u>

• A CONSTANT RATE OF GROWTH PLOTS AS A STRAIGHT LINE.

<u>KEY OBSERVATIONS</u>

• THE HORIZONTAL SCALE WILL ALMOST ALWAYS BE AN
  ARITHMETIC SCALE, WITH EQUAL DISTANCE BETWEEN
  THE DATES OF DATA OBSERVATIONS.

• SEMI-LOGARITHMIC FORMAT MEANS THAT THE ONLY
  THE VERTICAL SCALE IS LOGARITHMIC; THE HORIZONTAL
  SCALE IS ARITHMETIC.

20

ARITHMETIC AND SEMI-LOGARITHMIC PLOTS

ARITHMETIC PLOT

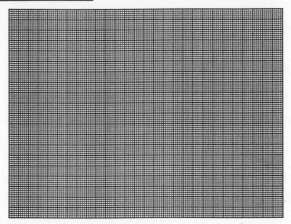

SEMI-LOGARITHMIC PLOT

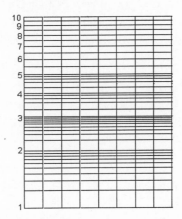

TRANSACTIONS AND THE FINANCIAL STATEMENTS

KEY IDEAS

- TRANSACTIONS AFFECT THE BALANCE SHEET AND/OR THE INCOME STATEMENT.

- THE BALANCE SHEET MUST BE IN BALANCE AFTER EVERY TRANSACTION.

- THE RETAINED EARNINGS ACCOUNT ON THE BALANCE SHEET INCLUDES NET INCOME FROM THE INCOME STATEMENT.

- BALANCE SHEET ACCOUNTS MAY HAVE BALANCES AT THE END OF A FISCAL PERIOD, AND BEFORE TRANSACTIONS OF THE SUBSEQUENT PERIOD ARE RECORDED.

KEY TERMINOLOGY

- EACH INDIVIDUAL ASSET, LIABILITY, OWNERS' EQUITY, REVENUE, OR EXPENSE "ACCOUNT" MAY ADDITIONALLY BE DESCRIBED WITH ITS CATEGORY TITLE. EXAMPLES:
    - "CASH ASSET ACCOUNT"
    - "ACCOUNTS PAYABLE LIABILITY ACCOUNT"
    - "COMMON STOCK OWNERS' EQUITY ACCOUNT"
    - "SALES REVENUE ACCOUNT"
    - "WAGES EXPENSE ACCOUNT"

KEY RELATIONSHIP

- TRANSACTIONS DURING A FISCAL PERIOD CAUSE THE BALANCE OF THE AFFECTED ACCOUNT(S) TO INCREASE OR DECREASE. BOOKKEEPING IS THE PROCESS OF KEEPING TRACK OF THESE CHANGES.

BOOKKEEPING PROCEDURES

WHAT THE BOOKS ARE CALLED

- THE **JOURNAL** IS A CHRONOLOGICAL RECORD OF EACH TRANSACTION.

- THE **LEDGER** IS A BOOK OF ALL OF THE ACCOUNTS; ACCOUNTS ARE USUALLY ARRANGED IN THE SEQUENCE FOUND ON THE BALANCE SHEET AND INCOME STATEMENT, RESPECTIVELY.

HOW TRANSACTIONS ARE RECORDED

- ACCOUNTS ARE FREQUENTLY IN THE SHAPE OF A T

- THE LEFT-HAND SIDE OF THE "T ACCOUNT" IS CALLED THE **DEBIT** SIDE.

- THE RIGHT-HAND SIDE OF THE "T ACCOUNT" IS CALLED THE **CREDIT** SIDE.

- AN INCREASE IN AN ASSET OR AN EXPENSE ACCOUNT IS RECORDED AS A DEBIT; A DECREASE IN EITHER AN ASSET OR AN EXPENSE ACCOUNT IS RECORDED AS A CREDIT.

- AN INCREASE IN A LIABILITY, OWNERS' EQUITY OR REVENUE ACCOUNT IS RECORDED AS A CREDIT; A DECREASE IN EITHER A LIABILITY, OWNERS' EQUITY, OR REVENUE ACCOUNT IS RECORDED AS A DEBIT.

BOOKKEEPING PROCEDURES

- A TRANSACTION IS INITIALLY RECORDED IN A JOURNAL ENTRY.

- THE JOURNAL ENTRY IS THEN **POSTED** TO THE LEDGER ACCOUNTS THAT HAVE BEEN AFFECTED BY THE TRANSACTION.

KEY IDEAS

- A TRANSACTION WILL AFFECT AT LEAST TWO ACCOUNTS, AND CAN AFFECT MANY ACCOUNTS.

- BECAUSE THE BALANCE SHEET MUST BALANCE AFTER EVERY TRANSACTION, THE DEBIT(S) AND CREDIT(S) AMOUNTS OF EACH JOURNAL ENTRY MUST BE EQUAL.

> **DEBITS = CREDITS**

KEY OBSERVATION

- EACH ACCOUNT HAS A **"NORMAL BALANCE"** SIDE - DEBIT OR CREDIT - THAT IS CONSISTENT WITH THE KIND OF ENTRY THAT CAUSES THE ACCOUNT BALANCE TO **INCREASE**.

DEBIT	CREDIT
ASSETS	LIABILITIES
EXPENSES	OWNERS' EQUITY
	REVENUES

TRANSACTION ANALYSIS METHODOLOGY

FIVE QUESTIONS OF TRANSACTION ANALYSIS

<u>KEY IDEA</u>

- TO UNDERSTAND EITHER THE BOOKKEEPING
  PROCEDURE FOR A TRANSACTION, OR THE EFFECT
  OF A TRANSACTION ON THE FINANCIAL STATEMENTS,
  THE FOLLOWING QUESTIONS MUST BE ANSWERED:

  1. WHAT'S GOING ON?
     (WHAT IS THE NATURE OF THE TRANSACTION?)

  2. WHAT ACCOUNTS ARE AFFECTED?
     (WHAT IS THE FINANCIAL STATEMENT CATEGORY
     OF EACH ACCOUNT - ASSET, LIABILITY, OWNERS'
     EQUITY, REVENUE OR EXPENSE?)

  3. HOW IS EACH ACCOUNT AFFECTED?
     (IS THE BALANCE INCREASING OR DECREASING?)

  4. DOES THE BALANCE SHEET BALANCE?
     (DO THE DEBITS EQUAL THE CREDITS? IS THE
     BALANCE SHEET EQUATION STILL IN BALANCE
     AFTER RECORDING THE TRANSACTION?)

  > **DEBITS = CREDITS?**
  >
  > **ASSETS = LIABLIITIES + OWNERS' EQUITY?**

  5. DOES MY ANALYSIS MAKE SENSE?
     (DO THE ACCOUNT BALANCES OR THE FINANCIAL
     STATEMENTS REFLECT THE EFFECT OF THE
     TRANSACTION?)

25

AN ALTERNATIVE ___ T AND CREDIT BOOKKEEPING

THE FINAN___ ___ NT RELATIONSHIP MODEL

BALANCE SHEET	INCOME STATEMENT

ASSETS = LIABILITIES + OWNERS' EQUITY ← NET INCOME = REVENUES − EXPENSES

KEY POINTS

- SHOW THE EFFECT OF EACH TRANSACTION IN THE APPROPRIATE COLUMN OF THE MODEL. SHOW ACCOUNT NAMES FOR ADDITIONAL PRECISION.

- BECAUSE NET INCOME INCREASES OWNERS' EQUITY, INCREASES IN REVENUES APPEAR AS POSITIVE AMOUNTS, AND INCREASES IN EXPENSES (WHICH DECREASE NET INCOME) APPEAR AS NEGATIVE AMOUNTS.

- KEEP THE EQUATION IN BALANCE FOR EACH TRANSACTION BY ENTERING (OR VISUALIZING) AN EQUAL SIGN BETWEEN ASSETS AND LIABILITIES.

KEY IDEA

- USE OF THIS MODEL FOCUSES ON THE IMPACT OF TRANSACTIONS ON THE FINANCIAL STATEMENTS WITHOUT CONCERN FOR BOOKKEEPING JARGON.

ADJUSTING ENTRIES

<u>WHAT ARE THEY? WHY DO THEM?</u>

- ADJUSTING ENTRIES, OR ADJUSTMENTS, ARE "UPDATES" AND "CORRECTIONS" MADE TO INCREASE THE ACCURACY OF THE INFORMATION IN THE FINANCIAL STATEMENTS.

- **RECLASSIFICATIONS:**
  THE BOOKKEEPING FOR THE ORIGINAL TRANSACTION WAS APPROPRIATE WHEN IT WAS RECORDED, BUT THE PASSAGE OF TIME REQUIRES A RECLASSIFICATION OF THE ORIGINAL BOOKKEEPING TO REFLECT CORRECT ACCOUNT BALANCES AS OF THE DATE OF THE FINANCIAL STATEMENTS.

- **ACCRUALS:**
  REVENUES WERE EARNED OR EXPENSES WERE INCURRED DURING THE PERIOD, BUT NO TRANSACTION WAS RECORDED, (BECAUSE NO CASH WAS RECEIVED OR PAID). THEREFORE, IT IS NECESSARY TO **ACCRUE** THE EFFECT OF THE TRANSACTION AS OF THE DATE OF THE FINANCIAL STATEMENTS.

<u>KEY IDEAS</u>

- ACCRUAL ACCOUNTING MEANS THAT REVENUES ARE RECOGNIZED WHEN <u>EARNED</u> (NOT WHEN CASH IS RECEIVED) AND THAT EXPENSES ARE REFLECTED IN THE PERIOD IN WHICH THEY ARE <u>INCURRED</u> (NOT WHEN CASH IS PAID).

- ADJUSTING ENTRIES RESULT IN MATCHING REVENUES AND EXPENSES, WHICH IS THE OBJECTIVE OF ACCRUAL ACCOUNTING.

CURRENT ASSETS

DEFINITION

- CURRENT ASSETS ARE CASH AND THOSE ASSETS
EXPECTED TO BE CONVERTED TO CASH OR USED
UP IN THE OPERATING ACTIVITIES OF THE ENTITY
WITHIN ONE YEAR.

ACCOUNTS THAT COMPRISE CURRENT ASSETS

- CASH

- MARKETABLE (OR SHORT-TERM) SECURITIES

- ACCOUNTS AND NOTES RECEIVABLE

- INVENTORIES

- PREPAID EXPENSES

KEY IDEA

- EVERY ENTITY HAS AN OPERATING CYCLE IN WHICH
PRODUCTS AND SERVICES ARE PURCHASED, SERVICES
ARE PERFORMED ON ACCOUNT (USUALLY), PAYMENT IS
MADE TO EMPLOYEES AND SUPPLIERS, AND FINALLY
CASH IS RECEIVED FROM CUSTOMERS. IF THE ENTITY
IS A MANUFACTURER, PRODUCT IS MADE AND HELD AS
INVENTORY BEFORE IT IS SOLD. CURRENT ASSETS
REFLECT THE INVESTMENT REQUIRED TO SUPPORT
THIS CYCLE.

28

CASH AND MARKETABLE SECURITIES

<u>KEY IDEAS</u>

- THE CASH AMOUNT ON THE BALANCE SHEET IS THE AMOUNT OF CASH OWNED BY THE ENTITY ON THE BALANCE SHEET DATE.

  THUS THE LEDGER ACCOUNT BALANCE OF CASH MUST BE RECONCILED WITH THE BANK STATEMENT ENDING BALANCE, AND THE LEDGER ACCOUNT BALANCE MUST BE ADJUSTED AS NECESSARY.

  THE ADJUSTMENT WILL REFLECT BANK TIMING DIFFERENCES AND BOOK ERRORS.

- SHORT-TERM MARKETABLE SECURITIES THAT WILL BE HELD UNTIL MATURITY ARE SHOWN ON THE BALANCE SHEET AT COST, WHICH IS USUALLY ABOUT THE SAME AS MARKET VALUE.

- SECURITIES EXPECTED TO BE HELD FOR SEVERAL MONTHS AFTER THE BALANCE SHEET DATE ARE SHOWN AT THEIR MARKET VALUE.

- INTEREST INCOME FROM MARKETABLE SECURITIES THAT HAS NOT BEEN RECEIVED MUST BE ACCRUED.

<u>ACCOUNTS RECEIVABLE</u>

<u>KEY ISSUES</u>

- ACCOUNTS RECEIVABLE ARE REPORTED ON THE BALANCE SHEET AT THEIR "NET REALIZABLE VALUE," WHICH IS THE AMOUNT OF CASH EXPECTED TO BE COLLECTED FROM THE ACCOUNTS RECEIVABLE .

- WHEN SALES ARE MADE ON ACCOUNT, THERE IS A VERY HIGH PROBABILITY THAT SOME ACCOUNTS RECEIVABLE WILL NOT BE COLLECTED.

- THE MATCHING OF REVENUES AND EXPENSES CONCEPT REQUIRES THAT THE "COST" OF UNCOLLECTIBLE ACCOUNTS RECEIVABLE BE REPORTED IN THE SAME PERIOD AS THE REVENUE THAT WAS RECOGNIZED WHEN THE ACCOUNT RECEIVABLE WAS CREATED.

<u>KEY POINTS</u>

- THE "COST" OF UNCOLLECTIBLE ACCOUNTS (BAD DEBTS EXPENSE) MUST BE ESTIMATED. THIS LEADS TO A VALUATION ADJUSTMENT.

- THE AMOUNT OF ACCOUNTS RECEIVABLE NOT EXPECTED TO BE COLLECTED IS RECORDED AND REPORTED IN AN "ALLOWANCE FOR BAD DEBTS" ACCOUNT.

- THE ALLOWANCE FOR BAD DEBTS ACCOUNT IS A "CONTRA ASSET" REPORTED IN THE BALANCE SHEET AS A SUBTRACTION FROM ACCOUNTS RECEIVABLE.

INTERNAL CONTROL STRUCTURE

KEY IDEA

- INTERNAL CONTROLS ARE DESIGNED TO PROVIDE REASONABLE ASSUARANCE THAT OBJECTIVES ARE BEING ACHIEVED WITH RESPECT TO:

    1. THE EFFECTIVENESS AND EFFICIENCY OF THE OPERATIONS OF THE ORGANIZATION.

    2. THE RELIABILITY OF THE ORGANIZATION'S FINANCIAL REPORTING.

    3. THE ORGANIZATION'S COMPLIANCE WITH APPLICABLE LAWS AND REGULATIONS.

FINANCIAL CONTROLS

- ASSURE ACCURACY OF BOOKKEEPING RECORDS AND FINANCIAL STATEMENTS AND PROTECT ASSETS FROM UNAUTHORIZED USE OR LOSS.

ADMINISTRATIVE CONTROLS

- ENCOURAGE ADHERENCE TO MANAGEMENT'S POLICIES AND PROVIDE FOR EFFICIENT OPERATIONS.

KEY OBSERVATIONS

- ALL ORGANIZATIONS NEED TO HAVE INTERNAL CONTROLS TO SUPPORT THE ACHIEVEMENT OF THEIR GOALS AND OBJECTIVES.

- INTERNAL CONTROLS ARE POSITIVE.

INVENTORIES

<u>WHAT'S GOING ON?</u>

• THE INVENTORY ASSET ACCOUNT CONTAINS THE
COST OF ITEMS THAT ARE BEING HELD FOR SALE.
WHEN AN ITEM OF INVENTORY IS SOLD, ITS COST
IS TRANSFERRED FROM THE INVENTORY ASSET
ACCOUNT (IN THE BALANCE SHEET) TO THE COST
OF GOODS SOLD EXPENSE ACCOUNT (IN THE
INCOME STATEMENT).

```
Dr.   Cost of Goods Sold ...................    $ xx
      Cr.   Inventory...........................          $ xx
```

THIS IS A TRANSACTION SEPARATE FROM THE SALE
TRANSACTION, WHICH RESULTS IN AN INCREASE IN
AN ASSET ACCOUNT IN THE BALANCE SHEET (EITHER
ACCOUNTS RECEIVABLE OR CASH), AND AN INCREASE
IN SALES, A REVENUE ACCOUNT IN THE INCOME
STATEMENT.

```
Dr.   Cash (or Accounts Receivable)......    $ xx
      Cr.   Sales...............................          $ xx
```

<u>KEY ISSUE</u>

• WHEN THE INVENTORY INCLUDES THE COST OF
SEVERAL UNITS OF THE ITEM SOLD, HOW IS THE
COST OF THE ITEM SOLD DETERMINED?

INVENTORY COST FLOW ASSUMPTIONS

<u>ALTERNATIVE COST FLOW ASSUMPTIONS</u>

• SPECIFIC IDENTIFICATION

• WEIGHTED AVERAGE

• FIFO - <u>F</u>IRST COST <u>IN</u> TO INVENTORY,
         <u>F</u>IRST COST <u>O</u>UT TO COST OF GOODS SOLD

• LIFO - <u>L</u>AST COST <u>IN</u> TO INVENTORY,
         <u>F</u>IRST COST <u>O</u>UT TO COST OF GOODS SOLD

<u>KEY ISSUES</u>

• HOW DO CHANGES IN THE <u>COST</u> OF INVENTORY
  ITEMS OVER TIME AFFECT COST OF GOODS SOLD
  UNDER EACH OF THE COST FLOW ASSUMPTIONS?

• HOW DO CHANGES IN THE <u>QUANTITY</u> OF INVENTORY
  ITEMS AFFECT COST OF GOODS SOLD UNDER
  EACH OF THE COST FLOW ASSUMPTIONS?

<u>KEY POINT</u>

• ROI, ROE, AND MEASURES OF LIQUIDITY WILL BE
  AFFECTED BY THE INVENTORY COST FLOW
  ASSUMPTION USED WHEN THE COST OF
  INVENTORY ITEMS CHANGES OVER TIME.

PREPAID EXPENSES

<u>WHAT'S GOING ON?</u>

• PREPAID EXPENSES RESULT FROM THE APPLICATION OF ACCRUAL ACCOUNTING. SOME EXPENDITURES MADE IN ONE PERIOD ARE NOT PROPERLY RECOGNIZABLE AS EXPENSES UNTIL A SUBSEQUENT PERIOD.

IN THESE SITUATIONS, EXPENSE RECOGNITION IS **DEFERRED** UNTIL THE PERIOD IN WHICH THE EXPENSE APPLIES.

<u>PREPAID EXPENSES FREQUENTLY INCLUDE</u>:

• INSURANCE PREMIUMS

• RENT

LONG-LIVED ASSETS

KEY TERMINOLOGY

- DEPRECIATION EXPENSE / ACCUMULATED DEPRECIATION

  DEPRECIATION EXPENSE REFERS TO THAT PORTION OF
  THE COST OF A LONG-LIVED ASSET RECORDED AS AN
  EXPENSE IN AN ACCOUNTING PERIOD. DEPRECIATION
  IN ACCOUNTING IS THE SPREADING OF THE COST OF A
  LONG-LIVED ASSET OVER ITS ESTIMATED USEFUL LIFE
  TO THE ENTITY. THIS IS AN APPLICATION OF THE
  MATCHING CONCEPT.

  ACCUMULATED DEPRECIATION IS A CONTRA ASSET
  ACCOUNT. THE BALANCE IN THIS ACCOUNT IS THE
  ACCUMULATED TOTAL OF ALL OF THE DEPRECIATION
  EXPENSE RECOGNIZED TO DATE ON THE RELATED
  ASSET(S).

- CAPITALIZE / EXPENSE

  TO **CAPITALIZE** AN EXPENDITURE MEANS TO RECORD
  THE EXPENDITURE AS AN ASSET. A LONG-LIVED ASSET
  THAT HAS BEEN CAPITALIZED WILL BE DEPRECIATED.

  TO **EXPENSE** AN EXPENDITURE MEANS TO RECORD
  THE EXPENDITURE AS AN EXPENSE.

- NET BOOK VALUE

  THE DIFFERENCE BETWEEN AN ASSET'S COST AND ITS
  ACCUMULATED DEPRECIATION IS ITS **NET BOOK VALUE**.

DEPRECIATION OF LONG-LIVED ASSETS

KEY POINT

- THE RECOGNITION OF DEPRECIATION EXPENSE DOES NOT AFFECT CASH.

DEPRECIATION EXPENSE CALCULATION ELEMENTS

- ASSET COST

- ESTIMATED SALVAGE VALUE

- ESTIMATED USEFUL LIFE TO ENTITY

ALTERNATIVE CALCULATION METHODS

- STRAIGHT-LINE
  - BASED ON YEARS OF LIFE
  - BASED ON UNITS OF PRODUCTION

- ACCELERATED
  - SUM-OF-THE-YEARS-DIGITS
  - DECLINING-BALANCE

DEPRECIATION METHOD ALTERNATIVES

KEY POINTS

- ACCELERATED DEPRECIATION RESULTS IN GREATER DEPRECIATION EXPENSE DURING THE EARLY YEARS OF THE ASSET'S LIFE THAN STRAIGHT-LINE DEPRECIATION. MOST FIRMS USE STRAIGHT-LINE DEPRECIATION FOR FINANCIAL REPORTING PURPOSES.

- DEPRECIATION EXPENSE DOES NOT AFFECT CASH, BUT BECAUSE DEPRECIATION IS DEDUCTIBLE FOR INCOME TAX PURPOSES, MOST FIRMS USE AN ACCELERATED METHOD FOR CALCULATING INCOME TAX DEPRECIATION.

- THE DEPRECIATION METHOD SELECTED FOR FINANCIAL REPORTING PURPOSES WILL HAVE AN EFFECT ON ROI AND ROE. TO MAKE VALID COMPARISONS BETWEEN COMPANIES, IT IS NECESSARY TO KNOW WHETHER OR NOT COMPARABLE DEPRECIATION CALCULATION METHODS HAVE BEEN USED.

- IF AN EXPENDITURE HAS BEEN INAPPROPRIATELY CAPITALIZED OR EXPENSED, BOTH ASSETS AND NET INCOME WILL BE AFFECTED, IN THE CURRENT YEAR AND IN FUTURE YEARS OF THE ASSET'S LIFE.

PRESENT VALUE ANALYSIS

KEY IDEAS

- MONEY HAS VALUE OVER TIME.

- AN AMOUNT TO BE RECEIVED OR PAID IN THE
  FUTURE HAS A VALUE TODAY (PRESENT VALUE)
  THAT IS LESS THAN THE FUTURE VALUE.

  WHY? BECAUSE OF THE INTEREST THAT CAN BE
  EARNED BETWEEN THE PRESENT AND THE FUTURE.

KEY RELATIONSHIP

- A TIME LINE APPROACH CREATES A VISUAL IMAGE
  THAT MAKES THE TIME VALUE OF MONEY CONCEPT
  EASY TO WORK WITH.

  WHAT IS THE PRESENT VALUE OF $ 4,000 TO BE
  RECEIVED OR PAID IN 4 YEARS, AT AN INTEREST
  RATE OF 8%?

```
                          Interest Rate = 8%
        TODAY        1         2          3          4
        -----------------------------------------------------
        AMOUNT DUE IN 4 YEARS                     $ 4,000
        PRESENT VALUE FACTOR (TABLE 6-2)    * .7350

        $2,940 <----------------------------------------
```

THE VALUE TODAY OF $4,000 TO BE PAID OR RECEIVED
IN 4 YEARS, ASSUMING AN INTEREST RATE OF 8%, IS
$2,940.

38

CURRENT LIABILITIES

DEFINITION

- CURRENT LIABILITIES ARE THOSE THAT MUST BE
  PAID WITHIN ONE YEAR OF THE BALANCE SHEET DATE.

ACCOUNTS THAT COMPRISE CURRENT LIABILITIES

- SHORT-TERM DEBT

- ACCOUNTS PAYABLE

- VARIOUS ACCRUED LIABILITIES, INCLUDING:

    - WAGES   · OPERATING EXPENSES
    - INTEREST · TAXES

- CURRENT MATURITIES OF LONG-TERM DEBT

KEY IDEAS

- A PRINCIPAL CONCERN ABOUT LIABILITIES IS THAT
  THEY ARE NOT UNDERSTATED. IF LIABILITIES ARE TOO
  LOW, EXPENSES ARE PROBABLY UNDERSTATED ALSO,
  WHICH MEANS THAT NET INCOME IS OVERSTATED.

- THE AMOUNT OF CURRENT LIABILITIES IS RELATED
  TO THE AMOUNT OF CURRENT ASSETS TO MEASURE
  THE FIRM'S **LIQUIDITY** -- ITS ABILITY TO PAY ITS BILLS
  WHEN THEY COME DUE.

INTEREST CALCULATION METHODS

<u>BASIC MODEL FOR CALCULATING INTEREST</u>

INTEREST = **PRINCIPAL** * ANNUAL **RATE** * **TIME** IN YEARS

<u>KEY ISSUE</u>

* IS THE PRINCIPAL AMOUNT USED IN THE INTEREST
  CALCULATION EQUAL TO THE CASH ACTUALLY
  AVAILABLE FOR THE BORROWER TO USE?

<u>STRAIGHT INTEREST</u>

* PRINCIPAL USED IN THE INTEREST CALCULATION IS
  EQUAL TO THE CASH RECEIVED BY THE BORROWER.

* INTEREST IS PAID TO THE LENDER PERIODICALLY
  DURING THE TERM OF THE LOAN, OR AT THE LOAN
  MATURITY DATE.

<u>DISCOUNT</u>

* PRINCIPAL USED IN THE INTEREST CALCULATION IS
  THE "AMOUNT BORROWED", BUT THEN INTEREST IS
  SUBTRACTED FROM THAT PRINCIPAL TO GET THE
  AMOUNT OF CASH MADE AVAILABLE TO THE
  BORROWER. THIS RESULTS IN AN EFFECTIVE
  INTEREST RATE (APR) GREATER THAN THE RATE
  USED IN THE INTEREST CALCULATION.

* BECAUSE INTEREST WAS PAID IN ADVANCE, ONLY
  THE PRINCIPAL AMOUNT IS REPAID AT THE LOAN
  MATURITY DATE.

FINANCIAL LEVERAGE

<u>KEY IDEAS</u>

- WHEN MONEY IS BORROWED AT A FIXED INTEREST
  RATE, THE DIFFERENCE BETWEEN THE ROI EARNED
  ON THAT MONEY AND THE INTEREST RATE PAID
  AFFECTS THE WEALTH OF THE BORROWER. THIS
  IS CALLED FINANCIAL LEVERAGE.

- FINANCIAL LEVERAGE IS POSITIVE WHEN THE ROI
  EARNED ON BORROWED MONEY IS GREATER THAN
  THE INTEREST RATE PAID ON THE BORROWED MONEY.
  FINANCIAL LEVERAGE IS NEGATIVE WHEN THE
  OPPOSITE OCCURS.

- FINANCIAL LEVERAGE INCREASES THE RISK THAT A
  FIRM'S ROI WILL FLUCTUATE, BECAUSE ROI CHANGES
  AS BUSINESS CONDITIONS AND THE FIRM'S OPERATING
  RESULTS CHANGE, BUT THE INTEREST RATE ON
  BORROWED FUNDS IS USUALLY FIXED.

LONG-TERM DEBT (BONDS PAYABLE)

KEY IDEA

- FIRMS ISSUE LONG-TERM DEBT (BONDS PAYABLE) TO GET SOME OF THE FUNDS NEEDED TO INVEST IN ASSETS. THE OWNERS DO NOT USUALLY PROVIDE ALL OF THE NECESSARY FUNDS BECAUSE IT IS USUALLY DESIRABLE TO HAVE SOME FINANCIAL LEVERAGE.

BOND CHARACTERISTICS

- A FIXED INTEREST RATE (USUALLY) CALLED THE **STATED** RATE OR **COUPON** RATE.

    - INTEREST USUALLY PAYABLE SEMI-ANNUALLY.

    - INDIVIDUAL BONDS USUALLY HAVE A FACE AMOUNT (PRINCIPAL) OF $1,000.

    - BOND PRICES ARE STATED AS A % OF THE FACE AMOUNT; FOR EXAMPLE, A PRICE QUOTE OF 98.3 MEANS 98.3% OF $1000, OR $983.

    - MOST BONDS HAVE A STATED MATURITY DATE - BUT MOST BONDS ARE ALSO **CALLABLE**; THEY CAN BE REDEEMED PRIOR TO MATURITY AT THE OPTION OF THE ISSUER.

    - FREQUENTLY SOME COLLATERAL IS PROVIDED BY THE ISSUER.

BOND MARKET VALUE

KEY POINT

- THE MARKET VALUE OF A BOND IS A FUNCTION OF
  THE RELATIONSHIP BETWEEN MARKET INTEREST
  RATES AND THE BOND'S STATED OR COUPON
  RATE OF INTEREST.

  - AS MARKET INTEREST RATES FALL, THE MARKET
    VALUE OF A BOND RISES.

  - AS MARKET INTEREST RATES RISE, THE MARKET
    VALUE OF A BOND FALLS.

WHAT'S GOING ON?

- A BOND'S STATED OR COUPON RATE OF INTEREST IS
  FIXED AND STAYS THE SAME REGARDLESS OF WHAT
  HAPPENS TO MARKET INTEREST RATES.   THEREFORE,
  IF MARKET INTEREST RATES RISE ABOVE THE STATED
  OR COUPON RATE, THE BOND BECOMES LESS VALUABLE
  TO INVESTORS.

KEY RELATIONSHIP

- THE MARKET VALUE OF A BOND IS THE PRESENT
  VALUE OF THE FUTURE PAYMENTS OF INTEREST AND
  PRINCIPAL, BASED ON (i.e., DISCOUNTED AT) MARKET
  INTEREST RATES.

BOND PREMIUM AND DISCOUNT

<u>KEY IDEA</u>

- WHEN THE MARKET INTEREST RATE AT THE
  DATE A BOND IS ISSUED IS DIFFERENT FROM
  THE STATED OR COUPON RATE OF THE BOND,
  THE BOND WILL BE ISSUED AT:

    - A PREMIUM (MARKET INTEREST RATE <
      STATED OR COUPON RATE)

    - OR A DISCOUNT (MARKET INTEREST RATE >
      STATED OR COUPON RATE).

<u>KEY POINTS</u>

- WHEN A BOND IS ISSUED AT A PREMIUM, THE
  PREMIUM IS AMORTIZED TO INTEREST EXPENSE
  OVER THE TERM OF THE BOND, RESULTING IN
  LOWER ANNUAL INTEREST EXPENSE THAN
  THE INTEREST PAID ON THE BOND.

- WHEN A BOND IS ISSUED AT A DISCOUNT, THE
  DISCOUNT IS AMORTIZED TO INTEREST EXPENSE
  OVER THE TERM OF THE BOND, RESULTING IN
  HIGHER ANNUAL INTEREST EXPENSE THAN THE
  INTEREST PAID ON THE BOND.

- THE AMORTIZATION OF PREMIUM OR DISCOUNT
  RESULTS IN REPORTING AN ACTUAL INTEREST
  EXPENSE FROM THE BONDS THAT IS A FUNCTION
  OF THE MARKET INTEREST RATE WHEN THE BONDS
  WERE ISSUED -- AN APPROPRIATE RESULT.

DEFERRED INCOME TAXES

<u>WHAT'S GOING ON?</u>

- DIFFERENCES BETWEEN BOOK AND TAXABLE INCOME ARISE BECAUSE FINANCIAL ACCOUNTING METHODS DIFFER FROM ACCOUNTING METHODS PERMITTED FOR INCOME TAX PURPOSES.

  <u>EXAMPLE</u>: BOOK DEPRECIATION IS USUALLY CALCULATED ON A STRAIGHT-LINE BASIS, AND TAX DEPRECIATION IS USUALLY BASED ON AN ACCELERATED METHOD.

<u>KEY ISSUE</u>

- WHEN TAXABLE INCOME IS DIFFERENT FROM FINANCIAL ACCOUNTING (i.e., BOOK) INCOME, INCOME TAX EXPENSE SHOULD BE A FUNCTION OF BOOK INCOME BEFORE TAXES, NOT TAXABLE INCOME. THIS IS AN APPLICATION OF THE MATCHING CONCEPT.

<u>KEY IDEA</u>

- INCOME TAX EXPENSE BASED ON BOOK INCOME CAN BE MORE OR LESS THAN THE INCOME TAXES CURRENTLY PAYABLE. WHEN THIS OCCURS,

    - "DEFERRED INCOME TAX LIABILITIES" and/or

    - "DEFERRED INCOME TAX ASSETS"

  ARE REPORTED.

OWNERS' EQUITY - PAID-IN CAPITAL

ACCOUNTS INCLUDED IN PAID-IN CAPITAL

- COMMON STOCK (SOMETIMES CALLED CAPITAL STOCK)

- PREFERRED STOCK (IF AUTHORIZED BY THE CORPORATION'S CHARTER)

- ADDITIONAL PAID-IN CAPITAL

KEY TERMINOLOGY FOR NUMBER OF SHARES OF STOCK

- AUTHORIZED - BY THE CORPORATION'S CHARTER

- ISSUED - SOLD IN THE PAST TO STOCKHOLDERS

- OUTSTANDING - STILL HELD BY STOCKHOLDERS

- TREASURY STOCK - SHARES OF ITS OWN STOCK PURCHASED AND HELD BY THE CORPORATION. THE NUMBER OF SHARES OF TREASURY STOCK IS THE DIFFERENCE BETWEEN THE NUMBER OF SHARES ISSUED AND THE NUMBER OF SHARES OUTSTANDING.

KEY TERMINOLOGY FOR STOCK VALUE

- PAR VALUE - AN ARBITRARY AMOUNT ASSIGNED TO EACH SHARE AT INCORPORATION. THE FIRM CAN ISSUE NO-PAR VALUE STOCK. IF NO-PAR VALUE STOCK HAS A "STATED VALUE", THE STATED VALUE IS LIKE A PAR VALUE.

48

COMMON STOCK AND PREFERRED STOCK

KEY IDEAS

- COMMON STOCK REPRESENTS THE BASIC OWNERSHIP OF A CORPORATION.

- PREFERRED STOCK REPRESENTS OWNERSHIP, BUT HAS SOME PREFERENCES RELATIVE TO COMMON STOCK. THESE INCLUDE:

    - PRIORITY CLAIM TO DIVIDENDS, AND

    - PRIORITY CLAIM TO ASSETS IN LIQUIDATION.

    - HOWEVER, PREFERRED STOCKHOLDERS ARE NOT USUALLY ENTITLED TO VOTE FOR DIRECTORS.

KEY POINTS ABOUT DIVIDENDS ON PREFERRED STOCK

- DIVIDENDS ARE USUALLY "CUMULATIVE," WHICH MEANS THAT DIVIDENDS NOT PAID DURING ONE YEAR (IN ARREARS) MUST BE PAID IN A FUTURE YEAR BEFORE DIVIDENDS CAN BE PAID ON COMMON STOCK.

- DIVIDEND AMOUNT IS EXPRESSED AS A CERTAIN AMOUNT PER SHARE ($3.50), OR AS A PERCENT OF PAR VALUE (7% OF PAR VALUE OF $50).

PAID-IN CAPITAL AMOUNTS ON THE BALANCE SHEET

WHAT'S GOING ON?

- IF THE STOCK HAS A PAR VALUE, THE AMOUNTS OPPOSITE THE STOCK CAPTIONS ARE ALWAYS PAR VALUE MULTIPLIED BY THE NUMBER OF SHARES ISSUED.

- THE DIFFERENCE BETWEEN THE PAR VALUE AND THE AMOUNT RECEIVED PER SHARE WHEN THE STOCK WAS ISSUED IS RECORDED AS ADDITIONAL PAID-IN CAPITAL.

- IF THE STOCK IS NO-PAR VALUE STOCK (WITHOUT A STATED VALUE), THE AMOUNT OPPOSITE THE CAPTION IS THE TOTAL AMOUNT RECEIVED WHEN THE STOCK WAS ISSUED.

RETAINED EARNINGS AND DIVIDENDS

KEY IDEAS

- RETAINED EARNINGS INCREASES EACH PERIOD BY THE AMOUNT OF NET INCOME FOR THAT PERIOD. (NET LOSSES DECREASE RETAINED EARNINGS.)

- DIVIDENDS ARE DISTRIBUTIONS OF RETAINED EARNINGS TO THE STOCKHOLDERS, AND ARE A REDUCTION IN RETAINED EARNINGS.

    - CASH DIVIDENDS ARE DECLARED BY THE BOARD OF DIRECTORS AS AN AMOUNT PER SHARE.

    - STOCK DIVIDENDS ARE DECLARED BY THE BOARD OF DIRECTORS AS A PERCENTAGE OF THE PREVIOUSLY ISSUED SHARES. STOCK DIVIDENDS AFFECT ONLY RETAINED EARNINGS AND PAID-IN CAPITAL; ASSETS AND LIABILITIES ARE NOT AFFECTED.

    - CASH DIVIDENDS ARE NOT PAID ON TREASURY STOCK. STOCK DIVIDENDS ARE USUALLY ISSUED ON TREASURY STOCK.

STOCK SPLITS

<u>KEY IDEA</u>

- A STOCK SPLIT INVOLVES ISSUING ADDITIONAL SHARES OF STOCK IN PROPORTION TO THE NUMBER OF SHARES CURRENTLY OWNED BY EACH STOCKHOLDER. THE RELATIVE OWNERSHIP INTEREST OF EACH STOCKHOLDER DOES NOT CHANGE.

- BECAUSE THERE ARE MORE SHARES OF STOCK OUTSTANDING, THE MARKET PRICE OF EACH SHARE WILL FALL TO REFLECT THE SPLIT.

<u>BALANCE SHEET EFFECT OF STOCK SPLIT</u>

- DOLLAR AMOUNTS ON THE BALANCE SHEET ARE NOT AFFECTED. THE PAR VALUE IS REDUCED, AND THE NUMBER OF SHARES ISSUED IS INCREASED.

INCOME STATEMENT

MULTIPLE-STEP MODEL

Exhibit 9-6

CRUISERS, INC., AND SUBSIDIARIES
Consolidated Income Statement
For the Year Ended August 31, 1999, and 1998
(000 omitted)

	1999	1998
Net sales	$77.543	$62,531
Cost of goods sold	48,077	39,870
Gross profit	$29,466	$22,661
Selling, general, and administrative expenses	23,264	18,425
Income from operations	$ 6,202	$ 4,236
Other income (expense):		
Interest expense	(3,378)	(2,679)
Other income (net)	385	193
Minority interest	(432)	(356)
Income before taxes	$ 2,777	$ 1,394
Provision for income taxes	1,250	630
Net income	$ 1,527	$ 764
Basic earnings per share of common stock	$ 5.56	$ 2.42

KEY OBSERVATIONS

- THERE IS A GREAT DEAL OF SUMMARIZATION.

- CAPTIONS REFLECT THE REVENUE AND EXPENSE CATEGORIES THAT ARE MOST SIGNIFICANT TO UNDERSTANDING RESULTS OF OPERATIONS.

- INCOME FROM OPERATIONS IS SOMETIMES MORE MEANINGFUL FOR TREND COMPARISONS THAN NET INCOME.

LINKAGE BETWEEN BALANCE SHEET AND INCOME STATEMENT ACCOUNTS

BALANCE SHEET	INCOME STATEMENT
ACCOUNTS RECEIVABLE -------->	SALES / REVENUES
NOTES RECEIVABLE AND -------> SHORT-TERM INVESTMENTS	INTEREST INCOME
INVENTORIES ------------------------>	COST OF GOODS SOLD
PREPAID EXPENSES AND -------> ACCRUED LIABILITIES	OPERATING EXPENSES
ACCUMULATED ---------------------> DEPRECIATION	DEPRECIATION EXPENSE
	(REPORTED IN COST OF GOODS SOLD AND OPERATING EXPENSES)
NOTES PAYABLE AND -------------> BONDS PAYABLE	INTEREST EXPENSE
INCOME TAXES PAYABLE -------> AND DEFERRED TAX LIABILITY	INCOME TAX EXPENSE

STATEMENT OF CASH FLOWS

<u>WHAT'S GOING ON?</u>

- THE INCOME STATEMENT REPORTS ACCRUAL BASIS
  NET INCOME. FINANCIAL STATEMENT USERS ALSO
  WANT TO KNOW ABOUT THE FIRM'S CASH FLOWS.

- THE REASONS FOR THE CHANGE IN CASH FROM
  THE BEGINNING TO THE END OF THE PERIOD ARE
  SUMMARIZED IN THREE CATEGORIES:

    - CASH FLOWS FROM **OPERATING** ACTIVITIES

    - CASH FLOWS FROM **INVESTING** ACTIVITIES

    - CASH FLOWS FROM **FINANCING** ACTIVITIES

INTERPRETING THE STATEMENT OF CASH FLOWS

KEY QUESTIONS

- WHAT HAPPENED TO THE CASH BALANCE DURING THE YEAR?

- WHAT IS THE RELATIONSHIP BETWEEN CASH FLOWS FROM OPERATING, INVESTING, AND FINANCING ACTIVITIES?

KEY RELATIONSHIPS TO OBSERVE

- DID CASH FLOWS FROM OPERATING ACTIVITIES EXCEED CASH USED FOR INVESTING ACTIVITIES?

    - DID FINANCING ACTIVITIES CAUSE A NET INCREASE OR NET DECREASE IN CASH?

    - IN OPERATING ACTIVITIES, WHAT WERE THE EFFECTS OF ACCOUNTS RECEIVABLE, INVENTORY, AND ACCOUNTS PAYABLE CHANGES?

    - IN INVESTING ACTIVITIES, WHAT WAS THE RELATIONSHIP BETWEEN THE INVESTMENT IN NEW ASSETS AND THE SALE OF OLD ASSETS?

    - IN FINANCING ACTIVITIES, WHAT WERE THE NET EFFECTS OF LONG-TERM DEBT AND CAPITAL STOCK CHANGES? WHAT WAS THE EFFECT OF CASH DIVIDENDS PAID?

EXPLANATORY NOTES TO FINANCIAL STATEMENTS

KEY POINT

- FINANCIAL STATEMENT READERS MUST BE ABLE TO LEARN ABOUT THE FOLLOWING KEY ISSUES THAT AFFECT THEIR ABILITY TO UNDERSTAND THE STATEMENTS:

    - DEPRECIATION METHODS
    - INVENTORY COST FLOW ASSUMPTIONS
    - CURRENT AND DEFERRED INCOME TAXES
    - EMPLOYEE BENEFIT INFORMATION
    - EARNINGS PER SHARE OF COMMON STOCK DETAILS
    - STOCK OPTION AND STOCK PURCHASE PLAN INFORMATION

OTHER KEY DISCLOSURES

- MANAGEMENT'S STATEMENT OF RESPONSIBILITY
- MANAGEMENT'S DISCUSSION AND ANALYSIS

KEY IDEA

- THE EXPLANATORY NOTES TO THE FINANCIAL STATEMENTS MUST BE REVIEWED TO HAVE A REASONABLY COMPLETE UNDERSTANDING OF WHAT THE NUMBERS MEAN.

FIVE-YEAR (OR LONGER) SUMMARY OF FINANCIAL DATA

KEY IDEAS

- LOOK AT TREND OF DATA.

- NOTICE THE EFFECT OF STOCK DIVIDENDS AND STOCK SPLITS ON PER SHARE DATA.

- USE THE DATA REPORTED FOR PRIOR YEARS TO MAKE RATIO CALCULATIONS FOR EVALUATIVE PURPOSES.

INDEPENDENT AUDITORS' REPORT

KEY IDEA

- FINANCIAL STATEMENTS PRESENT FAIRLY, **IN ALL MATERIAL RESPECTS**, THE FINANCIAL POSITION AND RESULTS OF OPERATIONS.

KEY POINT

- AUDITORS GIVE NO GUARANTEE THAT FINANCIAL STATEMENTS ARE FREE FROM ERROR OR FRAUD.

LIQUIDITY ANALYSIS

<u>KEY QUESTION</u>

- IS THE FIRM LIKELY TO BE ABLE TO PAY ITS
  OBLIGATIONS WHEN THEY COME DUE?

<u>LIQUIDITY MEASURES</u>

- WORKING CAPITAL

- CURRENT RATIO

- ACID-TEST RATIO

<u>KEY ISSUE</u>

- THE INVENTORY COST FLOW ASSUMPTION USED
  BY THE FIRM (FIFO, LIFO, WEIGHTED AVERAGE, OR
  SPECIFIC IDENTIFICATION) WILL AFFECT THESE
  MEASURES.

ACTIVITY MEASURES

<u>KEY QUESTION</u>

- HOW EFFICIENTLY ARE THE FIRM'S ASSETS BEING USED?

<u>ACTIVITY MEASURES</u>

- ACCOUNTS RECEIVABLE TURNOVER (OR NUMBER OF DAYS' SALES IN ACCOUNTS RECEIVABLE)

- INVENTORY TURNOVER (OR NUMBER OF DAYS' SALES IN INVENTORY)

- PLANT AND EQUIPMENT TURNOVER

- TOTAL ASSET TURNOVER

<u>GENERAL MODEL</u>

$$\text{TURNOVER} = \frac{\text{SALES FOR PERIOD}}{\text{AVERAGE ASSET BALANCE FOR PERIOD}}$$

<u>KEY IDEAS</u>

- INVENTORY ACTIVITY CALCULATIONS USE COST OF GOODS SOLD INSTEAD OF SALES.

- NUMBER OF DAYS' SALES CALCULATIONS USE THE ENDING BALANCE OF THE ASSET ACCOUNT DIVIDED BY AVERAGE DAILY SALES OR AVERAGE DAILY COST OF GOODS SOLD.

PROFITABILITY MEASURES

<u>KEY QUESTIONS</u>

- WHAT RATE OF RETURN HAS BEEN EARNED ON ASSETS OR OWNERS' EQUITY?

- HOW EXPENSIVE IS THE FIRM'S COMMON STOCK RELATIVE TO OTHER COMPANIES, AND WHAT HAS BEEN THE DIVIDEND EXPERIENCE?

<u>PROFITABILITY MEASURES</u>

- ROI - RETURN ON INVESTMENT

- ROE - RETURN ON EQUITY

- PRICE / EARNINGS RATIO (EARNINGS MULTIPLE)

- DIVIDEND YIELD

- DIVIDEND PAYOUT RATIO

<u>KEY IDEAS</u>

- FACTORS IN ROI CALCULATION MAY DIFFER AMONG COMPANIES (NET INCOME OR OPERATING INCOME IN THE NUMERATOR); WHAT IS IMPORTANT IS THE CONSISTENCY OF DEFINITION, AND **TREND** OF ROI.

- ROE IS BASED ON THE NET INCOME APPLICABLE TO, AND THE EQUITY OF, **COMMON STOCKHOLDERS**.

FINANCIAL LEVERAGE RATIOS

KEY IDEA

- FINANCIAL LEVERAGE REFERS TO THE USE OF DEBT (INSTEAD OF OWNERS' EQUITY) TO FINANCE THE ACQUISITION OF ASSETS FOR THE FIRM.

  THE INTEREST RATE ON DEBT IS FIXED, SO IF THE ROI EARNED ON THE BORROWED FUNDS IS GREATER THAN THE INTEREST RATE OWED, ROE WILL INCREASE. THIS IS REFERRED TO AS "POSITIVE" FINANCIAL LEVERAGE.

  IF THE ROI EARNED ON BORROWED FUNDS IS LESS THAN THE INTEREST RATE OWED, ROE WILL DECREASE. THIS IS REFERRED TO AS "NEGATIVE" FINANCIAL LEVERAGE.

KEY QUESTIONS

- HOW MUCH FINANCIAL LEVERAGE IS THE FIRM USING?

- HOW MUCH RISK OF FINANCIAL LOSS TO CREDITORS AND OWNERS IS THERE?

FINANCIAL LEVERAGE RATIOS

- DEBT RATIO

- DEBT / EQUITY RATIO

- TIMES INTEREST EARNED RATIO

62

OTHER ANALYTICAL TECHNIQUES

BOOK VALUE PER SHARE OF COMMON STOCK

KEY IDEA

- AN EASILY CALCULATED AMOUNT BASED ON THE
  BALANCE SHEET AMOUNT OF OWNERS' EQUITY, BUT
  NOT VERY USEFUL IN MOST CASES BECAUSE BALANCE
  SHEET AMOUNTS DO NOT REFLECT MARKET VALUES
  OR REPLACEMENT VALUES.

COMMON SIZE FINANCIAL STATEMENTS

KEY IDEA

- COMPARISONS BETWEEN FIRMS (OR BETWEEN
  PERIODS FOR THE SAME FIRM) CAN BE MORE
  EASILY UNDERSTOOD IF FINANCIAL STATEMENT
  AMOUNTS ARE EXPRESSED AS PERCENTAGES
  OF TOTAL ASSETS OR TOTAL REVENUES.

OTHER OPERATING STATISTICS

KEY IDEA

- NOT ALL DECISIONS AND INFORMED JUDGMENTS
  ABOUT AN ENTITY ARE BASED ON FINANCIAL DATA.
  NONFINANCIAL STATISTICS ARE FREQUENTLY
  RELEVANT AND USEFUL.

63

MANAGERIAL ACCOUNTING COMPARED TO FINANCIAL ACCOUNTING

KEY CHARACTERISTICS THAT DIFFER

- SERVICE PERSPECTIVE

- BREADTH OF CONCERN

- REPORTING FREQUENCY AND PROMPTNESS

- DEGREE OF PRECISION OF DATA USED

- REPORTING STANDARDS

COST CLASSIFICATIONS

KEY IDEA

- DIFFERENT COSTS FOR DIFFERENT PURPOSES.

COST CLASSIFICATIONS

- FOR COST ACCOUNTING PURPOSES:

    - PRODUCT COST
    - PERIOD COST

- RELATIONSHIP TO PRODUCT OR ACTIVITY:

    - DIRECT COST
    - INDIRECT COST

- RELATIONSHIP BETWEEN TOTAL COST AND VOLUME OF ACTIVITY:

    - VARIABLE COST
    - FIXED COST

- TIME-FRAME PERSPECTIVE:

    - CONTROLLABLE COST
    - NONCONTROLLABLE COST

- FOR OTHER ANALYTICAL PURPOSES:

    - DIFFERENTIAL COST
    - ALLOCATED COST
    - SUNK COST
    - OPPORTUNITY COST

COST ACCOUNTING SYSTEMS

KEY IDEAS

- PERIOD COSTS (SELLING, GENERAL, AND ADMIN-ISTRATIVE) ARE ACCOUNTED FOR AS EXPENSES IN THE PERIOD INCURRED.

- PRODUCT COSTS FLOW THROUGH INVENTORY (ASSET) ACCOUNTS, AND THEN TO THE COST OF GOODS SOLD (EXPENSE) ACCOUNT.

  RAW MATERIAL, DIRECT LABOR, AND **MANUFACTURING OVERHEAD** COSTS ARE CAPITALIZED AS INVENTORY → UNTIL THE PRODUCT THEY RELATE TO IS SOLD.

    - RAW MATERIAL AND DIRECT LABOR COSTS ARE RATHER EASILY IDENTIFIED WITH THE PRODUCT.

    - MANUFACTURING OVERHEAD IS "APPLIED" TO PRODUCTION BASED ON A **PREDETERMINED OVERHEAD APPLICATION RATE**, DETERMINED AS FOLLOWS:

$$\frac{\text{ESTIMATED OVERHEAD COSTS FOR THE YEAR}}{\text{ESTIMATED ACTIVITY FOR THE YEAR}}$$

KEY POINT

- BECAUSE THE PREDETERMINED OVERHEAD APPLI-CATION RATE IS BASED ON ESTIMATES, THERE WILL PROBABLY BE "OVERAPPLIED" OR "UNDERAPPLIED" OVERHEAD AT THE END OF THE YEAR. THIS AMOUNT USUALLY BECOMES PART OF COST OF GOODS SOLD.

COST OF GOODS MANUFACTURED AND COST OF GOODS SOLD

KEY IDEA

- BECAUSE OF THE INVENTORY ACCOUNTS, COST OF GOODS MANUFACTURED AND COST OF GOODS SOLD ARE NOT SIMPLY THE TOTALS OF COSTS INCURRED DURING THE PERIOD.

KEY MODELS

- COST OF GOODS MANUFACTURED:

      RAW MATERIALS INVENTORY, BEGINNING
  + RAW MATERIALS PURCHASES
  - <u>RAW MATERIALS INVENTORY, ENDING</u>
  = COST OF RAW MATERIALS USED
  + WORK-IN-PROCESS INVENTORY, BEGINNING
  + DIRECT LABOR COSTS INCURRED
  + MANUFACTURING OVERHEAD APPLIED
  - <u>WORK-IN-PROCESS INVENTORY, ENDING</u>
  = COST OF GOODS MANUFACTURED

- COST OF GOODS SOLD:

      FINISHED GOODS INVENTORY, BEGINNING
  + COST OF GOODS MANUFACTURED
  - <u>FINISHED GOODS INVENTORY, ENDING</u>
  = COST OF GOODS SOLD

         67

RELATIONSHIP OF TOTAL COST TO VOLUME OF ACTIVITY

KEY IDEA

- **COST BEHAVIOR PATTERN** DESCRIBES HOW TOTAL COST VARIES WITH CHANGES IN ACTIVITY.

KEY RELATIONSHIPS

- VARIABLE COST
- FIXED COST

Exhibit 12–10   Cost Behavior Patterns

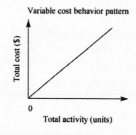
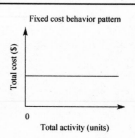

KEY ASSUMPTIONS

- RELEVANT RANGE
- LINEARITY

COST FORMULA

KEY POINT

- A **COST FORMULA** DESCRIBES THE EXPECTED TOTAL COST FOR ANY VOLUME OF ACTIVITY, USING COST BEHAVIOR INFORMATION.

KEY RELATIONSHIP

- TOTAL COST = FIXED COST + VARIABLE COST

    = FIXED COST + (VARIABLE RATE
                    PER UNIT * ACTIVITY)

KEY IDEA

- WHENEVER POSSIBLE, AVOID UNITIZING FIXED COSTS, BECAUSE THEY DO NOT BEHAVE THAT WAY!

ACTIVITY BASED COSTING

- AN ABC SYSTEM INVOLVES IDENTIFYING THE KEY ACTIVITIES THAT CAUSE THE INCURRANCE OF COST; THESE ACTIVITIES ARE KNOWN AS **COST DRIVERS.**

- EXAMPLES OF COST DRIVERS INCLUDE: MACHINE SETUP, QUALITY INSPECTION, PRODUCTION ORDER PREPARATION, AND MATERIALS HANDLING ACTIVITIES.

KEY RELATIONSHIPS

- THE NUMBER OF TIMES EACH ACTIVITY IS TO BE PERFORMED DURING THE YEAR AND THE TOTAL COST OF EACH ACTIVITY ARE ESTIMATED, AND A PREDETERMINED COST PER ACTIVITY IS CALCULATED.

- "ACTIVITY BASED COSTS" ARE THEN APPLIED TO PRODUCTS, RATHER THAN USING A TRADITIONAL METHOD OF OVERHEAD APPLICATION SUCH AS DIRECT LABOR HOURS OR MACHINE HOURS.

KEY IDEA

- ABC SYSTEMS OFTEN LEAD TO MORE ACCURATE PRODUCT COSTING AND MORE EFFECTIVE COST CONTROL, BECAUSE MANAGEMENT'S ATTENTION IS DIRECTED TO THE ACTIVITIES THAT *CAUSE* THE INCURRANCE OF COST.

INCOME STATEMENT MODELS

TRADITIONAL MODEL

REVENUES
- COST OF GOODS SOLD
GROSS PROFIT
- OPERATING EXPENSES
OPERATING INCOME

CONTRIBUTION MARGIN MODEL

REVENUES
- VARIABLE EXPENSES
CONTRIBUTION MARGIN
- FIXED EXPENSES
OPERATING INCOME

KEY IDEAS

- THE TRADITIONAL MODEL CLASSIFIES EXPENSES BY FUNCTION, AND THE CONTRIBUTION MARGIN MODEL CLASSIFIES EXPENSES BY COST BEHAVIOR PATTERN

- THE CONTRIBUTION MARGIN MODEL IS USEFUL FOR DETERMINING THE EFFECT ON OPERATING INCOME OF CHANGES IN THE LEVEL OF ACTIVITY.

EXPANDED CONTRIBUTION MARGIN MODEL

	PER UNIT	X	VOLUME	=	TOTAL	%
REVENUE	$ 1.				$	100%
VARIABLE EXP.	1.					
CONT. MARGIN	$ 1.	X	2.	=	2.	
FIXED EXPENSES					3.	
OPERATING INCOME					$ 3.	

KEY IDEAS

• THE PREFERRED ROUTE THROUGH THE MODEL IS:

1. TO ENTER PER UNIT REVENUE AND VARIABLE
   EXPENSES TO GET UNIT CONTRIBUTION MARGIN.

2. THEN MULTIPLY UNIT CONTRIBUTION MARGIN
   BY VOLUME (QUANTITY SOLD) TO GET TOTAL
   CONTRIBUTION MARGIN.

3. FIXED EXPENSES ARE NOT EXPRESSED ON A PER
   UNIT BASIS; THEY ARE SUBTRACTED FROM TOTAL
   CONTRIBUTION MARGIN TO GET OPERATING
   INCOME.

• THE CONTRIBUTION MARGIN RATIO EXPRESSES
CONTRIBUTION MARGIN AS A PERCENTAGE OF
REVENUES, ON EITHER A PER UNIT OR TOTAL BASIS.

BREAK-EVEN POINT ANALYSIS

KEY IDEA

- MANAGERS FREQUENTLY WANT TO KNOW THE
  NUMBER OF UNITS THAT MUST BE SOLD, OR THE
  TOTAL SALES DOLLARS REQUIRED, TO BREAK-EVEN
  (HAVE ZERO OPERATING INCOME).

BREAK-EVEN GRAPH

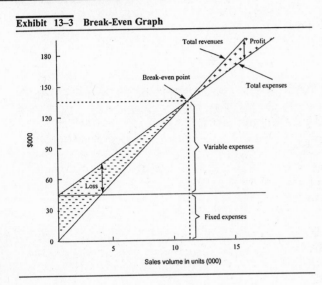

Exhibit 13–3   Break-Even Graph

KEY POINT

- ONCE THE BREAK-EVEN POINT HAS BEEN REACHED,
  OPERATING INCOME INCREASES BY THE AMOUNT
  OF CONTRIBUTION MARGIN FROM EACH ADDITIONAL
  UNIT SOLD.

73

KEY ASSUMPTIONS TO REMEMBER WHEN USING CONTRIBUTION MARGIN ANALYSIS

- COST BEHAVIOR PATTERNS CAN BE IDENTIFIED.

- COSTS ARE LINEAR WITHIN THE RELEVANT RANGE.

- ACTIVITY REMAINS WITHIN THE RELEVANT RANGE.

- SALES MIX OF THE FIRM'S PRODUCTS WITH DIFFERENT CONTRIBUTION MARGIN RATIOS DOES NOT CHANGE.

KEY POINT

- IF THESE SIMPLIFYING ASSUMPTIONS ARE NOT VALID, THE ANALYSIS IS MADE MORE COMPLICATED BUT THE CONCEPTS ARE STILL APPLICABLE.

BUDGETING

BUDGET CATEGORIES

- OPERATING BUDGET

- CAPITAL BUDGET

APPROACHES TO BUDGETING

- TOP-DOWN

- PARTICIPATIVE

- ZERO-BASED

BUDGET TIME FRAMES

- SINGLE-PERIOD BUDGET

- ROLLING (CONTINUOUS) BUDGET

OPERATING BUDGET PREPARATION SEQUENCE

- SALES / REVENUE BUDGET, OR SALES FORECAST

- PURCHASES / PRODUCTION BUDGET

- OPERATING EXPENSE BUDGET

- BUDGETED INCOME STATEMENT

- CASH BUDGET

- BALANCE SHEET BUDGET

KEY POINT

- THE ENTIRE BUDGET BUILDS ON THE SALES/ REVENUE BUDGET, SOMETIMES CALLED THE SALES FORECAST.

PERFORMANCE REPORTING

<u>KEY IDEAS</u>

- IF TIME AND EFFORT HAVE BEEN EXPENDED PREPARING A BUDGET, IT IS APPROPRIATE TO COMPARE ACTUAL RESULTS WITH BUDGETED RESULTS. THIS IS DONE IN THE PERFORMANCE REPORT.

- IF ACTUAL RESULTS APPROXIMATE BUDGETED RESULTS, THEN NO SIGNIFICANT FURTHER EVALUATION OF PERFORMANCE NEEDS TO BE MADE.

- MANAGEMENT ATTENTION IS GIVEN ONLY TO THOSE ACTIVITIES FOR WHICH ACTUAL RESULTS VARY SIGNIFICANTLY FROM BUDGETED RESULTS. THIS IS **MANAGEMENT BY EXCEPTION.**

SEGMENT REPORTING

<u>KEY IDEAS</u>

- WHEN A FIRM HAS SEVERAL IDENTIFIABLE SEGMENTS (DIVISIONS, SALES TERRITORIES, PRODUCTS, ETC.) MANAGEMENT FREQUENTLY WANTS TO EVALUATE THE OPERATING RESULTS OF EACH SEGMENT.

- SEGMENTS MAY BE REFERRED TO AS:

    - COST CENTERS

    - PROFIT CENTERS

    - INVESTMENT CENTERS

<u>KEY ISSUES</u>

- SALES, VARIABLE EXPENSES, AND CONTRIBUTION MARGIN FOR EACH SEGMENT CAN USUALLY BE EASILY ACCUMULATED FROM THE ACCOUNTING RECORDS.

- FIXED EXPENSES INCLUDE AMOUNTS ASSOCIATED DIRECTLY WITH EACH SEGMENT, AND AMOUNTS THAT ARE COMMON TO THE FIRM AS A WHOLE.

- TO REPORT SENSIBLE RESULTS FOR EACH SEGMENT, **<u>COMMON FIXED EXPENSES SHOULD NEVER BE ARBITRARILY ALLOCATED TO THE SEGMENTS</u>** BECAUSE THEY ARE NOT INCURRED DIRECTLY BY ANY OF THE SEGMENTS.

FLEXIBLE BUDGETING

KEY ISSUES

- BUDGET AMOUNTS ARE BASED ON EXPECTED LEVELS OF ACTIVITY. ACTUAL ACTIVITY IS UNLIKELY TO BE THE SAME AS BUDGETED ACTIVITY.

- SOME MANAGER IS RESPONSIBLE FOR THE DIFFERENCE BETWEEN BUDGETED AND ACTUAL ACTIVITY LEVELS, BUT IT IS USUALLY ANOTHER MANAGER WHO IS RESPONSIBLE FOR THE COSTS INCURRED.

- REVENUES ARE A FUNCTION OF UNITS SOLD, AND COSTS INCURRED ARE A FUNCTION OF COST BEHAVIOR PATTERNS.

KEY IDEA

- AT THE END OF A PERIOD, WHEN THE ACTUAL LEVEL OF ACTIVITY IS KNOWN, THE ORIGINAL BUDGET SHOULD BE **FLEXED** SO THAT THE PERFORMANCE REPORT COMPARES ACTUAL RESULTS WITH BUDGET AMOUNTS BASED ON ACTUAL ACTIVITY.

KEY POINT

- ONLY REVENUES AND VARIABLE EXPENSES ARE FLEXED. FIXED EXPENSES ARE NOT A FUNCTION OF THE LEVEL OF ACTIVITY (UNLESS ACTIVITY FALLS OUTSIDE OF THE RELEVANT RANGE).

STANDARD COSTS

WHAT ARE THEY?

- UNIT BUDGETS FOR MATERIALS, LABOR, AND OVERHEAD COST COMPONENTS OF A PRODUCT OR PROCESS.

- STANDARD COSTS ARE USED FOR PLANNING AND CONTROL.

KEY IDEAS

- STANDARD COSTS CAN BE BASED ON:

    - IDEAL, OR ENGINEERED, PERFORMANCE

    - ATTAINABLE PERFORMANCE

    - PAST EXPERIENCE

- THE STANDARD COST OF PRODUCT OR PROCESS COMPONENTS CAN BE USED TO BUILD UP THE TOTAL COST OF A PRODUCT OR PROCESS.

VARIABLE COST VARIANCE ANALYSIS

KEY IDEAS

- IT IS APPROPRIATE TO EVALUATE PERFORMANCE BY COMPARING ACTUAL COSTS WITH STANDARD COSTS, AND ANALYZING WHY ANY VARIANCES OCCURRED.

- THE REASON FOR CALCULATING VARIANCES IS TO ENCOURAGE ACTION TO ELIMINATE UNFAVORABLE VARIANCES AND CAPTURE FAVORABLE VARIANCES.

KEY POINTS

- VARIANCE TERMINOLOGY:

INPUT	QUANTITY VARIANCE	COST PER UNIT OF INPUT VARIANCE
RAW MATERIALS	USAGE	PRICE
DIRECT LABOR	EFFICIENCY	RATE
VAR. OVERHEAD	EFFICIENCY	SPENDING

- DIFFERENT MANAGERS ARE USUALLY RESPONSIBLE FOR THE QUANTITY AND COST PER UNIT OF INPUT VARIANCES. THAT IS WHY THEY ARE CALCULATED AND REPORTED SEPARATELY.

- THE REPORTING OF VARIANCES SHOULD LEAD TO BETTER COMMUNICATION AND COORDINATION OF ACTIVITIES.

FIXED COST VARIANCE ANALYSIS

KEY ISSUE

- FOR MANY FIRMS, FIXED MANUFACTURING OVERHEAD HAS BECOME MORE SIGNIFICANT THAN VARIABLE MANUFACTURING COSTS. THEREFORE, MANY FIRMS ARE INCREASING EFFORTS TO CONTROL FIXED OVERHEAD.

KEY POINTS

- VARIANCE TERMINOLOGY:

    - **BUDGET VARIANCE** IS THE DIFFERENCE BETWEEN BUDGETED FIXED OVERHEAD COSTS AND ACTUAL FIXED OVERHEAD COSTS.

    - **VOLUME VARIANCE** IS CAUSED BY THE DIFFERENCE BETWEEN THE PLANNED LEVEL OF ACTIVITY USED IN THE CALCULATION OF THE PREDETERMINED OVERHEAD APPLICATION RATE, AND THE ACTUAL LEVEL OF ACTIVITY.

    - THE SUM OF THE BUDGET VARIANCE AND THE VOLUME VARIANCE EQUALS THE OVERAPPLIED OR UNDERAPPLIED FIXED MANUFACTURING OVERHEAD.

CAPITAL BUDGETING

<u>WHAT'S GOING ON?</u>

- PROPOSED CAPITAL EXPENDITURES USUALLY INVOLVE
  RETURNS RECEIVED OVER EXTENDED PERIODS OF TIME,
  SO IT IS APPROPRIATE TO RECOGNIZE THE TIME VALUE
  OF MONEY WHEN EVALUATING WHETHER OR NOT THE
  INVESTMENT WILL GENERATE THE DESIRED ROI.

<u>KEY POINT</u>

- PRESENT VALUE ANALYSIS RECOGNIZES THE TIME
  VALUE OF MONEY.

<u>KEY ISSUE</u>

- PRESENT VALUE ANALYSIS USES:

    1. THE INVESTMENT AMOUNT
    2. THE EXPECTED CASH RETURNS, AND
    3. AN INTEREST RATE (COST OF CAPITAL),

    TO ANSWER THE FOLLOWING QUESTION:

> IS THE PRESENT VALUE OF THE FUTURE CASH
> FLOWS FROM THE INVESTMENT, DISCOUNTED
> AT THE COST OF CAPITAL, AT LEAST EQUAL TO
> THE AMOUNT THAT MUST BE INVESTED?

IF THE ANSWER IS "YES", THEN THE ROI ON THE
CAPITAL EXPENDITURE IS AT LEAST EQUAL TO THE
COST OF CAPITAL, AND THE INVESTMENT SHOULD
BE MADE.

83

CAPITAL BUDGETING ANALYSIS TECHNIQUES

METHODS THAT USE PRESENT VALUE ANALYSIS

- NET PRESENT VALUE (NPV) METHOD:

  - GIVEN A COST OF CAPITAL, COMPUTE THE PRESENT
    VALUE OF THE CASH RETURNS FROM THE INVESTMENT
    AND THEN SUBTRACT THE INVESTMENT REQUIRED.
    THIS DIFFERENCE IS THE NET PRESENT VALUE (NPV)
    OF THE PROJECT:

    > - IF THE NPV IS POSITIVE, ROI > COST OF CAPITAL,
    >   SO THE INVESTMENT SHOULD BE MADE.
    >
    > - IF THE NPV IS NEGATIVE, ROI < COST OF CAPITAL,
    >   SO THE INVESTMENT SHOULD NOT BE MADE.
    >
    > - IF THE NPV IS ZERO, ROI = COST OF CAPITAL,
    >   SO THE FIRM WOULD BE INDIFFERENT ABOUT
    >   THE INVESTMENT PROPOSAL.

- INTERNAL RATE OF RETURN (IRR) METHOD:

  - SOLVE FOR THE INTEREST RATE AT WHICH THE
    PRESENT VALUE OF THE CASH RETURNS EQUALS
    THE INVESTMENT REQUIRED. THIS IS THE PROPOSED
    INVESTMENT'S ROI -- REFERRED TO AS THE INTERNAL
    RATE OF RETURN (IRR).

  - THE INVESTMENT DECISION IS MADE BASED ON THE
    RELATIONSHIP BETWEEN THE PROJECT'S INTERNAL
    RATE OF RETURN (IRR) AND THE FIRM'S DESIRED ROI
    (COST OF CAPITAL).

CAPITAL BUDGETING ANALYSIS TECHNIQUES

METHODS THAT DO NOT USE PRESENT VALUE ANALYSIS

- PAYBACK METHOD:

    HOW LONG DOES IT TAKE FOR THE CASH FLOWS
    TO EQUAL THE AMOUNT OF THE INVESTMENT?

- ACCOUNTING RATE OF RETURN METHOD:

    WHAT IS THE ROI BASED ON FINANCIAL STATEMENT
    REPORTING OF THE INVESTMENT AND OPERATING
    RESULTS?

KEY ISSUE

- THESE METHODS ARE SIGNIFICANTLY FLAWED BECAUSE
  THEY IGNORE THE TIME VALUE OF MONEY.

Solutions to Odd-Numbered Problems

CHAPTER 1. *Accounting—Present and Past*

1-5. The principal factors Paul Alberga must consider are his competence and independence. Is he competent to prepare financial statements for a company that operates in a different industry than the one in which he works? A contingent fee arrangement would normally be considered an impairment of his independence because he would directly benefit if the loan were to be approved.

CHAPTER 2. *Financial Statements and Accounting Concepts/Principles*

2-1.

	Category	*Financial Statement(s)*
Cash	A	BS
Accounts payable	L	BS
Common stock	OE	BS,SOE
Depreciation expense	E	IS
Net sales	R	IS
Income tax expense	E	IS
Short-term investments	A	BS
Gain on sale of land	G	IS
Retained earnings	OE	BS,SOE
Dividends payable	L	BS
Accounts receivable	A	BS
Short-term debt	L	BS

2-3. Use the accounting equation to solve for the missing information.

Firm A:

```
    A    =    L    +   PIC   + ( Beg. RE  + NI -   DIV    = End. RE )
$420,000 = $215,000 + $75,000 + ( $78,000  +  ? - $50,000 =    ?     )
```

In this case, the ending balance of retained earnings must be determined first:
$420,000 = $215,000 + $75,000 + End. RE.
Retained earnings, 12/31/99 = **$130,000**
Once the ending balance of retained earnings is known, net income can be determined:
$78,000 + NI - $50,000 = $130,000
Net income for 1999 = **$102,000**

2-3. Firm B:

```
    A      =     L      +   PIC   +  (Beg.RE  +    NI     -    DIV    =  End. RE)
$540,000 = $145,000 +    ?    +  (   ?     + $83,000 - $19,000 = $310,000)
```

$540,000 = $145,000 + PIC + $310,000
Paid-in capital, 12/31/99 = **$85,000**
Beg. RE + $83,000 – $19,000 = $310,000
Retained earnings, 1/1/99 = **$246,000**

Firm C:

```
    A      =   L   +    PIC   + (  Beg.RE   +    NI     -    DIV    =  End. RE)
$325,000 =   ?   + $40,000 + ( $42,000  + $113,000 - $65,000 =    ?      )
```

In this case, the ending balance of retained earnings must be determined first:
$42,000 + $113,000 - $65,000 = End. RE
Retained earnings, 12/31/99 = **$90,000**

Once the ending balance of retained earnings is known, liabilities can be determined:
$325,000 = L + $40,000 + $90,000
Total liabilities, 12/31/99 = **$195,000**

2-5. Prepare the retained earning portion of a statement of changes in owners' equity for the year ended December 31, 1999:

Retained earnings, December 31, 1998.	$311,800
Less: Net loss for the year ended December 31, 1999..	(4,700)
Less: Dividends declared and paid in 1999	(18,500)
Retained earnings, December 31, 1999.	**$288,600**

2-7.

```
                                                   OE
                  A     =     L     +   PIC   +     RE
Beginning:   $12,400  =   $7,000  + $   0   +  $5,400
Changes:         ?    =   -1,200  +     0   +   3,000  (net income)
                                                        (dividends)
Ending:          ?    =     ?     +     0   +  $6,000
```

Solution approach:
*(Remember that **net assets** = Assets – Liabilities = Owners' equity = PIC + RE).*
Since paid-in capital did not change during the year, assume that the beginning and ending balances are $0. Thus, beginning retained earnings = $12,400 – $7,000 = **$5,400**, and ending

retained earnings = net assets at the end of the year = **$6,000**. By looking at the RE column, it can be seen that dividends must have been **$2,400**. Also by looking at the liabilities column, it can be seen that ending liabilities are **$5,800**, and therefore ending assets must be **$11,800**. Thus, total assets decreased by **$600** during the year ($12,400 − $11,800), which is equal to the net decrease on the right-hand side of the balance sheet (−$1,200 liabilities + $3,000 net income −$2,400 dividends = $600 net decrease in assets).

2-9. Set up the accounting equation and show the effects of the transactions described. Since total assets must equal total liabilities and owners' equity, the *unadjusted* owners' equity can be calculated by subtracting liabilities from the total of the assets given.

	Cash	+ Inventory	+ Accounts Receivable	+ Plant & Equipment =	Liabilities	+	Owners' Equity
				A =	**L**	**+**	**OE**
Data given	$ 22,800	+ 61,400	+ 114,200	+ 265,000 =	305,600	+	157,800
Liquidation of inventory *	+49,120	−61,400					−12,280
Collection of acc. rec. *	+108,490		−114,200				−5,710
Sale of plant & equipment *	+190,000			−265,000			−75,000
Payment of liabilities	−305,600				−305,600		
Balance	$ 64,810	+ 0	+ 0	+ 0 =	0	+	$ 64,810

* The effects of these transactions on owners' equity represent losses from the sale (or collection) of the non-cash assets.

2-11. a. Accounts receivable .... $ 33,000
Cash 9,000
Supplies 6,000
Merchandise inventory 31,000
Total current assets .... **$ 79,000**

b. Accounts payable .... $ 23,000
Long-term debt 40,000
Common stock... 10,000
Retained earnings.. 59,000
Total liabilities and owners' equity **$132,000**

2-11. c.

Sales revenue	$140,000
Cost of goods sold	(90,000)
Gross profit	$ 50,000
Service revenue	20,000
Depreciation expense	(12,000)
Supplies expense	(14,000)
Earnings from operations (operating income)	**$ 44,000**

d.

Earnings from operations (operating income)	$ 44,000
Interest expense	(4,000)
Earnings before taxes	$ 40,000
Income tax expense	(12,000)
Net income	**$ 28,000**

e. $12,000 income tax expense / $40,000 earnings before taxes = **30% tax rate**

f.

Retained earnings, January 1, 1999	?
Net income for the year	$ 28,000
Dividends declared and paid during the year	(16,000)
Retained earnings, December 31, 1999	$ 59,000

Solving the model, the beginning retained earnings balance must have been **$47,000**, because the account balance increased by $12,000 during the year to an ending balance of $59,000.

2-13. a.

BREANNA, INC.
Income Statement
For the Year Ended December 31, 1999

Sales	$200,000
Cost of goods sold	(128,000)
Gross profit	$ 72,000
Selling, general, and administrative expenses	(34,000)
Earnings from operations (operating income)	$ 38,000
Interest expense	(6,000)
Earnings before taxes	$ 32,000
Income tax expense	(8,000)
Net income	$ 24,000

2-13. a.

BREANNA, INC.
Statement of Changes in Owners' Equity
For the Year Ended December 31, 1999

Paid-in capital:

Common stock		$ 90,000
Retained earnings:		
Beginning balance	$ 23,000	
Net income for the year	24,000	
Less: Dividends declared and paid during the year	(12,000)	
Ending balance		35,000
Total owners' equity		$125,000

BREANNA, INC.
Balance Sheet
December 31, 1999

Assets:

Cash	$ 65,000	
Accounts receivable	10,000	
Merchandise inventory	37,000	
Total current assets		$112,000
Equipment	120,000	
Less: Accumulated depreciation	(52,000)	68,000
Total assets		$180,000

Liabilities:

Accounts payable	$ 15,000	
Long-term debt	40,000	
Total liabilities		$ 55,000

Owners' Equity:

Common stock	$ 90,000	
Retained earnings	35,000	
Total owners' equity		$125,000
Total liabilities and owners' equity		$180,000

b. $8,000 income tax expense / $32,000 earnings before taxes = **25% tax rat**e.

c. $6,000 interest expense / $40,000 long-term debt = **15% interest rate.** This assumes that the year-end balance of long-term debt is representative of the *average* long-term debt account balance throughout the year.

d. $90,000 common stock / 9,000 shares = **$10 per share par value.**

e. $12,000 dividends declared and paid/ $24,000 net income = **50%**. This assumes that the board of directors has a policy to pay dividends in proportion to earnings.

2-15. a. Retained earnings, January 1, 1999 .... $ 75,000
 Net income for the year ....   ?
 Dividends declared and paid during the year ....   (17,000)
 Retained earnings, December 31, 1999 .... $ 70,000

Solving for the missing amount, net income for the year is **$12,000.**

 Revenues..... .... $120,000
 Expenses..... ....   ?
 Net income.. .... $ 12,000

Solving for the missing amount, total expenses for the year are **$108,000.**

GARBER, INC.
Statement of Cash Flows
For the Year Ended December 31, 1999

 Cash flows from operating activities .... $ 27,000
 Cash flows from investing activities   0
 Cash flows from financing activities ....   (12,000)
 Net increase in cash for the year .... $ 15,000
 Cash balance, January 1, 1999   35,000
 Cash balance, December 31, 1999 .. .. $ 50,000

c. Depreciation expense of $15,000 was added back to net income to arrive at the cash
 flows from operating activities. (Since no production equipment was purchased or sold
 during the year, the $15,000 decrease in net production equipment is attributable to
 depreciation expense.)

d. Issuance of common stock............. .... $ 10,000
 Repayment of long-term debt ....   (5,000)
 Payment of cash dividends............. ....   (17,000)
 Net cash used for financing activities .... $(12,000)

e. Garber, Inc., is better off at the end of the year. Although total assets did not change
 during the year, liabilities decreased by $5,000 and total owners' equity increased by
 $5,000. Net income of $12,000 was earned, and this is the bottom-line measure of
 profitability. In addition, the firm generated $27,000 in cash flows from operations
 and $10,000 from the sale of common stock (a financing activity). These cash flows
 allowed Garber, Inc., to reduce its long-term debt by $5,000, pay dividends of $17,000,
 and still have a net increase in cash of $15,000.

2-17.

	Assets =	Liabilities +	Owners' Equity
a. Borrowed cash on a bank loan	+	+	NE
b. Paid an account payable	–	–	NE
c. Sold common stock	+	NE	+
d. Purchased merchandise inventory on account	+	+	NE
e. Declared and paid dividends	–	NE	–
f. Collected an account receivable	NE	NE	NE
g. Sold inventory on account at a profit	+	NE	+
h. Paid operating expenses in cash	–	NE	–
i. Repaid principal and interest on a bank loan	–	–	–

2-19. Amounts shown in the balance sheet below reflect the following use of the data given:

a. An asset should have a "probable future economic benefit"; therefore the accounts receivable are stated at the amount expected to be collected from customers.

b. Assets are reported at original cost, not current "worth." Depreciation in accounting reflects the spreading of the cost of an asset over its estimated useful life.

c. Assets are reported at original cost, not at an assessed or appraised value.

d. The amount of the note payable is calculated using the accounting equation, $A = L + OE$. Total assets can be determined based on items (a), (b), and (c); total owners' equity is known after considering item (e); and the note payable is the difference between total liabilities and the accounts payable.

e. Retained earnings is the difference between cumulative net income and cumulative dividends.

Assets:			Liabilities and Owners' Equity:	
Cash		$ 700	Note payable	$ 2,200
Accounts receivable		3,400	Accounts payable	3,400
Land		7,000	Total liabilities	$ 5,600
Automobile	$9,000		Common stock	8,000
Less: Accumulated depreciation	(3,000)	6,000	Retained earnings	3,500
			Total owners' equity	11,500
Total assets		$17,100	Total liabilities and owners' equity	$17,100

2-21.

OPTICO, INC.
Balance Sheet
December 31, 1999

Assets		Liabilities	
Current assets:		Current liabilities:	
Cash	$ 10,000	Short-term debt	$ 0
Accounts receivable	10,000	Accounts payable	20,000
Merchandise inventory	45,000	Other accrued liabilities	9,000
Total current assets	$ 65,000	Total current liabilities	$ 29,000
Plant and Equipment:		Long-term debt	39,000
Land	$ 8,000	Total liabilities	$ 68,000
Building	122,000	**Owners' Equity**	
Less: Accumulated depreciation	(51,000)	Common stock, no par	$ 10,000
Total plant and equipment	$ 79,000	Retained earnings *	66,000
		Total owners' equity	$ 76,000
Total assets	$144,000	Total liabilities and owners' equity	$144,000

* Retained earnings, 12/31/98	$ 41,000
Add: Net income	37,000
Less: Dividends	(12,000)
Retained earnings, 12/31/99	$ 66,000

2-23. a.

	1997	1996
Net sales and other income	$106,146	$ 94,749
Less: Other income	(1,287)	(1,122)
Net sales	$104,859	$ 93,627
Less: Cost of goods sold	(83,663)	(74,564)
Gross profit	$ 21,196	$ 19,063
Gross profit/net sales	20.21%	20.36%

The change in the gross profit/net sales ratio during the year ended January 31, 1997 was insignificant, suggesting that Wal-Mart's sales mix and pricing strategies have been remarkably consistent.

b.

	1997	1996
Gross profit	$ 21,196	$ 19,063
Operating, selling, and general and administrative expenses	(16,788)	(14,951)
Operating income	$ 4,408	$ 4,112
Operating income/net sales	4.20%	4.39%

2-23. b. The change in operating income as a percentage of net sales during the fiscal year ended on January 31, 1997 was slightly unfavorable, due primarily to higher operating expenses of nearly $2 billion as compared to the prior year.

c.

	1997	1996
Operating income	$ 4,408	$ 4,112
Other income	1,287	1,122
Interest costs	(845)	(888)
Income before taxes	$ 4,850	$ 4,346
Provision for income taxes	(1,794)	(1,606)
Net income	$ 3,056	$ 2,740

Solution approach: The key to answering part *c* correctly is to recast the income statement data as shown above, remembering to include "Other income" as a source of non-operating revenue.

2-25. You should be prepared to share the different kinds of assets and liabilities that you have identified, and to discuss what you regard to be the characteristics of assets and liabilities.

CHAPTER 3. *Fundamental Interpretations Made from Financial Statement Data*

3-1. a.

$$ROI = \frac{\text{Amount of return}}{\text{Amount invested}} \qquad \text{Julie:} \quad \frac{\$50}{\$560} = \textbf{8.93\%} \qquad \text{Sam:} \quad \frac{\$53}{\$620} = \textbf{8.55\%}$$

Julie's investment is preferred because it has the higher ROI.

b. Risk is a principal factor to be considered.

3-3. *Solution approach:* Calculate the amount of return from each alternative, then calculate the ROI of the additional return from the higher paying investment relative to the $50 that must be invested to get the higher return.

ROI * amount invested = amount of return.
Alternative # 1...   10% * $500 = **$50 return.**
Alternative # 2...   10.5% * $550 = **$57.75 return.**

The extra amount of return of $7.75 on an additional investment of $50 is an ROI of 15.5%. **($7.75 / $50 = 15.5%)**. Therefore, do not pay an interest rate of more than 15.5% to borrow the additional $50 needed for the higher yield investment.

3-5. The following model can be used to help answer any questions related to ROI:

ROI	=	MARGIN	x	TURNOVER

$$\frac{\text{NET INCOME}}{\text{AVERAGE TOTAL ASSETS}} = \frac{\text{NET INCOME}}{\text{SALES}} \quad x \quad \frac{\text{SALES}}{\text{AVERAGE TOTAL ASSETS}}$$

a. 18% ROI = 12% Margin * ($600,000 Sales / Average total assets)
Average total assets = **$400,000**

b. ROI = ($78,000 Net income / $950,000 Average total assets) = **8.21%**

   1.3 Turnover =   (Sales / $950,000 Average total assets)
              Sales = **$1,235,000**

   Margin = ($78,000 Net income / $1,235,000 Sales) = **6.32%**

   ROI = (6.32% Margin * 1.3 Turnover) = 8.21%

c. 7.37% ROI = (Margin * 2.1 Turnover)
    Margin = **3.5%**

3-7. Remember that "net assets" is the same as "owners' equity."

Beginning net assets	$346,800
Add: Net income	42,300
Less: Dividends	(12,000)
Ending net assets	$377,100

ROE = Net income / Average owners' equity
    = $42,300 / (($346,800 + $377,100) / 2) = **11.7%**

3-9. a. ROI = (32% Margin * 0.4 Turnover) = **12.8%**

   0.4 Turnover = (Sales / $800,000 Average total assets)
   Sales = **$320,000**

b. 12.8% ROI = (20% Margin * Turnover)
   Turnover = **0.64**

   0.64 Turnover = (Sales / $800,000 Average total assets)
   Sales = **$512,000**

3-11. a. ROI = Margin * Turnover

= (Net income / Net revenues) * (Net revenues / Average total assets)

= ($5,157 / $20,847) * ($20,847 / (($17,504 + $23,735) / 2))

= (24.7% Margin * 1.01 Turnover) = **25.0%**

b. ROE = Net income / Average stockholders' equity

= $5,157 / (($12,140 + $16,872) / 2) = **35.6%**

c. Working capital = Current assets - Current liabilities

	12/28/96	12/30/95
Current assets.......	$13,684	$ 8,097
- Current liabilities..	(4,863)	(3,619)
= Working capital....	**$ 8,821**	**$ 4,478**

d. Current ratio = Current assets / Current liabilities

	12/28/96	12/30/95
Current assets.......	$13,864	$ 8,097
/ Current liabilities..	4,863	3,619
= Current ratio	**2.85**	**2.24**

e. Acid-test ratio = <u>(Cash + Short-term securities + Accounts and Notes receivable)</u>
Current liabilities

	12/28/96	12/30/95
Cash and cash equivalents	$ 4,165	$ 1,463
Short-term investments................	3,742	995
Trading assets	87	--
Accounts receivable, net.............	3,723	3,116
Total (quick assets)	$11,717	$ 5,574
Total (quick assets)	$11,717	$ 5,574
/ Current liabilities..	4,873	3,619
= Acid-test ratio	**2.40**	**1.54**

3-13. a. Working capital = Current assets - Current liabilities

	1/31/99	1/31/98
Current assets (A)	$ 14	$ 18
Current liabilities (B)...................	(9)	(6)
Working capital (A - B)................	**$ 5**	**$ 12**
Current ratio (A / B)	**1.56**	**3.0**

b. Even though the firm has more cash at January 31, 1999, it is less liquid based on the working capital and current ratio measures. The firm owes more on accounts payable, and has less inventory to sell and fewer accounts receivable to collect, as compared to January 31, 1998.

c. Accounts receivable were collected, inventories were reduced, and current liabilities increased. These changes and the increase in cash are all possible, because changes in a firm's cash position and its profitability are not directly related.

3-15. a.

	Do Not Prepay *Accounts Payable*	*Prepay* *Accounts Payable*
Current assets (A) ..	$ 12,639	$ 8,789
Current liabilities (B)	(7,480)	(3,630)
Working capital (A - B)	**$ 5,159**	**$ 5,159**
Current ratio (A / B)	**1.69**	**2.42**

Payment of the accounts payable does not affect working capital, but does improve the current ratio. Is this balance sheet "window dressing" worth the opportunity cost of not being able to invest the cash? Remember, once the payment is made, the cash is in someone else's hands.

b.

	Without Loan	*With Loan*
Current assets (A) ...	$ 12,639	$ 17,639
Current liabilities (B)	(7,480)	(12,480)
Working capital (A - B)	**$ 5,159**	**$ 5,159**
Current ratio (A / B)	**1.69**	**1.41**

If the loan is taken after the end of the fiscal year, the current ratio on the year-end balance sheet will be higher than if the loan is taken before the end of the year. Working capital is not affected. Thus, it makes sense to wait until after the end of the year to borrow on a short-term basis, unless cash is needed immediately.

3-17. a.

	1996	*1995*
Cash and cash equivalents	$ 516,360	$ 169,429
Accounts receivable, net	449,723	405,283
Total quick assets for acid-test ratio (A)	$ 966,083	$ 574,712
Inventory	278,043	224,916
Other current assets.	74,216	66,561
Total current assets (B)	$1,318,342	$ 866,189

3-17. a. Notes payable... $ 15,041 $ 13,564
(cont.) Accounts payable...   411,788   235,064
           Accrued liabilities..   190,762   108,976
           Accrued royalties payable...   125,270   123,385
           Customer prepayments...   16,574   16,397
           Income taxes payable..   40,334   27,905
           Total current liabilities (C).. $ 799,769 $ 525,291

           Working capital (B + C).. $ **518,573** $ **340,898**
           Current ratio (B / C) **1.65**   **1.65**
           Acid-test ratio (A / C) **1.21**   **1.09**

   b.   *1996*   *1995*
           Common stock and additional paid-in capital.................. $ 290,280 $ 281,193
           Retained earnings...   524,712   274,033
           Total stockholders' equity... $ 814,992 $ 555,226

           ROE = Net income / Average stockholders' equity
           1996 = $250,679 / (($555,226 + $814,992) / 2) = **36.6%**
           1995 = $172,981 / (($376,035 + $555,226) / 2) = **37.1%**

   c. ROI = Margin * Turnover
               = (Net income / Net sales) * (Net sales / Average total assets)

           1996 = ($250,679 / $5,035,228) * ($5,035,228 / (($1,124,011 + $1,673,411) / 2))
                  = **(5.0% Margin * 3.60 Turnover) = 17.9% ROI**
           1995 = ($172,981 / $3,676,328) * ($3,676,328 / (($770,580 + $1,124,011) / 2))
                  = **(4.7% Margin * 3.88 Turnover) = 18.3% ROI**

   d. Gateway 2000's liquidity ratios have been well managed, and are not of great concern.
        Working capital expanded rapidly during 1996, especially with respect to cash and cash
        equivalents which is likely to be a reflection of the company's tremendous sales growth.
        Gateway 2000's profitability has been outstanding! Although the personal computer
        market continues to grow each year, an ROI in the range of 18% may be difficult to
        maintain for an extended period of time. Gateway 2000's ROE was significantly higher
        than ROI during both years, which indicates that the company is making effective use of
        borrowed funds—that is, the company is using borrowed funds to increase the return to
        its owners. (The idea of *financial leverage* will be introduced in Chapter 7 and
        expanded upon in Chapter 11.) In Gateway 2000's case, nearly all of the company's
        liabilities are current, and non-interest bearing—which effectively means that the
        company is able to borrow money for free and then put it to use to enhance their
        stockholders' ROE.

e. If stockholders were to have received dividends from Gateway 2000, they would not have been likely to earn an ROI of 17.9% in 1996, or 18.3% in 1995, by investing in other firms. Thus, stockholders of highly profitable firms such as Gateway 2000, Inc., are not inclined to place strong dividend pressures on the board of directors. This is especially true if the firm can further enhance their ROE through the positive use financial leverage. Many stockholders also wish to avoid the tax consequences of current dividends, and generally favor "growth" oriented stocks.

CHAPTER 4. *The Bookkeeping Process and Transaction Analysis*

4-1.

		ASSETS			=	LIABILITIES	+		OWNERS' EQUITY		
Trans-action	Cash +	Accounts Receivable +	Merchandise Inventory +	Equipment =		Notes Payable +	Accounts Payable +	Paid-In Capital +		Revenues –	Expenses
a.	+8,000							+8,000			
b.	+5,000					+5,000					
c.	–1,750			+1,750							
d.	–1,400										–1,400
e.	–9,000		+15,000				+6,000				
f.	+6,500		–4,000							+6,500	–4,000
g.							+100				–100
h.	–1,200		+4,200				+3,000				
i.	+3,900	+9,600	–9,000							+13,500	–9,000
j.							+3,500*				–3,500
k.	+3,160	–3,160									
l.	–4,720						–4,720				

$$\underline{8,490} + \underline{6,440} + \underline{6,200} + \underline{1,750} = \underline{5,000} + \underline{7,880} + \underline{8,000} + \underline{20,000} - \underline{18,000}$$

Month-end totals: **Assets $22,880 = Liabilities $12,880 + Owners' equity $10,000**

Net income for the month: **Revenues $20,000 – Expenses $18,000 = Net income $2,000**

* Ordinarily, the Wages Payable account would be increased for employee wage expense that has been incurred but not yet paid.

4-3. a. Dr. Cash.. $ 8,000
Cr. Paid-In Capital .... $ 8,000

4-3. b. Dr. Cash... $ 5,000
      Cr.   Note Payable... $ 5,000

  c. Dr. Equipment.. 1,750
      Cr.   Cash.. 1,750

  d. Dr. Rent Expense.. 1,400
      Cr.   Cash.. 1,400

  e. Dr. Merchandise Inventory................................... 15,000
      Cr.   Cash.. 9,000
      Cr.   Accounts Payable... 6,000

  f. Dr. Cash... 6,500
      Cr.   Sales Revenue.. 6,500

      Dr.   Cost of Goods Sold... 4,000
      Cr.   Merchandise Inventory................................... 4,000

  g. Dr. Advertising Expense... 100
      Cr.   Accounts Payable... 100

  h. Dr. Merchandise Inventory................................... 4,200
      Cr.   Cash.. 1,200
      Cr.   Accounts Payable... 3,000

  i. Dr. Cash... 3,900
      Dr.   Accounts Receivable....................................... 9,600
      Cr.   Sales Revenue.. 13,500

      Dr.   Cost of Goods Sold... 9,000
      Cr.   Merchandise Inventory................................... 9,000

  j. Dr. Wages Expense... 3,500
      Cr.   Accounts (or Wages) Payable......................... 3,500

  k. Dr. Cash... 3,160
      Cr.   Accounts Receivable....................................... 3,160

  l. Dr. Accounts Payable.. 4,720
      Cr.   Cash.. 4,720

4-5.	*Transaction/Situation*	*A*	=	*L*	+	*OE*	*Net Income*
	a. Example transaction.	Supplies -1,400					Supplies Exp -1,400
	b. Paid an insurance premium of $480 for the coming year. An asset, prepaid insurance, was debited	Prepaid Insurance +480 Cash -480					
	c. Paid $3,200 of wages for the current month	Cash -3,200					Wages Exp -3,200
	d. Received $250 of interest income for the current month	Cash +250					Interest Inc +250
	e. Accrued $700 of commissions payable to sales staff for the current month ...			Commissions Payable +700			Commissions Expense -700
	f. Accrued $130 of interest expense at the end of the month....................			Interest Pay +130			Interest Exp -130
	g. Received $2,100 on accounts receivable accrued at the end of the prior month	Cash +2,100 Accounts Rec -2,100					
	h. Purchased $600 of merchandise inventory from a supplier on account	Merch Inventory +600		Accounts Payable +600			
	i. Paid $160 of interest expense for the month......	Cash -160					Interest Exp -160
	j. Accrued $800 of wages at the end of the current month..			Wages Pay +800			Wages Exp -800
	k. Paid $500 of accounts payable.........	Cash -500		Accounts Pay -500			

a. Dr. Supplies Expense...................		$1,400	
Cr. Supplies			$1,400
b. Dr. Prepaid Insurance.................		480	
Cr. Cash..........			480

4-5. c. Dr. Wages Expense $3,200
          Cr. Cash $3,200

     d. Dr. Cash 250
          Cr. Interest Income 250

     e. Dr. Commissions Expense 700
          Cr. Commissions Payable 700

     f. Dr. Interest Expense 130
          Cr. Interest Payable 130

     g. Dr. Cash 2,100
          Cr. Accounts Receivable 2,100

     h. Dr. Merchandise Inventory 600
          Cr. Accounts Payable 600

     i. Dr. Interest Expense 160
          Cr. Cash 160

     j. Dr. Wages Expense 800
          Cr. Wages Payable 800

     k. Dr. Accounts Payable 500
          Cr. Cash 500

4-7.

Transaction/Situation	*A*	=	*L*	+	*OE*	*Net Income*
a. Example transaction	+550					+550
b. Paid an insurance premium of $360 for the coming year. An asset, "prepaid insurance" was debited	−360 +360					
c. Recognized insurance for one month from the above premium via a reclassification adjusting entry	−30					−30
d. Paid $800 of wages accrued at the end of the prior month	−800		−800			

Transaction/Situation	A	=	L	+	OE	Net Income
e. Paid $2,600 of wages for the current month	-2,600					-2,600
f. Accrued $600 of wages at the end of the current month..			+600			-600
g. Received cash of $1,500 on accounts receivable accrued in prior month	+1,500 -1,500					

a. Dr. Accounts Receivable .... $ 550
      Cr. Service Revenue .... $ 550

b. Dr. Prepaid Insurance.................   360
      Cr. Cash..........   360

c. Dr. Insurance Expense.................   30
      Cr. Prepaid Insurance.................   30

d. Dr. Wages Payable   800
      Cr. Cash..........   800

e. Dr. Wages Expense.   2,600
      Cr. Cash   2,600

f. Dr. Wages Expense.   600
      Cr. Wages Payable   600

g. Dr. Cash   1,500
      Cr. Accounts Receivable   1,500

4-9. a. Dr. Cash..... .... $1,000,000
      Cr. Common Stock $1,000,000

b. Dr. Cash.....   500,000
      Cr. Notes Payable.................   500,000

c. Dr. Salaries Expense   380,000
      Cr. Cash..........   380,000

d. Dr. Merchandise Inventory...........   640,000
      Cr. Accounts Payable.............   640,000

4-9. e. Dr. Accounts Receivable $910,000
　　　　　Cr.　Sales $910,000
　　　　Dr. Cost of Goods Sold... 580,000
　　　　　Cr. Merchandise Inventory 580,000

　　f. Dr. Rent Expense 110,000
　　　　　Cr.　Cash.. 110,000

　　g. Dr. Equipment.. 150,000
　　　　　Cr.　Cash.. 50,000
　　　　　Cr.　Accounts Payable 100,000

　　h. Dr.　Accounts Payable... 720,000
　　　　　Cr.　Cash.. 720,000

　　i. Dr. Utilities Expense 36,000
　　　　　Cr.　Cash.. 36,000

　　j. Dr. Cash.. 825,000
　　　　　Cr.　Accounts Receivable 825,000

　　k. Dr. Interest Expense 60,000
　　　　　Cr.　Interest Payable.. 60,000

　　l. Dr. Rent Expense 10,000
　　　　　Cr.　Rent Payable (or Accounts Payable) 10,000

Balance Sheet			Income Statement		
Assets	=	Liabilities + Owners' Equity	← Net income	= Revenues −	Expenses
a. Cash		Common Stock			
+1,000,000		+1,000,000			
b. Cash		Notes Payable			
+500,000		+500,000			
c. Cash					Salaries Exp
−380,000					−380,000
d. Merchandise		Accounts			
Inventory		Payable			
+640,000		+640,000			

Balance Sheet				**Income Statement**	
Assets	**= Liabilities**	**+ Owners' Equity**	**← Net income**	**= Revenues**	**− Expenses**
e. Accounts Rec				Sales	
+910,000				+910,000	Cost of
Merchandise Inv					Goods Sold
−580,000					−580,000
f. Cash					Rent Exp
−110,000					−110,000
g. Equipment	Accounts				
+150,000	Payable				
Cash	+100,000				
−50,000					
h. Cash	Accounts				
−720,000	Payable −720,000				
i. Cash					Utilities Exp
−36,000					−36,000
j. Cash					
+825,000					
Accounts Rec					
−825,000					
k.	Interest Pay				Interest Exp
	+60,000				−60,000
l.	Rent Payable				Rent Exp
	+10,000				−10,000

4-11. Prepare an analysis of the change in stockholders' equity for the month, showing the effects of the net loss and dividends:

Balance, February 1, 1999		$ 630,000
Revenues	$123,000	
Expenses	(131,000)	(8,000)
Dividends		(12,000)
Balance, February 28, 1999		**$ 610,000**

4-13. a. Net sales $741,000
Cost of goods sold ... . (329,000)
Gross profit.. 412,000
General and administrative expenses .... (83,000)
Advertising expense . ... (76,000)
Other selling expenses .... (42,000)
Income from operations (operating income) **$211,000**

b. Income from operations (operating income). $211,000
Income tax expense.. .... (83,000)
Income before extraordinary items... 128,000
Extraordinary loss from earthquake, net of tax savings of $25,000. .... (61,000)
Net income... .... **$ 67,000**

4-15. a. *4/1/1999*
Dr. Note Receivable $6,000
  Cr. Accounts Receivable $6,000

b. *12/31/1999*
Dr. Interest Receivable..................... 675
  Cr. Interest Revenue ($6,000 * 15% * 9/12)... 675

c. *3/31/2000*
Dr. Cash..... 6,900
  Cr. Note Receivable 6,000
  Cr. Interest Receivable 675
  Cr. Interest Revenue.............. 225

In entry *c*, only $675 of the total interest of $900 had been accrued, so the Interest Receivable account is reduced by the $675 that had been accrued in 1999; the other $225 that is received is recorded as interest revenue for 2000, the year in which it was earned.

Balance Sheet			Income Statement		
Assets	**= Liabilities**	**+ Owners' Equity**	**← Net income**	**= Revenues**	**– Expenses**

a. *Receipt of note on April 1, 1999*:
Notes Receivable
+6,000
Account Receivable
−6,000

Balance Sheet	Income Statement
Assets = Liabilities + Owners' Equity	**← Net income = Revenues − Expenses**

b. *Accrual of 9 month's interest at December 31, 1999*:

Interest
Receivable
+675

Interest
Revenue
+675

c. *Collection of note and interest at March 31, 2000*:

Cash
+6,900
Note Receivable
−6,000
Interest Receivable
−675

Interest
Revenue
+225

4-17. a. *1/10/99*

Dr. Paper Napkin Expense (or Supplies Expense)............	$4,800	
Cr. Cash........		$4,800

To record as an expense the cost of paper napkins purchased for cash.

b. *1/31/99*

Dr. Paper Napkins on Hand (or Supplies).........	3,850	
Cr. Paper Napkin Expense (or Supplies Expense)...		3,850

To remove from the expense account and set up as an asset the cost
of paper napkins on hand January 31.

c. *1/10/99*

Dr. Paper Napkins on Hand (or Supplies).........	4,800	
Cr. Cash		4,800

To set up as an asset the cost of paper napkins purchased for cash.

d. *1/31/99*

Dr. Paper Napkin Expense (or Supplies Expense).........	950	
Cr. Paper Napkins on Hand. (or Supplies)..		950

To record the cost of paper napkins used in January.

Balance Sheet	Income Statement
Assets = Liabilities + Owners' Equity	**← Net income = Revenues − Expenses**

a. *1/10/99. Record as an expense the cost of paper napkins purchased for cash:*

Cash
−4,800

Supplies
Expense
−4,800

4-17.

<u>Balance Sheet</u>	<u>Income Statement</u>
Assets = Liabilities + Owners' Equity	← **Net income = Revenues – Expenses**

b. *1/31/99. Remove from the expense account and set up as an asset the cost of the paper napkins on hand January 31.*

Supplies
+3,850

(Note: A reduction in Supplies Expense.)

Supplies
Expense
+3,850

c. *1/10/99. Set up as an asset the cost of paper napkins purchased for cash.*

Supplies
+4,800
Cash
−4,800

d. *1/31/99. Record the cost of paper napkins used in January.*

Supplies
−950

Supplies
Expense
−950

e. Each approach results in the same expense for January ($950) and the same asset amount ($3,850) reported on the January 31 balance sheet.

4-19.

BIG BLUE RENTAL CORP. **Income Statement—August 1999**		*Adjustments / Corrections*		
	Preliminary	*Debit*	*Credit*	*Final*
Commission revenue	$ 4,500	$	$a) 200	$ 4,700
Interest revenue.........	850		f) 140	990
Total revenues	$ 5,350	$	$ 340	$ 5,690
Rent expense..	$ 510	$	$e) 340	$ 170
Wages expense.........	1,190	d) 130		1,320
Supplies expense........	--	b) 180		180
Interest expense	--	c) 20		20
Total expenses	$ 1,700	$ 330	$ 340	$ 1,690
Net income.....	$ 3,650	$ 330	$ 680	$ 4,000

BIG BLUE RENTAL CORP.
Balance Sheet—August 31, 1999

Cash....	$ 400	$	$	$ 400
Notes receivable....	13,000			13,000
Commissions receivable....	--	a) 200		200
Interest receivable....	--	f) 140		140
Prepaid rent....	--	e) 340		340
Supplies....	650		b) 180	470
Total assets....	$ 14,050	$ 680	$ 180	$14,550
Accounts payable....	$ 120	$	$	$ 120
Note payable....	2,400			2,400
Interest payable....	40		c) 20	60
Wages payable....	--		d) 130	130
Dividend payable....	--		g)1,400	1,400
Total liabilities....	$ 2,560	$	$ 1,550	$ 4,110
Paid-in capital....	$ 2,400	$	$	$ 2,400
Retained earnings:				
Balance, August 1....	$ 5,440	$	$	$ 5,440
Net income....	3,650	330	680	4,000
Dividends....	--	g) 1,400		(1,400)
Balance, August 31....	$ 9,090	$ 1,730	$ 680	$ 8,040
Total owners' equity....	$ 11,490	$ 1,730	$ 680	$10,440
Total liabilities and owners' equity....	$ 14,050	$ 1,730	$ 2,230	$14,550

Note: The net income line from the income statement is transferred down to the retained earnings section of the balance sheet. Remember, net income increases retained earnings, and net income is the link between the income statement and balance sheet. **This is an excellent self study / review problem because it requires an understanding of much of the material that has been presented to this point in the course.**

Calculation for part c:
$2,400 Notes payable * 10% interest rate * 1/12 = **$20 accrued interest, one month.**
Thus, the $40 preliminary balance in the Interest Payable account makes sense because it represents interest for two months on the note payable that had been accrued between the last interest payment date (May 31) and the end of last month (July 31).

Calculation for part e:
Too much was recorded as Rent Expense in August because the $510 rent payment included a prepayment of the rent for September and October. Thus, the Prepaid Rent (asset) account should be recorded for $340 (2/3 * $510), and only $170 should be included as Rent Expense in the final August income statement.

4-21. a.

Accounts Receivable			
Beginning balance	$ 1,200	February collections	
February sales revenue	12,000	from customers	?
Ending balance	$ 900		

Solution: $1,200 + $12,000 - ? = $900
Cash collected from customers in February = **$12,300**

Dr. Accounts Receivable...........	$12,000	
Cr. Sales Revenue		$12,000
Revenue from credit sales.		

Dr. Cash...........	$12,300	
Cr. Accounts Receivable		$12,300
Collections from customers.		

b.

Supplies on Hand			
Beginning balance	$ 540	Cost of supplies used	$2,340
Cost of supplies purchased	?		
Ending balance	$ 730		

Solution: $540 + ? - $2,340 = $730
Cost of supplies purchased in February = **$2,530**

Dr. Supplies on Hand...............	$2,530	
Cr. Cash or Accounts Payable		$2,530
Supplies purchased during month.		

Dr. Supplies Expense	$2,340	
Cr. Supplies on Hand		$2,340
Supplies used during month		

c.

Wages Payable			
		Beginning balance	$ 410
Wages paid	$3,800	Wages accrued	4,100
		Ending balance	$?

Solution: $410 + $4,100 - $3,800 = ?
Wages payable at February 28 = **$710**

Dr. Wages Expense $4,100
    Cr. Wages Payable $4,100
    Wage expense accrued during month.

Dr. Wages Payable $3,800
    Cr. Cash..... .... $3,800
    Wages paid during month.

4-23. a. Net income for October would be overstated, because an expense was not recorded.

b. Net income for November would be understated, because November expenses would include an expense from October.

c. There wouldn't be any effect on net income for the two months combined, because the overstatement and understatement offset.

d. To match revenues and expenses, which results in more accurate financial statements.

4-25. a. Commissions expense. Since DeBauge Realtors, Inc., is a service firm, the company would not report cost of goods sold, and the other costs of operating the business are likely to be less than the commissions expense that would be paid to Jeff and Kristi, and to any non-owner sales associates employed by the firm.

b. Advertising expense is material in amount. The owners of the firm would be interested in knowing how much was spent on advertising so that an assessment could be made of the relative value received (i.e., commissions revenue per dollar spent on advertising).

c. $5 Interest Expense / $50 Note Payable = **10% effective interest rate**.

d. Operating income .... $ 55,000
Interest expense .... (5,000)
Earnings before taxes .... $ 50,000

    Average income tax rate = Income tax expense / Earnings before taxes
            = $16,000 / $50,000 = **32%**

e. Since there were no changes in paid-in capital during the year, the beginning paid-in capital would also be $20,000. Thus, the beginning retained earnings would be $30,000 (total owners' equity at December 31, 1998 of $50,000 less $20,000 paid-in capital).

4-25. e. Retained earnings, December 31, 1998 .... $ 30,000
       Add: Net income for the year ended December 31, 1999 34,000
       Less: Dividends declared and paid in 1999.. .... (34,000)
       Retained earnings, December 31, 1999 .... $ 30,000

      The company's dividend policy must be to distribute 100% of net income as dividends to its two stockholders. This is not uncommon for a closely-held corporation. In effect, this provides additional income to the owners besides the compensation included in the "Cost of services provided" on the income statement.

    f. The corporate form of organization protects the owners by providing *limited liability*, such that their personal assets that have not been invested in the business are free from the reach of the business creditors—even in corporate bankruptcy proceedings. The primary disadvantage of the corporate form is that business *profits are taxed twice*— once at the corporate level, and a second time at the individual level when dividends are paid to stockholders. For DeBauge Realty, Inc., the *corporation* incurred $16,000 of Income Tax Expense (based on $50,000 of earnings before taxes), and Jeff and Kristi will have to pay additional *individual* income taxes on the $34,000 received as dividends (at their marginal tax rate). In the partnership form of organization, the income earned by the business passes through to the owners, and no taxes are paid by the partnership.

    g. Businesses are often required to make quarterly tax payments based on their estimated annual taxable income, so DeBauge Realty, Inc., has probably already paid a substantial portion of its 1999 tax bill.

    h. Working capital = CA - CL   Current ratio = CA / CL

	12/31/99
Cash and short-term investments	$ 30,000
Accounts receivable, net..............	40,000
Total current assets (A).....:.........	$ 70,000
Accounts payable	$ 90,000
Income taxes payable	5,000
Total current liabilities (B).............	$ 95,000
Working capital (A - B).................	**$(25,000)**
Current ratio (A / B)	**0.74**

With negative working capital and a current ratio of less than 1.0, this company is experiencing a major liquidity crisis. Money will have to be borrowed on a long-term basis in order to pay current obligations unless the owners discontinue their practice of distributing 100% of net income as dividends.

i.

	ROI	=	MARGIN	x	TURNOVER
	$\dfrac{\text{NET INCOME}}{\text{AVERAGE TOTAL ASSETS}}$	=	$\dfrac{\text{NET INCOME}}{\text{SALES*}}$	x	$\dfrac{\text{SALES*}}{\text{AVERAGE TOTAL ASSETS}}$
	$\dfrac{\$34{,}000}{(\$205{,}000 + \$195{,}000)/2}$	=	$\dfrac{\$34{,}000}{\$142{,}000}$	x	$\dfrac{\$142{,}000}{(\$205{,}000 + \$195{,}000)/2}$
	17%	=	23.9%	x	0.71

* Commissions revenue is used for sales.

ROE = Net income / Average owners' equity
     = $34,000 / (($50,000 + $50,000) / 2)
     = **68%**

Trend comparisons of ROI and ROE cannot be made with data for only one year. For service firms such as DeBauge Realty, Inc., ROE is more significant to analysts than ROI because the investment in assets is relatively small (as compared to that required for merchandising and manufacturing firms). Thus, the ROI measure may be distorted by the small amount of "Average total assets" in the denominator. ROE provides a better measure for closely-held service firms because the stockholders are interested in their personal return.

CHAPTER 5. *Accounting for and Presentation of Current Assets*

5-1.

Balance per bank...........	$373	Balance per books.	$844
Less: Outstanding checks		Less: NSF check	(75)
($13 + $50)...	(63)	Error in recording check	
Add: Deposit in transit	450	(as $56 instead of $65).	(9)
Reconciled balance.......	$760	Reconciled balance	$760

5-3. a. Dr. Accounts Receivable *(for NSF check)*.. .... $75

Dr. Expense (or other account originally debited *for error*) 9

Cr. Cash........... .... $84

Balance Sheet			Income Statement		
Assets = **Liabilities** + **Owners' Equity** ←			**Net income** = **Revenues** −		**Expenses**
Accounts					Expense
Receivable					(or other
+75					account)
Cash −84					−9

b. The cash amount to be shown on the balance sheet is the $760 reconciled amount.

5-5. *Solution approach:* Set up a bank reconciliation in the usual format, enter the known information, and then work backwards to solve for the beginning balances in the company's Cash account and on the bank statement (these are referred to as the "Indicated balance" amounts in Exhibit 5-1 in the text).

Indicated balance (per bank)... $?		Indicated balance (per books)...... $?	
Less: Outstanding checks .... (3,000)		Less: NSF check . ... (400)	
Add: Deposits in transit.......... 2,100		Bank service charge........ .... (50)	
		Add: Check recording error........ 90	
Reconciled balance..... .... $4,800		Reconciled balance........ .... $4,800	

Key: To solve for the beginning (i.e., indicated) balances, the effects of reconciling items must be reversed out of the known ending (i.e., reconciled) balances.

a. Balance per Cash account before reconciliation = $4,800 - 90 + 400 + 50 = **$5,160**

b. Balance per bank before reconciliation = $4,800 - 2,100 + 3,000 = **$5,700**

5-7. a.

Allowance for Bad Debts		
Bad debt write-offs	1/1/99 balance	$13,400
(from 1/1 to 11/30) .... ?	Bad debt expense	
	(from 1/1 to 11/30)	21,462
	1/30/99 balance......	9,763
Adjustment required.................... ?		
	12/31/99 balance....	$ 9,500

Solution approach: The bad debt write-offs from January through November can be determined by subtracting the November 30 balance from the total of the beginning balance and the bad debts expense recognized for the first 11 months.

Bad debt write-offs = $13,400 + $21,462 - $9,763 = **$25,099**

b. The adjustment required at December 31, 1999 can be determined by comparing the November 30 balance in the allowance account to the desired ending balance.

Bad debt expense adjustment = $9,763 - $9,500 = **$263**

Dr. Allowance for Bad Debts	$263	
Cr. Bad Debts Expense		$263

To adjust the allowance account to the appropriate balance, and to correct the overstatement of expense recorded in the January through November period.

Balance Sheet			Income Statement		
Assets =	**Liabilities** +	**Owners' Equity** ←	**Net income** =	**Revenues** -	**Expenses**
Allowance	*(Note: A reduction in an expense increases net*				Bad Debts
for Bad Debts	*income, and a reduction in a contra-asset account*				Expense
+263	*increases total assets.)*				+263

c. The write-off will not have any effect on 1999 net income, because the write-off decreases both the accounts receivable asset and the allowance account contra-asset for equal amounts. Net income was affected when the expense was recognized.

5-9. a.

	Allowance for Bad Debts		
Bad debt write-offs		12/31/98 balance	$17,900
(during the year)....... $11,800		Bad debt expense..	?
		12/31/99 balance...	$ 9,500

Bad debt expense = $11,800 - $17,900 + $9,500 = **$3,400**

b. 1. Working capital would not be affected because the write-off entry decreases both the accounts receivable asset and the allowance account contra-asset by equal amounts.

Dr. Allowance for Bad Debts $3,100

    Cr. Accounts Receivable $3,100

To write off a past due account as uncollectible.

Balance Sheet			Income Statement		
Assets =	**Liabilities** +	**Owners' Equity** ←	**Net income** =	**Revenues** -	**Expenses**
Accounts					
Receivable					
-3,100					
Allowance					
for Bad Debts					
+3,100					

2. Net income would not be affected by the write-off entry because it does not adjust any expense or revenue accounts. ROI would not be affected because net income and total assets are not changed.

c. Sales were *probably* lower in 1999 because the accounts receivable balance has decreased during the year-−but this cannot be determined for sure without information about the cash collections of accounts receivable.

5-11 *Solution approach:* Net realizable value = Accounts receivable - Allowance for bad debts. The balance sheet presentation of this information at December 31, 1999 (ending balances) is provided with the problem information. Your task is to work backwards to determine the balances in these accounts at December 31, 1998 (beginning balances).

Accounts Receivable

12/31/98 balance	$?		Cash collections	$410,000
Sales on account	400,000		Accounts written off	15,000
12/31/99 balance	$ 50,000			

December 31, 1998 balance = $410,000 + $15,000 - $400,000 + $50,000 = **$75,000.** This makes sense because the credits to accounts receivable during the year for cash collections and write-offs exceeded the debit for sales on account.

Allowance for Bad Debts

Bad debt write-offs		12/31/98 balance	$?
(during the year) $15,000		Bad debt expense	12,000
		12/31/99 balance.	$ 7,000

December 31, 1998 balance = $7,000 + $15,000 - $12,000 = **$10,000.** This makes sense because Carr Co. wrote-off more accounts during the year than it added to the allowance account with the bad debts expense adjustment.

At December 31, 1998:

Accounts receivable	$75,000
Less: Allowance for bad debts....	(10,000) $65,000

5-13. a. 2% * $340,000,000 * 90% = **$6,120,000,** or $6.12 million.

b. Sales during last 10 days of the year = ($340,000,000 / 365) average day's sales *10 days = $9,315,000. Discount expected = 2% * $9,315,000 * 90%= **$167,670.** This should be the balance in the allowance for cash discounts.

c. By paying within 10 days instead of 30 days, the customers are "investing" funds for 20 days, and receiving slightly more than a 2 percent return on their investment (for a $100 obligation, the return is $2 on an investment of $98). But ROI is expressed as an annual percentage rate, and there are slightly more than 18 twenty-day periods in a year. The annual ROI is a little more than 36 percent. *See Business in Practice—Cash Discounts.*

5-15. a.

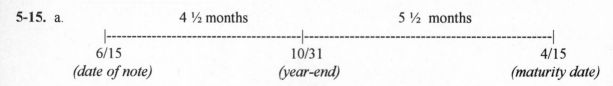

4 ½ months		5 ½ months
6/15	10/31	4/15
(date of note)	*(year-end)*	*(maturity date)*

Interest earned = $4,500 principal * 13.8% rate * 4½/12 time = **$232.88**

Dr. Interest Receivable................. .... $232.88
 Cr. Interest Revenue.............. .... $232.88
 To accrue interest earned on a short-term note.

Balance Sheet			Income Statement		
Assets =	**Liabilities** +	**Owners' Equity**	← **Net income** =	**Revenues** -	**Expenses**
Interest Receivable +232.88				Interest Revenue +232.88	

b. *Solution approach*: What accounts are affected, and how are they affected? Cash is being received for note principal and 10 month's interest. Notes receivable is reduced because the note is being paid off. Interest receivable accrued at 10/31 is being collected. Interest revenue for 5 ½ months from 10/31 to 4/15 has been earned.

Dr. Cash ($4,500 + ($4,500 * 13.8% * 10/12)) $5,017.50
 Cr. Note Receivable $4,500.00
 Cr. Interest Receivable (accrued at 10/31)..... .... 232.88
 Cr. Interest Revenue ($4,500 * 13.8% * 5 ½ /12)...... .... 284.62
 To record the collection of principal and interest at the maturity date of a short-term note (for which some interest had been previously accrued).

Balance Sheet			Income Statement		
Assets =	**Liabilities** +	**Owners' Equity**	← **Net income** =	**Revenues** -	**Expenses**
Cash +5,017.50 Note Receivable -4,500 Interest Receivable -232.88				Interest Revenue +284.62	

5-17. a. *Ending inventory calculations:*

	- - - - - - - - - FIFO - - - - - - - - - -	- - - - - - - - - - LIFO - - - - - - - - - -
Blowers........	10 of 11/7 @ 200 = $2,000	10 of 1/21 @ 200 = $2,000
Mowers........	20 of 9/20 @ 210 = $4,200 5 of 8/15 @ 215 = 1,075 $5,275	20 of 4/6 @ 210 = $4,200 5 of 5/22 @ 215 = 1,075 $5,275

5-17. a. ***Analysis of results:*** In this problem, there is no difference between ending inventories, and therefore there won't be any difference between cost of goods sold under either alternative. Neither the amount of goods available for sale (the sum of the beginning inventory and purchases amounts) nor the amount of ending inventory are affected by the inventory cost flow assumption used. Why? Look carefully at the cost per unit of inventory items that were purchased during the year. Notice that the costs per unit of the beginning inventory and the cost per unit of items purchased on September 20 and November 7 are the same.

    b. Probably LIFO, because the higher cost of the most recent (last-in) purchase will become part of the cost of goods sold, thus increasing cost, decreasing profits, and decreasing the firm's income tax obligation.

5-19. ***Solution approach:*** Calculate goods available for sale in units and dollars, and ending inventory in units. These amounts are the same for both FIFO and LIFO under either a periodic or a perpetual inventory system.

Beginning inventory	150 @ $30 =	$ 4,500	
Purchases	70 @ 33 =	2,310	
	90 @ 35 =	3,150	
	140 @ 36 =	5,040	
	50 @ 38 =	1,900	
Goods available for sale	500	$16,900	
Sales	(300)		
Ending inventory	200 units		

FIFO periodic cost of goods sold	150 @ $30 =	$ 4,500	
	70 @ 33 =	2,310	
	80 @ 35 =	2,800	$ 9,610
FIFO periodic ending inventory	10 @ 35 =	350	
	140 @ 36 =	5,040	
	50 @ 38 =	1,900	7,290
			$16,900
LIFO periodic cost of goods sold	50 @ $38 =	$1,900	
	140 @ 36 =	5,040	
	90 @ 35 =	3,150	
	20 @ 33 =	660	$10,750
LIFO periodic ending inventory	150 @ 30 =	$4,500	
	50 @ 33 =	1,650	6,150
			$16,900

b. FIFO perpetual cost of goods sold... ....

3/7 sale	100 @	$30 =	$3,000	
9/28 sale	50 @	30 =	1,500	
	50 @	33 =	1,650	
12/4 sale	20 @	33 =	660	
	80 @	35 =	2,800	$ 9,610

FIFO perpetual ending inventory ....

10 @	35 =	350	
140 @	36 =	5,040	
50 @	38 =	1,900	7,290
			$16,900

LIFO perpetual cost of goods sold .. ..

3/7 sale	70 @	$33 =	$2,310	
	30 @	30 =	900	
9/28 sale	100 @	36 =	3,600	
12/4 sale	50 @	38 =	1,900	
	40 @	36 =	1,440	
	10 @	35 =	350	$10,500

LIFO perpetual ending inventory.... ....

120 @	30 =	$3,600	
80 @	35 =	2,800	6,400
			$16,900

c. Under FIFO, the periodic and perpetual inventory systems *always* result in the same dollar amounts being assigned to ending inventory and cost of goods sold -- once first-in, always first-in -- and the timing of the application of the FIFO rules makes no difference. Under LIFO, the "last-in cost" changes each time another inventory item is purchased. Thus, the timing of the application of the LIFO rules is relevant, and different results will occur under the periodic and perpetual systems. These relationships are discussed in the Business in Practice—The Perpetual Inventory System.

5-21. a. Under LIFO, the most recent purchase costs are released to cost of goods sold. If the *purchase cost* of inventory items is changing, the *selling price* of these same items is likely to be changing in the same direction. Thus, releasing the most recent purchase costs to the Cost of Goods Sold account results in better matching of revenue and expense.

b. During periods of rising prices, LIFO results in a balance sheet valuation that is lower than current cost. This is considered consistent with the "original cost" concept usually used to record asset values. However, it understates the "value" of inventory items because it does not reflect the current cost of inventory items. The ending inventory under FIFO more accurately reflects the value of inventory items.

5-23. a.

Inventory		Cost of Goods Sold	
Balance is $5,000 too high	Credit to correct error	Debit to correct inventory error	

To correct the overstatement, inventory should be reduced (credited) $5,000, and cost of goods sold should be increased (debited) $5,000. If the error is not corrected, cost of goods sold will be too low and net income will be too high.

b. If ending inventory were understated (too low) cost of goods sold would be overstated (too high) and net income would be understated (too low).

5-25. a. *March 1*

Dr. Prepaid Insurance.................. .... $3,000
Cr. Cash.......... .... $3,000
To record the payment of a one-year insurance premium.

Balance Sheet			Income Statement		
Assets = Liabilities + Owners' Equity			← **Net income = Revenues - Expenses**		
Prepaid Insurance +3,000					
Cash −3,000					

b. *Each month-end:*

Dr. Insurance Expense............... .... $250
Cr. Prepaid Insurance........... .... $250
To record the expiration of prepaid insurance each month.

Balance Sheet			Income Statement		
Assets = Liabilities + Owners' Equity			← **Net income = Revenues - Expenses**		
Prepaid Insurance −250					Insurance Exp. −250

c. At August 31, 6 months of insurance coverage has been used, and 6 months is still to be used. So one-half of the original premium of $3,000, or $1,500 is prepaid and will be shown on the August 31 balance sheet as a current asset.

d. The prepaid amount is $4,500, for coverage for the 18 months. Only $3,000 of this amount is a current asset, because of the one-year time frame for current assets. Thus, $1,500 of the prepaid amount is technically a noncurrent asset.

e. To result in better matching of revenues and expenses, and a more meaningful net income amount. Although the expenditure of cash has been made, the item relates to the earning of revenue in a subsequent accounting period.

5-27.

	Current Assets	Current Liabilities	Owners' Equity	Net Income
b. Determined that the Allowance for Bad Debts balance should be increased by $2,200.	Allowance for Bad Debts −2,200			Bad Debts Expense −2,200
c. Recognized bank service $30 for the month.	Cash −30			Service Charge −30
d. Received $25 cash for interest receivable that had been accrued in a prior month.	Cash +25 Interest Receivable −25			
e. Purchased five units of a new item of inventory on account at a cost of $35 each.	Inventory +175	Accounts Payable +175		
f. Purchased 10 more units of the above item at a cost of $38 each.	Inventory +380	Accounts Payable * +380		

* Could also be recorded as: Cash −380 under the current assets category.

	Current Assets	Current Liabilities	Owners' Equity	Net Income
g. Sold eight of the items purchased (in *e* and *f* above), and recognized the cost of goods sold using the FIFO cost-flow assumption.	Inventory −289 *(5 units @ $35, 3 units @ $38)*			Cost of Goods Sold −289

5-29.

	Current Assets	Current Liabilities	Owners' Equity	Net Income
b. Recorded estimated bad debts in the amount of $700.	Allowance for Bad Debts −700			Bad Debts Expense −700
c. Wrote off an overdue account receivable of $520.	Accounts Receivable −520 Allowance for Doubtful Accounts +520			*(Net realizable value of accounts receivable is not affected.)*

5-29.

		Current Assets	Current Liabilities	Owners' Equity	Net Income
d.	Converted a customer's $1,200 overdue account receivable into a note.	Notes Receivable +1,200 Accounts Receivable -1,200			
e.	Accrued $48 of interest earned on the note (in *d* above).	Interest Receivable +48			Interest Revenue +48
f.	Collected the accrued interest (in *e* above).	Cash +48 Interest Receivable -48			
g.	Recorded $4,000 of sales, 80% of which were on account.	Cash +800 Accounts Receivable +3,200			Sales +4,000
h.	Recognized cost of goods sold in the amount of $3,200.	Inventory -3,200			Cost of Goods Sold -3,200

CHAPTER 6. Accounting for and Presentation of Property, Plant and Equipment, and OtherNoncurrent Assets

6-1. a. Allocate the purchase cost in proportion to appraised values.

Cost of land = ($20,000 / ($80,000 + $20,000)) * $90,000 = **$18,000**

b. Land is not a depreciable asset. Management would want as much of the purchase price as feasible to be assigned to assets whose cost will become a tax-deductible expense in future years—reducing taxable income and income taxes payable.

c. All ordinary and necessary costs incurred by Dorsey Co. in order to get the land ready for its intended use should be added to the Land account. Thus, the cost included in the Land account is the total amount paid, plus the cost of razing building. Note that no costs are added to Dorsey Co.'s Buildings account because the building was not acquired with the intent to be used as a building.

Cost of land = $90,000 + $10,000 = **$100,000**

d. Appraised values are be used because they represent the *current* asset values (at the time of purchase by Dorsey Co.). The old original cost data represent what the relative asset values were (at the time of purchase by Bibb Co.), which is not relevant to Dorsey Co.

6-3. a. Expense. Routine repair and maintenance costs would not increase the useful life or estimated salvage of the vehicles, so the "economic benefits" of these expenditures relate only to the current year.

6-3. b. Asset. The cost of developing the coal mine should be capitalized (as a natural resource) because the extraction of coal will generate revenues in future years. The $60,000 cost of developing the coal mine will be recorded as depletion expense (at a rate of six cents per ton extracted).

c. Asset. This cost should be added to the Building account because it will extend the useful life of the asset.

d. Expense. Advertising costs are *always* treated as expenses in the year incurred because it is impossible to determine to what extent, if any, future-period revenues will be affected by current-period advertising expenditures.

e. Asset. This cost should be added to the Land account because it is an ordinary and necessary cost incurred to get the land ready for its intended use.

6-5. a. Repair cost capitalized in error = $20,000.

Depreciation expense in current year on above amount:

To be depreciated	$20,000
Remaining life	5 years
Depreciation expense in current year	$ 4,000

To correct the error:

Operating income originally reported	$160,000
Increase in repair expense	(20,000)
Decrease in depreciation expense	4,000
Corrected operating income	**$144,000**

6-5. b. *ROI for current year based on original data:*
ROI = Operating income / Average total assets
= $160,000 / (($940,000 + $1,020,000) / 2) = **16.3%**

ROI for current year based on corrected data:

Year-end assets originally reported...		$1,020,000
Less net book value of mistakenly capitalized repair expense:		
Cost...	$20,000	
Less accumulated depreciation..	(4,000)	(16,000)
Corrected year-end assets..		$1,004,000

ROI = Operating income / Average total assets
= $144,000 / (($940,000 + $1,004,000) / 2) = **14.8%**

c. In subsequent years, depreciation expense will be too high, net income will be too low, and average assets will be too high. Thus, ROI will be too low.

6-7. a. Amount to be depreciated = Cost − Salvage value
Annual depreciation expense = Amount to be depreciated / Useful life
Annual depreciation expense = ($80,000 − $8,000) / 8 = $9,000 per year
After 5 years, accumulated depreciation = $9,000 * 5 = **$45,000**

b. Straight-line rate = 1 / 8 = 12.5%. Double-declining rate = 12.5% * 2 = **25%**

			At End of Year	
	Net Book Value	*Depreciation*	*Accumulated*	*Net Book*
Year	*at Beginning of Year*	*Expense*	*Depreciation*	*Value*
1	$80,000	$80,000 * 25% = $20,000	$20,000	$60,000
2	60,000	60,000 * 25% = 15,000	35,000	45,000
3	45,000	45,000 * 25% = **11,250**	46,250	33,750

c. Sum of the digits for an 8-year life = 8 + 7 + 6 + 5 + 4 + 3 + 2 + 1 = 36 digits
Amount to be depreciated = $80,000 cost − $8,000 salvage value = $72,000

Solution approach: Accumulated depreciation at the end of the fifth year equals the sum of the depreciation expense amounts recorded in the first five years.

After 5 years, accumulated depreciation = ((8 + 7 + 6 + 5 + 4) / 36) * $72,000
= (30 / 36) * $72,000 = **$60,000**

Under sum-of-the-years'-digits, accumulated depreciation after 5 years is $15,000 higher ($60,000 − $45,000), than under straight-line because of the accelerated depreciation pattern.

d. Net book value = Cost − Accumulated depreciation. After 8 years, the asset will have been fully depreciated to its estimated salvage value of $8,000 under each method. Accumulated depreciation will be $72,000, and net book value will be $8,000 ($80,000 − $72,000).

6-9. Estimated useful life...... .... 7 years
Cost of machine $9,600
Estimated salvage value. .... (1,200)
Amount to be depreciated $8,400

1. *Straight-line depreciation*:
Annual depreciation expense = $8,400 / 7 years = **$1,200 per year**
Depreciation expense for 1998 (9 months) = $1,200 * 9/12 = **$900**
Depreciation expense for 1999 (12 months) = **$1,200**

2. *Sum-of-the-years' digits depreciation:*
Sum of the digits for a 7-year life = (7 + 6 + 5 + 4 +3 +2 + 1) = 28 digits
Depreciation expense of first year of asset's life = 7/28 * $8,400 = $2,100
Depreciation expense of second year of asset's life = 6/28 * $8,400 = $1,800

Depreciation expense for 1998 = 9 months of the first year's expense
$$= \$2,100 * 9/12 = \textbf{\$1,575}$$

Depreciation expense for 1999 = (3 months of the first year's expense + 9 months
of the second year's expense)
$$= (3/12 * \$2,100) + (9/12 * \$1,800)$$
$$= \$525 + \$1,350 = \textbf{\$1,875}$$

6-11. Estimated useful life.... .... 4 years
Cost of machine $120,000
Estimated salvage value.................... .... (20,000)
Amount to be depreciated ....,......... .... $100,000

a.

Year	Net Book Value at Beginning of Year	Net Book Value at End of Year	Depreciation Expense	Accumulated Depreciation
1998	$120,000	$80,000	**$40,000**	$ 40,000
1999	80,000	50,000	**30,000**	70,000
2000	50,000	30,000	**20,000**	90,000
2001	30,000	20,000	**10,000**	100,000

The **sum-of-the-years'-digits method** is being used because the depreciation expense recorded each year is decreasing at a constant rate representing the 4/10, 3/10, 2/10, 1/10 pattern * $100,000.

6-11. b.

Year	Net Book Value at Beginning of Year	Net Book Value at End of Year	Depreciation Expense	Accumulated Depreciation
1998	$120,000	$98,000	**$22,000**	$ 22,000
1999	98,000	66,000	**32,000**	54,000
2000	66,000	38,000	**28,000**	82,000
2001	38,000	20,000	**18,000**	100,000

The **units of production method** is being used. At first glance, no clear pattern can be seen in the amount of depreciation expense recorded each year. However, based on the machine's productive capacity of 50,000 units and the actual production data provided for 1998-2001, the depreciation expense amounts shown above can be easily verified.

c.

Year	Net Book Value at Beginning of Year	Net Book Value at End of Year	Depreciation Expense	Accumulated Depreciation
1998	$120,000	$60,000	**$60,000**	$ 60,000
1999	60,000	30,000	**30,000**	90,000
2000	30,000	20,000	**10,000**	100,000
2001	20,000	20,000	**0**	100,000

The **double-declining balance (200%) method** is being used. Notice that the expense pattern is extremely accelerated in this case. Using the double-declining balance method for an asset with a 4-year useful life results in an annual depreciation rate of 50% (25% straight-line rate * 2) of the asset's net book value. In year 2000, the machine became fully depreciated after only $10,000 was recorded as depreciation expense, even though the calculated amount was higher (50% * $30,000 = $15,000).

d.

Year	Net Book Value at Beginning of Year	Net Book Value at End of Year	Depreciation Expense	Accumulated Depreciation
1998	$120,000	$95,000	**$25,000**	$ 25,000
1999	95,000	70,000	**25,000**	50,000
2000	70,000	45,000	**25,000**	75,000
2001	45,000	20,000	**25,000**	100,000

The **straight-line method** is being used because an equal amount of depreciation expense is recorded each year, which represents 1/4 * $100,000.

6-13. a. Estimated useful life . ... 5 years
Cost of machine $210,000
Estimated salvage value................... .... (20,000)
Amount to be depreciated $190,000

Straight-line depreciation:
Annual depreciation expense = $190,000 / 5 = **$38,000 per year**
Depreciation expense for 2000 = **$38,000**
Accumulated depreciation at December 31, 2000 = $38,000 * 2½ years = **$95,000**

6-13. b. *Double-declining balance method:*

Straight-line rate = 1 / 5 = 20%. Double-declining rate = 20% * 2 = **40%**

Year	Net Book Value at Beginning of Year #	Depreciation Expense	At End of Year Accumulated Depreciation	Net Book Value
1998	$210,000	$210,000 * 40% * ½ = $42,000	$ 42,000	$168,000
1999	168,000	168,000 * 40% = 67,200	109,200	100,800
2000	100,800	100,800 * 40% = **40,320**	149,520	**60,480**

July 1 for 1998, and January 1 for 1999 and 2000.

6-15. Straight-line depreciation is used for financial reporting purposes because depreciation expense will be lower than under any of the accelerated depreciation methods. Accelerated depreciation using the MACRS rates is probably used for tax purposes to minimize taxes payable.

6-17. Alpha, Inc. should have a higher ROI than Beta Co. Alpha, Inc.'s plant is older and will be depreciated to a greater extent than Beta Co.'s. Thus, Alpha, Inc.'s asset base will be lower, so its ROI will be higher.   The implication for Beta Co. is that because of its lower ROI, its ability to raise capital will be reduced unless it has production and/or technological advantages or efficiencies.

6-19. a. Depreciation expense for 1999 is the *increase* in the amount of accumulated depreciation from the beginning balance sheet to the ending balance sheet, or $18,000 ($42,000 – $24,000).

   b. 1. The cost of the asset is the net book value plus the accumulated depreciation, or $28,000 + $42,000 = **$70,000.**

   2. It is difficult to determine which depreciation *method* is being used because the acquisition date of the asset is not known. However, the *amount* to be depreciated can be determined, as follows:

Estimated useful life	4 years
Cost of machine	$70,000
Estimated salvage value	(10,000)
Amount to be depreciated	$60,000

   The straight-line method is not being used because the annual depreciation expense would be $15,000 ($60,000 / 4 years), and not $18,000 as determined in part *a*. The **sum-of the-years'-digits method** is being used because the balance of the accumulated depreciation account has increased from $24,000 to $42,000, which is consistent with the depreciation pattern under this method. For an asset with a 4-year useful life, the depreciation pattern would be: 4/10, 3/10, 2/10, 1/10.

6-19. b. 2.

Year	Depreciation Expense	At End of Year Accumulated Depreciation	Net Book Value
1	4/10 * $60,000 = **$24,000**	**$24,000**	**$46,000**
2	3/10 * 60,000 = **18,000**	**42,000**	**28,000**
3	2/10 * 60,000 = 12,000	54,000	16,000
4	1/10 * 60,000 = 6,000	60,000	10,000

3. At December 31, 1999, the accumulated depreciation of $42,000 represents 2 years of depreciation expense, so the acquisition date of the machine must have been on or near **January 1, 1998.**

c. Dr. Cash..... .... $23,600
Dr. Accumulated depreciation   42,000
Dr. Loss on sale of machine..........   4,400
  Cr. Machine $70,000
  To record the sale of a machine at a loss.

Balance Sheet			Income Statement		
Assets =	**Liabilities** +	**Owners' Equity** ←	**Net income** =	**Revenues** -	**Expenses**
Cash					Loss on Sale
+23,600					of Machine
Machine					−4,400
−70,000					
Accumulated	*(A decrease in a*				
Depreciation	*contra-asset account*				
+42,000	*increases assets).*				

6-21. a. List price of new computer............ .... $110,000
Less: Trade-in allowance................ ....   (12,000)
Cash to be paid....... .... $ 98,000

$21,000 net book value = ($85,000 cost − accumulated depreciation)
Accumulated depreciation = $64,000

Cost of new asset in trade-in transaction:
Net book value of old asset .... $ 21,000
Cash paid "to boot"   98,000
Cost of new computer....................... .... $119,000

b. Dr. Computer equipment (cost of new)..... .... $119,000
    Dr. Accumulated depreciation (on old)....   64,000
      Cr. Cash......... .... $98,000
      Cr. Computer Equipment (cost of old)   85,000
    To record the trade-in of an old computer for a new computer.

Balance Sheet			Income Statement		
Assets	= Liabilities	+ Owners' Equity ←	Net income =	Revenues -	Expenses

Computer   *(Note that the trade-in transaction effects <u>assets only</u>,*
Equipment (cost of old)   *and has no effect on the income statement because*
−85,000   *the earnings process of the old asset will continue*
Accumulated   *with the use of the new asset.)*
Depreciation (on old)
+64,000
Cash
−98,000
Computer
Equipment (cost of new)
+119,000

6-23. a. List price of new machine $40,000
       Less: Trade-in allowance......... ....   <u>(3,600)</u>
       Cash to be paid....... ....   <u>$36,400</u>
       Cost of new asset in trade-in transaction:
       Cost of old asset..... .... $25,000
       Accumulated depreciation on old asset...... .... (18,000)
       Current year's depreciation on old asset .... <u>(2,000)</u>
       Net book value of old asset .... $ 5,000
       Cash paid "to boot" ....   <u>36,400</u>
       Cost of new machine......... ....   **<u>$41,400</u>**

    b. Dr. Machine (cost of new)......... .... $41,400
       Dr. Accumulated Depreciation (on old)....   18,000
       Dr. Depreciation Expense (for current year on old) #......   2,000
          Cr. Cash......... .... $36,400
          Cr. Machine (cost of old)   25,000
       To record the current year's depreciation expense, and the trade-in of an
       old machine for a new machine.

    # A common bookkeeping practice is to record the entry for the current year's depreciation expense on
      the old asset first, and then record the trade-in (or sale) transaction separately. This approach brings the
      accumulated depreciation account up-to-date, which then makes it easier to determine what the net book
      value of the old asset was at the time it was traded in (or sold). The results are the same either way:

| Dr. | Depreciation Expense (for current year on old)... | $ 2,000 | |
| | Cr. Accumulated Depreciation (on old). .... | | $ 2,000 |

Dr.	Machine (cost of new)..	41,400	
Dr.	Accumulated Depreciation (on old)...	20,000	
	Cr. Cash..		36,400
	Cr. Machine (cost of old)..		25,000

Balance Sheet				Income Statement			
Assets	=	**Liabilities**	+ **Owners' Equity** ←	**Net income**	= **Revenues**	-	**Expenses**

Machine (cost of old)	Depreciation
− 25,000	Expense
Accumulated	− 2,000
Depreciation (old)	
+ 18,000	*(Note that the trade-in transaction effects <u>assets only</u>, and*
Cash	*has no effect on the income statement because the earnings*
− 36,400	*process of the old asset will continue with the use of the*
Machine (cost of new)	*new asset. <u>As explained above, the depreciation expense</u>*
+ 41,400	<u>*entry is really a separate transaction from the trade-in*</u>.

c. Installation costs for a machine that will be used in the firm's operations are ordinary and necessary costs incurred to get the machine ready for its intended purpose. Thus, the $700 should be capitalized (i.e., added to the Machine account).

6-25. a. If *any* of the four criteria listed in the text for capitalizing a lease are met, the lease should be accounted for as a capital lease rather than an operating lease.

1. Maybe. The problem does not state that *ownership* of the computer system is transferred to Carey, Inc. during the term of the lease, but it does state that the system was *acquired*. Thus, its not clear whether title to the asset transferred.
   2. Yes. The option to purchase the computer system for $1 at the end of four years is a "bargain purchase option."
   3. Yes. The 75% test is met because the lease term of 4 years is 100% of the economic life of the computer system.
   4. Yes. The 90% test is met because the present value of the lease payments is $10,197.95 which is 100% (rounded) of the $10,200 fair value of the asset.

b.

Annual lease payments (paid at the end of each year).....................................	$	3,500
Present value factor (Table 6-3, 4 periods, 14% discount rate).....................	*	2.9137
Present value of lease payments (amount to be capitalized)...........................		**$10,197.95**

Dr. Equipment... $10,200
    Cr. Capital Lease Liability.. $10,200
To record a capital lease transaction at the present value of future lease
payments (amount rounded to the nearest $10).

Balance Sheet			Income Statement		
Assets =	**Liabilities** +	**Owners' Equity**	← **Net income** =	**Revenues** -	**Expenses**
Equipment	Capital				
+ 10,200	Lease Liability				
	+ 10,200				

c. Annual lease payment $3,500
Beginning balance, capital lease liability............................. $10,200
Interest rate .... * 14%
Interest expense (for first year of lease term) .... **(1,428)**
Payment of principal (reduction of capital lease liability)............ **$2,072**

Dr. Interest Expense... $1,428
Dr. Capital Lease Liability.. 2,072
    Cr. Cash.. $3,500
To record the first annual lease payment on a capital lease.

Balance Sheet			Income Statement		
Assets =	**Liabilities** +	**Owners' Equity**	← **Net income** =	**Revenues** -	**Expenses**
Cash	Capital				Interest
− 3,500	Lease Liability				Expense
	− 2,072				− 1,428

d. In addition to the **$1,428 of Interest Expense** on the capital lease liability, **Depreciation Expense of $2,550** ($10,200 / 4 years) on the equipment should also be recognized in the income statement. Note that the amount of interest expense will *decrease* each year of the lease term because the capital lease liability is reduced each time an annual lease payment is made.

e. As discussed and illustrated in the text, the *economic effect* of a long-term capital lease is not any different than the purchase of an asset with borrowed funds. In substance, the firm has acquired virtually all of the rights and benefits of ownership—so the accounting for a capital lease should be consistent with that of an asset purchase.

6-27. a. Today   2 years

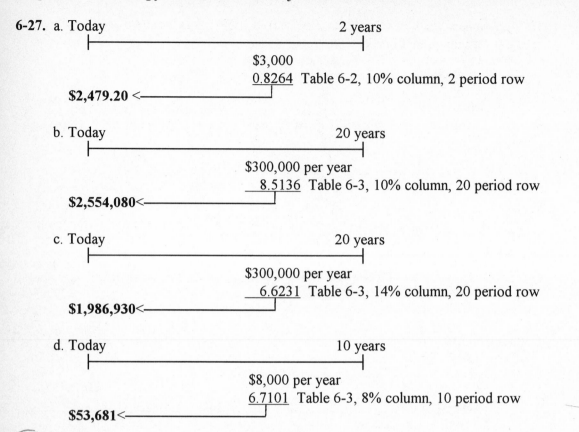

$3,000
0.8264 Table 6-2, 10% column, 2 period row
$2,479.20 <——

b. Today   20 years

$300,000 per year
8.5136 Table 6-3, 10% column, 20 period row
$2,554,080 <——

c. Today   20 years

$300,000 per year
6.6231 Table 6-3, 14% column, 20 period row
$1,986,930 <——

d. Today   10 years

$8,000 per year
6.7101 Table 6-3, 8% column, 10 period row
$53,681 <——

6-29. The present value factor for a single amount for 5 periods, at a discount rate of 16% in Table 6-2 is 0.4761. Thus, $100,000 * 0.4761 = **$47,610** present value.

a. Since interest will be compounded twice per year, the number of periods is 10 (5 years * 2) and the rate is 8% (16% / 2). The present factor for 10 periods at 8% from Table 6-2 is 0.4632. Thus, $100,000 * 0.4632 = **$46,320** present value.

b. The number of periods now becomes 20 (5 years * 4 quarters per year), and the rate becomes 4% (16% / 4 quarters per year). The present value factor for 20 periods at 4% from Table 6-2 is 0.4564. Thus, $100,000 * 0.4564 = **$45,640** present value.

c. The present value factor at 12% for 5 periods in Table 6-2 is 0.5674. Thus, $100,000 * 0.5674 = **$56,740** present value.

d. The present value factor at 20% for 5 periods in Table 6-2 is 0.4019. Thus, $100,000 * 0.4019 = **$40,190** present value.

e. The present value factor at 16% for 3 periods in Table 6-2 is 0.6407.
    Thus, $100,000 * 0.6407 = **$64,070** present value.

f. The present value factor at 16% for 7 periods in Table 6-2 is 0.3538.
    Thus, $100,000 * 0.3538 = **$35,380** present value.

6-31. a. Yes, because of the above-average ROI of 18%, I could afford to invest **$40,000** more
    than $200,000 and still earn a 15% ROI—which is the rate I'd expect to earn from an
    investment in this type of business. The excess earnings offered by this investment =
    ($200,000 * 18%) − ($200,000 * 15%) = $36,000 − $30,000 = **$6,000 per year** on a
    $200,000 investment. At an ROI of 15%, an investment of **$240,000** would be required
    to earn $36,000 of income, so that is the maximum price I'd be willing to pay for the
    business.

b. Each of the individual assets acquired would be recorded at their fair market values, and
    $40,000 would be recorded as "Goodwill."

6-33.

	Assets	**Liabilities**	**Net Income**
b. Sold land that had originally cost $9,000 for $14,000 in cash.	Land − 9,000 Cash + 14,000		Gain on Sale of Land + 5,000
c. Acquired a new machine under a capital lease. The present value of future lease payments, discounted at 10%, was $12,000.	Machine + 12,000	Capital Lease Liability + 12,000	
d. Recorded the first annual payment of $2,000 for the leased machine (in *c* above).	Cash − 2,000	Capital Lease Liability − 800	Interest Expense − 1,200
		*(Interest = $12,000 * 10%).*	
e. Recorded a $6,000 payment for the cost of developing and registering a trademark.	Trademark + 6,000 Cash − 6,000		
f. Recognized the periodic amortization on the trademark (in *e* above) using a 40-year useful life.	Trademark − 150		Amortization Expense − 150

6-33. *(continued)*

	Assets	Liabilities	Net Income
g. Sold used production equipment for $16,000 in cash. The equipment originally cost $40,000. The accumulated depreciation account had a balance of $22,000 before adjusting for a $1,000 year-to-date depreciation entry that must be recorded before the sale of the equipment is recorded.	Accumulated Depreciation − 1,000, Equipment − 40,000 Cash + 16,000	+ 23,000	Depreciation Expense − 1,000 Loss on Sale of Equipment − 1,000

	Assets	Liabilities	Net Income
h. Traded in an old tractor plus $12,000 for a new tractor having a $20,000 list price. The old tractor had cost $16,000 and had a net book value of $7,000 at the time of the exchange. A trade-in allowance of $8,000 was given for the old tractor.	Tractor (old) − 16,000 Cash − 12,000 Accumulated Depreciation (old) + 9,000 Tractor (new) + 19,000		*(Note: No gain or loss is recorded on the trade-in.)*

Cost of new asset in trade-in transaction:

Net book value of old asset	$ 7,000
Cash paid "to boot"..	12,000
Cost of new tractor	**$19,000**

CHAPTER 7. *Accounting for and Presentation of Liabilities*

7-1. Discount basis means interest is paid in advance.
   a. Proceeds = Face amount of note − Interest
   = $300,000 − ($300,000 * 9% * 6/12)
   = $300,000 − $13,500 = **$286,500**

April 15, 1999

Dr. Cash.....	$286,500	
Dr. Discount on Notes Payable......	13,500	
Cr. Notes Payable...................		$300,000

   To record the proceeds of a short-term note payable (discount basis).

7-1.

Balance Sheet			Income Statement		
Assets	=	**Liabilities**	+ **Owners' Equity**	← **Net income** = **Revenues**	- **Expenses**
Cash		Notes Payable		*(Note: The discount account is a contra liability,*	
+ 286,500		+ 300,000		*so the initial carrying value of the note is equal*	
		Discount on		*to the cash proceeds received—which is the*	
		Notes Payable		*approach taken when interest is calculated*	
		− 13,500		*on a straight basis.)*	

b. The note was dated April 15, 1999, so 2½ months have passed from the time the note was signed until the June 30, 1999 fiscal year-end. Interest = $300,000 * 9% * 2½/12 = **$5,625**

c. Current liability = Face amount less discount balance.
$$= \$300,000 - (\$13,500 - \$5,625)$$
$$= \$300,000 - \$7,875 = \mathbf{\$292{,}125}$$

7-3. a. *3/31/99*

    Dr. Payroll Tax Expense.................. .... $4,800
    Cr. Payroll Taxes Payable....... .... $4,800
    To accrue payroll taxes for the year.

Balance Sheet			Income Statement		
Assets	=	**Liabilities**	+ **Owners' Equity**	← **Net income** = **Revenues**	- **Expenses**
		Payroll Taxes			Payroll Tax
		Payable			Expense
		+ 4,800			− 4,800

b. Failure to make the accrual resulted in an understatement of expense and an overstatement of net income. On the 3/31/99 balance sheet, current liabilities are understated and retained earnings is overstated.

c.

    3/31/96   *3/31/97*

Paid taxes of prior year in April; debited expense for $4,800 this year.

Should have recognized $5,000 expense this year.

Effect on net income for year ended 3/31/00:
Expense is too high by amount applicable to prior year: $4,800
Expense is too low by accrual *not* made this year: $5,000
Net effect is that expense this year is $200 too low, and profits this year are $200 too high.

Effect on the 3/31/00 balance sheet:
Current liabilities are $5,000 understated, and retained earnings is $5,000 overstated.

7-5. *December 31:*

Dr. Advertising Expense ($2,700,000 * 60% * 5%)... .... $81,000

    Cr. Estimated Liability for Advertising Allowance $81,000

To accrue the estimated liability for advertising allowances offered.

Balance Sheet			Income Statement		
Assets =	**Liabilities** +	**Owners' Equity**	← **Net income** =	**Revenues** -	**Expenses**
	Estimated Liability for Advertising Allowance + 81,000				Advertising Expense − 81,000

7-7. a. Warranty Expense = ($3,600,000 sales * 0.4% estimated warranty expense) = **$14,400**

  b. Estimated Warranty Liability, 1/1/99 balance $35,200

      Less: Actual warranty costs during 1999 .... (15,600)

      Add: Warranty Expense accrued during 1999.........   14,400

      Estimated Warranty Liability, 12/31/99 balance...... .... $34,000

7-9. a. Keg deposits are a current liability on the balance sheet because they are amounts that are likely to be paid within a year.

  b. Dr. Keg Deposits.... .... $50

        Cr. Cash.......... .... $50

      To record the refund of keg deposits.

Balance Sheet			Income Statement		
Assets =	**Liabilities** +	**Owners' Equity**	← **Net income** =	**Revenues** -	**Expenses**
Cash − 50	Keg Deposits − 50				

  c. The Keg Deposits liability for the 200 kegs (200 * $50 = $10,000) should be eliminated with a debit; an income statement account (such as Keg Deposits Revenue) should be credited.

    Dr. Keg Deposits $10,000

       Cr. Keg Deposits Revenue $10,000

      To eliminate the liability for unreturned kegs.

	Balance Sheet				Income Statement		
Assets	=	**Liabilities**	+	**Owners' Equity**	← **Net income** =	**Revenues** -	**Expenses**

To eliminate the liability for unreturned kegs:

	Keg Deposits	Keg Deposits
	− 10,000	Revenue
		+10,000

7-11. a. *September 1, 1999*

Dr. Cash.. $4,200

    Cr. Unearned Rent Revenue.. .... $4,200

To record the receipt a six-month advance rent payment.

Each month-end:

Dr. Unearned Rent Revenue........ .... $700

    Cr. Rent Revenue.............. .... $700

To record a reduction in the liability account for rent earned each month.

	Balance Sheet				Income Statement		
Assets	=	**Liabilities**	+	**Owners' Equity**	← **Net income** =	**Revenues** -	**Expenses**
Cash		Unearned					
+ 4,200		Rent Revenue					
		+ 4,200					
		Unearned				Rent	
		Rent Revenue				Revenue	
		− 700				+ 700	

b. At December 31, 1999, 4 months of rent has been earned, and 2 months remains to be earned. So 2/6 of the original premium of $4,200, or $1,400 is unearned rent and will be shown on the December 31 balance sheet as a current liability.

c. At a rate of $700 per month, the receipt of an 18-month rent prepayment would have been for $12,600. The unearned amount at December 31, 1999, is $9,800 ($700 per month for the next 14 months). Only $8,400 ($700 * 12 months) of this amount is a current liability, because of the one-year time frame for current liabilities. Thus, $1,400 ($700 * 2 months) of the unearned amount is technically a noncurrent liability.

7-13. a. Gross Pay − Total Deductions = Net Pay

Gross Pay = (Net Pay + Total Deductions)

           = ($58,360 + $21,640) = **$80,000**

FICA Tax Withholdings = (Total Deductions − all other deductions)

                = ($21,640 − $13,760 − $1,120 − $640) = **$6,120**

7-13. a. FICA Tax Withholdings / Gross Pay = withholding percentage
$$\$6,120 / \$80,000 = \textbf{7.65\%}$$

b. Dr. Wages Expense $85,540
  Cr. Wages Payable (or Accrued Payroll)....... .... $63,900
  Cr. FICA Taxes Withheld...... 6,120
  Cr. Income Taxes Withheld... 13,760
  Cr. Medical Insurance Contributions 1,120
  Cr. Union Dues 640
  To record accrued payroll.

Balance Sheet			Income Statement		
Assets =	**Liabilities** +	**Owners' Equity**	← **Net income** =	**Revenues** -	**Expenses**
	Wages Payable				Wages
	+ 63,900				Expense
	Withholding Liabilities (as described above)				−85,540
	+ 6,120 + 13,760 + 1,120 + 640				

7-15. a. The market interest rate is lower than the stated interest rate, so the bonds will sell for more than their face amount. The lower the discount rate (i.e., market interest rate), the higher the *present value* of cash flows associated with the bond (for interest payments and principal) becomes.

b. Dr. Cash $1,080,000
  Cr. Bonds Payable................... .... $1,000,000
  Cr. Premium on Bonds Payable 80,000
  To record the issuance of bonds payable at a premium.

Balance Sheet			Income Statement		
Assets =	**Liabilities** +	**Owners' Equity**	← **Net income** =	**Revenues** -	**Expenses**
Cash	Bonds Payable				
+1,080,000	+1,000,000				
	Premium on				
	Bonds Payable				
	+80,000				

c.

4/1/99	6 months	9/30/99
Bonds issued.		End of fiscal year.

Accrued interest payable ($1,000,000 * 11% * 6/12)......... .... $55,000
Premium amortization ($80,000 / 20 years * 6/12). .... (2,000)
Interest expense for 6 months........ .... **$53,000**

Dr. Interest Expense	$53,000
Dr. Premium on Bonds Payable....	2,000
Cr. Interest Payable.................	$55,000

To record the accrual of interest and premium amortization for 6 months.

7-17. The semiannual interest on the bonds = 10% stated rate * $5,000 face amount * 6/12 = **$250**
The remaining term of the bonds is 12 years, or **24 semiannual periods.**
The semiannual market interest rate is = 8% * 6/12 = **4%**
The present value of an interest annuity of $250 for 24 periods at 4% =
$250 * 15.2470 = **$3,811.75**

The present value of the maturity value of $5,000 in 24 periods at 4% =
$5,000 * 0.3901 = **$1,950.50**

The market value of the bonds = PV of interest + PV of maturity value =
$3,811.75 + $1,950.50 = **$5,762.25**

7-19. a. Because the exchange ratio is five shares of common stock to one bond, bondholders would be interested in converting the bonds to common stock if the market price per share of common stock was at least 20% (or more) of the market price per bond. For example, when the bonds were issued on January 1, 1990 at their $1,000 face amount, the market rate of interest and the stated rate were both 12%, and the market price per bond was $1,000. At that time, bondholders would not have been willing to convert their bonds unless the common stock was trading at price of $200 per share or more.

b. ***Solution approach:*** Upon exercise of the conversion feature, the bonds have been retired and thus the Bonds Payable account must be reduced by the carrying value of $1,000 per bond retired (there was no discount or premium). Common stock has been issued for $215 per share and should be recorded in the usual way. The difference is a loss on the early retirement of bonds of $75 per bond retired (or $15 per share of common stock issued) because the company gave more in exchange for the bonds ($215 per share * 5 shares equals $1,075) than the carrying value of the bonds ($1,000 per bond).

Dr. Bonds Payable (400 bonds * $1,000 per bond)........	$400,000
Dr. Loss on Early Retirement of Bonds #	30,000
Cr. Common Stock (400 bonds * 5 shares * $10 par)..........	$ 20,000
Cr. Additional Paid-In Capital (400 * 5 * $205 per share)....	410,000

To record the conversion of bonds to common stock at a loss.

For financial reporting purposes, gains and losses on the early retirement of debt are reported as "extraordinary items" on the income statement, and are shown net of their tax effects. The accounting for extraordinary items is discussed in Chapter 9.

Balance Sheet			Income Statement		
Assets =	Liabilities +	Owners' Equity	← Net income = Revenues	-	Expenses
	Bonds	Common Stock			Loss on
	Payable	+ 20,000			Early
	− 400,000	Additional Paid-In			Retirement
		Capital			of Bonds
		+ 410,000			− 30,000

7-21. a. Annual interest payment = $40 million * 11% = **$4,400,000**

b. The bonds were issued at a discount because market interest rates were more than the stated rate when the bonds were issued. The higher the discount rate (i.e., the market interest rate), the lower the *present value* of cash flows for interest payments and principal (i.e., the lower the bond's selling price).

c. Interest expense will be more than the interest paid because the amortization of bond discount will increase interest expense.

7-23. a. The semiannual interest payments on the bonds =
14% stated rate * $3,000,000 face amount * 6/12 = **$210,000**
The term of the bonds is 10 years, or **20 semiannual periods.**
The semiannual market interest rate is = 12% * 6/12 = **6%**
The present value of an annuity of $210,000 for 20 periods at 6% =
$210,000 * 11.4699 = **$2,408,679**
The present value of the maturity value of $3,000,000 in 20 periods at 6% =
$3,000,000 * 0.3118 = **$935,400**
The proceeds (issue price) of the bonds = PV of interest + PV of maturity value =
$2,408,679 + $935,400 = **$3,344,079**

b. The semiannual discount amortization, straight-line basis = $50,000 / 20 periods = **$2,500**

Dr. Interest Expense................. .... $212,500
    Cr. Cash.......... .... $210,000
    Cr. Discount on Bonds Payable 2,500
    To record the semiannual cash payment and amortization of discount.

Balance Sheet			Income Statement		
Assets =	Liabilities +	Owners' Equity	← Net income = Revenues	-	Expenses
Cash	Discount on				Interest
− 210,000	Bonds Payable				Expense
	+ 2,500				− 212,500

c. Discount on bonds payable is amortized with a credit, and thus increases interest expense. Under the straight-line basis, the amount of discount amortization is the same each period. Under the compound (or *effective*) interest method, the amount of discount amortization increases each period. Thus, interest expense under the compound method will be lower in the early years of the bond's life, and higher in the later years, as compared to interest expense under the straight-line method of amortization.

Rationale of compound interest method: <u>Interest expense</u> under the compound interest method is calculated by multiplying the carrying value of the bond (face amount minus the unamortized discount) by the market rate of interest. This amount is then compared to the <u>*cash payment*</u> required (the face amount multiplied by the stated rate). Any difference between interest expense and the required cash payment represents the amortization of discount for the period. Because the carrying value of the bond *increases* over the life of the bond as discount is amortized, the *amount* of discount amortization also increases each period, causing interest expense to be higher each period. Thus, as compared to the straight-line basis, interest expense under the compound method will be lower in the first year.

7-25. The principal risk associated with financial leverage is that a decrease in the entity's operating income could result in a decrease in cash flows and an inability to make interest and required principal payments on the debt. A second risk is that as the amount of debt increases, lenders require a higher interest rate to compensate for the additional risk they are taking.

7-27. The amount of deferred income taxes has risen steadily because the excess of accelerated tax depreciation over straight-line book depreciation on recent asset additions exceeds the excess of book depreciation over tax depreciation for older asset additions. This occurs because as the company grows over time, asset additions increase in amount, and over time the cost of replacement assets rises because of inflation.

7-29.

Transaction/ Adjustment	Current Assets	Current Liabilities	Long-Term Debt	Net Income
a.		+ 867		− 867
b.		+ 170		− 170
c.		+ 1,700		− 1,700
d.			+ 50	− 50
e.	− 1,240	− 1,240		
f.		+ 1,500		− 1,500

a. Dr. Wages Expense $867
    Cr. Wages Payable $867

b. Dr. Interest Expense............................ .... $170
    Cr. Interest Payable............ .... $170

c. Dr. Interest Expense ($240,000 * 8.5% * 1/12).. .... $1,700
    Cr.   Interest Payable............. .... $1,700

d. Dr. Interest Expense $50
    Cr. Discount on Bonds Payable $50

e. Dr. Estimated Warranty Liability $1,240
    Cr. Cash......... .... $410
    Cr. Parts Inventory.......................   830

f. Dr. Sales $1,500
    Cr. Unearned Revenues......... .... $1,500

7-31.

Transaction/ Adjustment	Current Assets	Noncurrent Assets	Current Liabilities	Noncurrent Liabilities	Owners' Equity	Net Income
a.			Income Taxes Payable + 500	Deferred Income Taxes + 200		Income Tax Expense − 700
b.	Cash + 4,950			Bonds Payable + 5,000 Discount on Bonds Payable − 50		
c.	Cash − 3,000	Land + 3,000				
d.	Inventory − 64		Estimated Warranty Liability − 64			
e.	Cash + 19,400			Notes Payable + 20,000 Discount on Notes Payable − 600		
f.			Current Maturities of Long-Term Debt + 35,000	Serial Bonds Payable − 35,000		

7-31. a. Dr. Income Tax Expense $700
           Cr. Income Taxes Payable $500
           Cr. Deferred Income Taxes 200

     b. Dr. Cash... $4,950
           Dr. Discount on Bonds Payable 50
           Cr. Bonds Payable... $5,000

     c. Dr. Land.. $3,000
           Cr. Cash... $3,000

     d. Dr. Estimated Warranty Liability $64
           Cr. Inventory.. $64

     e. Dr. Cash ($20,000 − ($20,000 * 12% * 3/12))................ $19,400
           Dr. Discount on Notes Payable ($20,000 * 12% * 3/12)........ 600
           Cr. Notes Payable.. $20,000

     f. Dr. Serial Bonds Payable.. $35,000
           Cr. Current Maturities of Long-Term Debt.................. $35,000

CHAPTER 8. *Accounting for and Presentation of Owners' Equity*

8-1.

	A	=	L	+	PIC	+	RE	OE
Beginning..........	$ (4)		$ (3)		(1)		(2)	$520,000 OE
Changes	+260,000		+21,000		+40,000		+(7)	Net income
							−55,000	Dividends
Ending	(5)	=	$234,000	+	$175,000	+	(6)	

Steps:
1. $175,000 − $40,000 = $135,000
2. $520,000 − $135,000 = $385,000
3. $234,000 − $21,000 = $213,000
4. $213,000 + $520,000 = $733,000
5. $733,000 + $260,000 = $993,000
6. $993,000 − $234,000 − $175,000 = $584,000
7. $385,000 + Net income − $55,000 = $584,000
     Net income = **$254,000**

Short-cut approach:
$260,000 = + $21,000 + $40,000
            + Net income − $55,000

Net income = **$254,000**

8-3.

Retained earnings, December 31, 1998	$346,400
Add: Net income for the year	56,900
Less: Dividends for the year	(32,500)
Retained earnings, December 31, 1999	**$370,800**

8-5. a. Balance sheet amount equals number of shares issued * par value.
   1,400,000 shares * $5 = **$7,000,000**

   b. Cash dividends are paid on shares outstanding.
   1,250,000 shares * $0.15 = **$187,500**

   c. Treasury stock accounts for the difference between shares issued and shares outstanding.

8-7. a.

Number of shares issued	161,522
Less: Number of shares in treasury	(43,373)
Number of shares outstanding	118,149
Dividend requirement per share	* $3.75
Total annual dividends required to be paid	**$443,058.75**

   b.

Dividend per share (6% * $40 par value)	$2.40
Number of shares outstanding	73,621
Total annual dividends required to be paid	**$176,690.40**

   c.

Dividend per share (11.4% * $100 stated value)	$11.40
Number of shares outstanding	37,600
Total annual dividends required to be paid	**$428,640**

8-9. Preferred dividends for 1997, 1998, and 1999 would have to be paid before a dividend on the common stock could be paid. Annual dividend = $6.50 * 22,000 shares = $143,000
Dividends for 3 years = 3 * $143,000 = **$429,000**

8-11. a. 1. *January 1, 1998:*

Dr. Cash ((150,000 @ $19) + (60,000 @ $122))		$10,170,000
Cr. Common Stock (150,000 shares @ $19 per share)		$2,850,000
Cr. Preferred Stock (60,000 shares @ $100 per share)		6,000,000
Cr. Additional Paid-In Capital—Preferred (60,000 @ $22)		1,320,000
To record stock issuances.		

   2. *December 28, 1999:*

Dr. Retained Earnings		$1,800,000
Cr. Dividends Payable		$1,800,000
To record the declaration of dividends.		

8-11. a. 3. *February 12, 2000:*

Dr. Dividends Payable $1,800,000

Cr. Cash $1,800,000

To record the payment of dividends.

Balance Sheet			Income Statement		
Assets =	**Liabilities** +	**Owners' Equity**	← **Net income** =	**Revenues** -	**Expenses**

a. 1. *To record stock issuances:*

Cash	Common Stock
+ 10,170,000	+ 2,850,000
	Preferred Stock
	+ 6,000,000
	Additional
	Paid-In Capital
	+ 1,320,000

2. *To record the declaration of dividends:*

Dividends Payable	Retained Earnings
+ 1,800,000	− 1,800,000

3. *To record the payment of dividends:*

Cash	Dividends Payable
− 1,800,000	− 1,800,000

b. Preferred shareholders are entitled to one year of dividends in arrears (for 1998), as well as their current year preference (for 1999). 60,000 shares * $100 par per share * 9.5% = $570,000 per year * 2 years = **$1,140,000**

8-13. a. February 21 is the declaration date. Because this is a regular dividend of the same amount as prior dividends, the stock price would not be significantly affected.

b. March 12 is the ex-dividend date. On this date the market price of the stock is likely to fall by the amount of the dividend because purchasers will not receive the dividend.

c. March 15 is the record date. The market price of the stock should not be affected because for a publicly traded stock it is the ex-dividend date that affects who receives the dividend.

d. March 30 is the payment date. The market price of the stock should not be affected because the corporation is merely paying a liability (dividends payable).

8-15. To declare a dividend, the firm must have retained earnings and enough cash to pay the dividend. Of course the board of directors must approve a dividend.

8-17. If the company can reinvest its retained earnings at a higher ROI than I could earn on the money paid to me in dividends, I would prefer that the company *not* pay a cash dividend (Intel is a perfect example of this). If I needed current income from my investment, I would want cash dividends. As a common stock investor, I don't really care whether or not the company issues a stock dividend, because a stock dividend doesn't change my equity in the company, the total market value of my investment, or the company's ability to earn a return on my investment.

8-19. a. A 2-for-1 split means that for every share now owned, the stockholder will own 2 shares. Thus, I will own 200 shares.

b. Because there are now twice as many shares of stock outstanding, and the financial condition of the company hasn't changed, the market price per share should be half of what it was, or $20 per share. The total market value of my investment will not have changed.

8-21. a. *May 4, 1999:*

Dr. Treasury Stock	$14,600	
Cr. Cash..........		$14,600

To record the purchase of 800 shares of treasury stock @ $18.25 per share.

June 15, 1999:

Dr. Retained Earnings (36,200 – 800 = 35,400 shares * $0.35).	$12,390	
Cr. Cash..........		$12,390

To record the declaration and payment of a cash dividend.

September 11, 1999:

Dr. Cash (600 shares @ $19.50).........	$11,700	
Cr. Treasury Stock (600 shares @ $18.25).........		$10,950
Cr. Additional Paid-In Capital (600 shares @ $1.25).......		750

To record the sale of 600 shares of treasury stock @ $19.50 per share.

Balance Sheet	**Income Statement**
Assets = Liabilities + Owners' Equity	**← Net income = Revenues - Expenses**

To record the purchase of 800 shares of treasury stock @ $18.25 per share:

Cash	Treasury Stock
– 14,600	– 14,600

To record the declaration and payment of a cash dividend:

Cash	Retained
– 12,390	Earnings
	– 12,390

Balance Sheet	Income Statement
Assets = **Liabilities** + **Owners' Equity**	← **Net income** = **Revenues** - **Expenses**

To record the sale of 600 shares of treasury stock @ $19.50 per share.

Cash   Treasury Stock   *600 ✗ 18.25*

+ 11,700   + 10,950

                   Additional

                   Paid-in Capital   *extra*

                   + 750

8-23.

Transaction	Cash	Other Assets	Liabilities	Paid-in Capital	Retained Earnings	Treasury Stock *	Net Income
a.	+205,000			+205,000			
b.			+18,450		−18,450		
c.	−35,100					+35,100	
d.		+113,000		+113,000			
e.	+17,400			+1,200		−16,200	
f.	No entry is required for a stock split.						

    * Note that an increase in treasury stock (for a purchase transaction such as item c) decreases total owners' equity, and a decrease in treasury stock (for a sale transaction such as item f) increases total owners' equity. The effects shown are with respect to the Treasury Stock account, which is a contra owners' equity account.

a. Dr.   Cash ($50 par * 4,100 shares)... $205,000

      Cr.   Preferred Stock $205,000

b. Dr.   Retained Earnings ($50 par * 9% * 4,100 shares).   18,450

      Cr.   Dividends Payable   18,450

c. Dr.   Treasury Stock ($54 per share * 650 shares)........................   35,100

      Cr.   Cash...   35,100

d. Dr.   Land (market value)..   113,000

      Cr.   Common Stock ($1 par * 2,000 shares)........   2,000

      Cr.   Additional Paid-In Capital (excess over par)   111,000

e. Dr.   Cash ($58 per share * 300 shares)   17,400

      Cr.   Treasury Stock ($54 per share * 300 shares).   16,200

      Cr.   Additional Paid-In Capital ($4 excess * 300 shares)..   1,200

f. No entry is required for a stock split.

8-25.

Transaction	Cash	Other Assets	Liabilities	Paid-in Capital	Retained Earnings	Treasury Stock *	Net Income
a.	+ 90,000			+ 90,000			
b.		+ 40,000		+ 40,000			
c.	– 3,200				– 3,200		
d.	– 4,750					+ 4,750	
e.			+ 6,713		– 6,713		
f.	+ 2,600			+ 130		– 2,470	
g.				+ 28,350	– 28,350		

h.   No entry is required for a stock split.

* Note that an increase in treasury stock (for a purchase transaction such as item d) decreases total owners' equity, and a decrease in treasury stock (for a sale transaction such as item f) increases to owners' equity. The effects shown are with respect to the Treasury Stock account, which is a contra owners' equity account.

a. Dr. Cash... $90,000
　　　Cr. Common Stock ($1 per share * 5,000 shares)......................   　　　　$ 5,000
　　　Cr. Additional Paid-In Capital ($17 per share * 5,000 shares)......   　　　　85,000

b. Dr. Land and Building   40,000
　　　Cr. Preferred Stock ($40 per share * 1,000 shares)...........   　　　　40,000

c. Dr. Retained Earnings ($40 per share * 8% * 1,000 shares)..........   3,200
　　　Cr. Cash...   　　　　3,200

d. Dr. Treasury Stock ($4,750 / 250 shares = $19 per share)..........   4,750
　　　Cr. Cash...   　　　　4,750

e. Dr. Retained Earnings (40,000 + 5,000 – 250 = 44,750 shares)..........   6,713
　　　Cr. Dividends Payable ($0.15 per share * 44,750 shares outstanding)   　　　　6,713

f. Dr. Cash ($20 per share * 130 shares)...........................   2,600
　　　Cr. Treasury Stock ($19 per share * 130 shares)..................   　　　　2,470
　　　Cr. Additional Paid-In Capital ($1 per share * 130 shares)..........   　　　　130

g. Dr. Retained Earnings (45,000 shares *issued* * 3% = 1,350)............   28,350
　　　Cr. Common Stock ($1 per share * 1,350 dividend shares)............   　　　　1,350
　　　Cr. Additional Paid-In Capital ($20 per share * 1,350 per share)....   　　　　27,000

h. No entry is required for a stock split.

8-27. a. Annual dividend per share (12% * $60) .... $ 7.20
    Number of shares outstanding 1,500
    Annual dividend requirement **$10,800**

b. Balance sheet amount = ($60 par value * 1,500 shares issued) = **$90,000**

c. Number of shares issued = ($240,000 balance sheet amount / $8 par value) = **30,000**
    Number of shares outstanding = (30,000 shares issued − 2,000 treasury shares) = **28,000**

d.

	Common Stock	Additional Paid-in Capital
November 30, 1999.	$240,000	$540,000
January 1, 1999	(210,000)	(468,750)
Increase	**$ 30,000**	**$ 71,250**

Number of shares sold = ($30,000 increase in common stock / $8 par value) = **3,750**

Selling price per share = (($30,000 increase in common stock + $71,250 increase in additional paid-in capital) / 3,750 shares sold) = **$27 per share.**

e. Treasury stock was resold at a price greater than its cost.

f. Retained earnings, January 1, 1999. .... $90,300
    Add: Net income 24,000
    Less: Preferred stock dividends *(see answer to part a)* .... (10,800)
    Less: Common stock dividends .... ?
    Retained earnings, December 31, 1999 .... **$97,000**

Solving for the unknown amount, common stock dividends = **$6,500**

8-29. a. Par value per share of preferred stock = ($1,440,000 balance sheet amount / 24,000 shares issued) = **$60 par value per share.**
    Preferred stock dividend percentage = ($4.50 dividend per share / $60 par value per share) = **7.5 %**

b. Balance sheet amount for common stock = (820,000 shares issued * $5 par value per share) = **$4,100,000** (shown as $4,100).

c. Average issue price of common stock = (($4,100,000 common stock + $5,740,000 additional paid-in capital) / 820,000 shares issued) = **$12 per share issued.**

d. Treasury shares = (820,000 issued shares − 750,000 outstanding shares) = **70,000**

8-29. e. Balance sheet amount for treasury shares = (70,000 shares * $18 per share)
= **$1,260,000** (shown as $1,260).

f. Preferred stock	$ 1,440,000
Common stock	4,100,000
Additional paid-in capital	5,740,000
Retained earnings	?
Treasury stock	(1,260,000)
Total stockholders' equity	$15,000,000

Solving for the unknown amount, retained earnings = **$4,980,000** (shown as $4,980).

g. Retained earnings, July 1, 1997	$4,800,000
Add: Net income	288,000
Less: Preferred stock dividends (24,000 shares outstanding * $4.50 per share)	(108,000)
Retained earnings, June 30, 1998	**$4,980,000**

CHAPTER 9. *The Income Statement and the Statement of Cash Flows*

9-1. a. For the year end June 30, 1999, recognize 21/49 of summer school tuition, because that proportion of the summer session occurs within the first fiscal year. Summer session expenses will be accrued or deferred (i.e., recognized as incurred), so an appropriate matching of revenue and expense will occur in each fiscal year.

Amount of revenue for the year ended June 30, 1999 = (21/49 * $112,000) = **$48,000**

b. No. Revenues and expenses would still be allocated to each fiscal year to achieve the most appropriate matching (based on when revenues are *earned* and when expenses are *incurred*). Since revenues are earned as services are provided, the critical event is the offering of classes rather than the university's tuition refund policy. Thus, the amounts calculated in part *a* would still result in the most meaningful financial statements for each fiscal year.

9-3. *Solution approach:*   Use the cost of goods sold model with hypothetical data that are the same except for the item in error:

	"Error"	*"Correct"*
Beginning inventory	$100,000	$100,000
Add: Purchases	300,000	300,000
Goods available for sale	$400,000	$400,000
Less: Ending inventory	(125,000)	(75,000)
Cost of goods sold	$275,000	$325,000

The overstatement of ending inventory causes cost of good sold to be too low, so **gross profit and operating income are too high, or overstated, by $50,000.**

9-5. a.

	(in millions)		
	1996	*1995*	*1994*
Net revenues	$20,847	$16,202	$11,521
Cost of good sold	(9,164)	(7,811)	(5,576)
Gross profit	$11,683	$ 8,391	$ 5,945
Gross profit ratio	56.0%	51.8%	51.6%

b. Using the gross profit ratio for 1996 of 56.0%:

Net sales ($ millions)	$7,800
Cost of goods sold (44%)	**(3,432)**
Gross profit (56%)	**$4,368**

Alternative calculation: Some students may calculate a weighted average gross profit ratio for the three-year period from 1994-1996, as follows:

Total gross profit ($11,683 + $8,391 + $5,945)	$26,019
/ Total net revenues ($20,847 + $16,202 + $11,521)	$48,570
Weighted average gross profit ratio	**53.6%**

Net sales ($ millions)	$7,800
Cost of goods sold (46.4%)	**(3,619)**
Gross profit (53.6%)	**$4,181**

9-7. I would prefer to have operating income data, because this describes how well management has done operating the business. Net income is important, but includes non-recurring items such as discontinued operations and extraordinary items. Thus, trends in operating income data are more likely to reflect the firm's ability to generate future earnings than are trends in net income data.

9-9. a.

Net sales	$644,000
Cost of goods sold	(368,000)
Gross profit	$276,000
General and administrative expenses	(143,000)
Advertising expense	(45,000)
Other selling expenses	(13,000)
Operating income	**$ 75,000**

9-9. b. *Note:* Since Manahan Co. did not report any interest expense, or other income or expense, the operating income amount calculated in part *a* also represents the firm's "Income before taxes."

Income before taxes (operating income)	$ 75,000
Income tax expense	(26,000)
Earnings before extraordinary item	$ 49,000
Extraordinary loss from flood, net of taxes of $35,000	(105,000)
Net loss	**$ (56,000)**

9-11. *Solution approach:* Calculate ending inventory in the cost of goods sold model for the high (33%) and low (30%) gross profit ratios, and select the ratio that gives the highest ending inventory.

	Gross Profit Ratio			Calculation
	33%		**30%**	**Sequence**
Sales	$142,680		$142,680	Given
Cost of goods sold:				
Beginning inventory	$ 63,590		$ 63,590	Given
Add: Purchases	118,652		118,652	Given
Goods available for sale	$182,242		$182,242	
Less: Ending inventory	**(86,646)**		(82,366)	3rd
Cost of goods sold		$(95,596)	$(99,876)	2nd
Gross profit		**$ 47,084**	**$ 42,804**	1st *

* Gross profit percentage multiplied by sales.

Franklin Co.'s management would argue for using a 33% gross profit ratio for 1999 to the date of the tornado, because the higher the gross profit ratio, the higher the estimated ending inventory lost in the storm, and the greater the insurance claim.

9-13.

Net income	$473,400
Less: Dividends required on preferred stock (38,000 shares * $4.50 per share).	(171,000)
Net income available for common stockholders	$302,400
/ Number of common share outstanding	105,000
= Earnings per share—basic	**$2.88**

9-15. a. ($760,000 sales on account + $24,000 decrease in accounts receivable) = **$784,000** source of cash. Since accounts receivable decreased during the year, more accounts were collected in cash than were created by credit sales.

Accounts Receivable

Beginning balance	$???	
Sales on account	$760,000	
Ending balance	$??? - 24,000	

Cash collections from customers	$784,000

b. ($148,000 income tax expense + $34,000 decrease in income taxes payable) = **$182,000** use of cash. Tax payments exceeded the current year's income tax expense because the payable account decreased.

Income Taxes Payable

Cash payments for taxes	**$182,000**

Beginning balance	$	???
Income tax expense		$148,000
Ending balance	$???	- 34,000

c. ($408,000 cost of goods sold + $14,000 increase in inventory − $19,000 increase in accounts payable) = **$403,000** use of cash. Cost of goods sold reflects inventory uses. Inventory purchases were greater than inventory uses because inventory increased during the year, but part of the inventory purchases were not paid for in cash because accounts payable also increased during the year.

Inventory

Beginning balance	$???	
Inventory purchases	$422,000	
Ending balance	$??? + $14,000	

Cost of goods sold	$408,000

Accounts Payable

Beginning balance	$???	
Cash paid to suppliers	**$403,000**	

Inventory purchases	$422,000	
Ending balance	$??? + $19,000	

d. ($240,000 increase in net book value + $190,000 depreciation expense) = **$430,000** use of cash. Since depreciation is an expense that does not affect cash, the amount of cash paid to purchase new buildings exceeded the increase in net book value. *(Note: In some years, a firm may spend an enormous amount of cash to acquire new buildings and equipment, yet still report a <u>decrease</u> in net book value.)*

9-15. d.   **Buildings, net of Accumulated Depreciation**

Beginning balance	$???	
Purchase of buildings	**$430,000**	Depreciation expense $190,000
Ending balance	$??? + $240,000	

9-17. a. *Cash flows from operating activities:*   *($000 omitted)*

Net income...	$420
Add (deduct) items not affecting cash:	
Depreciation and amortization expense.......	320
Accounts receivable decrease	45
Inventory increase....	(20)
Accounts payable decrease......	(10)
Income tax payable increase	35
Net cash provided by operating activities....	**$790**

b. Net income is based on accrual accounting, and revenues may be *earned* before or after cash is received. Likewise, expenses may be *incurred* before or after cash payments are made. Thus, net income and cash flows provided by operations may differ because of the *timing* of cash receipts and payments. In addition to the timing issue, other adjustments to net income may be necessary to add back non-cash expenses (such as depreciation and amortization), or to remove the effects of non-operating transactions (such as the gains and losses from the sale of long-term assets). To adjust net income for timing differences, changes during the year in non-cash working capital items (i.e., current assets other than cash, and current liabilities) must be considered. If a current asset account increases or if a current liability account decreases during the year, the cash account balance is assumed to have decreased. If a current asset account decreases or if a current liability account increases, the cash account balance is assumed to have increased. *(Note: You should review the Business in Practice—Understanding Cash Flow Relationships—Indirect Method if you are having difficulty understanding these adjustments.)*

9-19. *Solution approach:* Prepare a statement of cash flows—direct method *(see Exhibit 9-8).*

a. **Cash flows from operating activities:**   *(in millions)*

Cash collected from customers.....	$1,350
Interest and taxes paid...............	(90)
Cash paid to suppliers and employees.......	(810)
Net cash provided by operating activities..	**$ 450**

b. **Cash flows from investing activities:**

Purchase of land and buildings.....	$(170)
Proceeds from the sale of equipment	40
Net cash used for investing activities	$(130)

c. **Cash flows from financing activities:**

Payment of long-term debt	$ (220)
Issuance of preferred stock..........	300
Cash dividends declared and paid	(340)
Net cash used for financing activities	$(260)

d. Net increase in cash for the year .. ..   **$ 60**

9-21. a. Intel uses the multiple-step format, but does not report gross profit separately. The multiple-step format seems easier to read and interpret because it provides intermediate captions and subtotals that are useful to investors.

b. The EPS disclosure is an important measure to investors because it expresses accrual accounting income on a per share basis. For Intel, this disclosure is straight-forward. As discussed in the text, however, additional disclosure about the significant elements of EPS is appropriate for any years during which a firm reports any of the "unusual" income statement items (i.e., the "net of tax" items—discontinued operations, extraordinary items, and/or cumulative effect of accounting changes). Knowledge about the impact of non-recurring items provides investors with a better basis for anticipating what may happen to EPS in the future.

9-23. a.-d. Answers vary depending upon the company being analyzed.

9-25. a.

HOEMAN, INC.
Balance Sheets
December 31, 1999, and 1998

Assets

	1999	1998
Current assets:		
Cash..........	$ 52,000	$ 46,000
Accounts receivable	(1)	134,000
Inventory	156,000	176,000
Total current assets	$ (2)	$ 356,000
Land	(3)	140,000
Buildings...	(4)	290,000
Less: Accumulated depreciation	(120,000)	(105,000)
Total land & buildings..........	$ (5)	$ 325,000
Total assets	$ (6)	$ 681,000

9-25. a. *(continued)* | | **Liabilities**

Current liabilities:

Note payable..	$ 155,000	$ 124,000
Accounts payable	(7)	197,000
Total current liabilities...	$ 322,000	$ 321,000
Long-term debt	$ (11)	$ 139,000

Owners' Equity

Common stock...	$ 50,000	$ 45,000
Retained earnings...	(9)	176,000
Total owners' equity..	$ (10)	$ 221,000
Total liabilities and owners' equity	$ (8)	$ 681,000

Calculations:

1. $134,000 – $10,000 = $124,000
2. $52,000 + $124,000 + $156,000 = $332,000
3. Land is carried at historical cost = $140,000
4. $290,000 + $125,000 = $415,000
5. $140,000 + $415,000 – $120,000 = $435,000
6. $332,000 + $435,000 = $767,000
7. $322,000 – $155,000 = $167,000
8. Same as total assets = $767,000
9. $176,000 + $94,000 – $67,000 = $203,000
10. $50,000 + $203,000 = $253,000
11. $767,000 – $253,000 – $322,000 = $192,000

b.
HOEMAN, INC.
Statement of Cash Flows
For the Year Ended December 31, 1999

Cash flows from operating activities:

Net income	$ 94,000
Add (deduct) items not affecting cash:	
Depreciation expense	15,000
Decrease in accounts receivable......................................	10,000
Decrease in inventory...	20,000
Increase in notes payable...	31,000
Decrease in accounts payable	(30,000)
Net cash provided by operating activities......................	**$ 140,000**

Cash flows from investing activities:

Cash paid to acquire new buildings	**$(125,000)**

Cash flows from financing activities:

Cash received from issuance of long-term debt	$ 53,000
Cash received from issuance of common stock	5,000
Payment of cash dividends on common stock	(67,000)
Net cash used for financing activities ...., ...	**(9,000)**
Net increase in cash for the year	**$ 6,000**

9-27. a.

HARRIS, INC.
Balance Sheet
December 31, 1999

Assets

Current assets:

Cash	$ 6,000	
Accounts receivable	67,000	
Merchandise inventory	46,000	
Total current assets		$ 119,000

Noncurrent assets:

Land	27,000	
Buildings...	208,000	
Less: Accumulated depreciation	(101,000)	
Total noncurrent assets...........		134,000
Total assets		$ 253,000

Liabilities and Owners' Equity

Current liabilities:

Short-term debt.....	$ 12,000	
Notes payable........	24,000	
Accounts payable	61,000	
Total current liabilities...........		$ 97,000
Long-term debt.....		65,000

Owners' equity:

Common stock, no par	$ 28,000	
Retained earnings..	63,000	
Total owners' equity		91,000
Total liabilities and owners' equity		$ 253,000

9-27. b.

HARRIS, INC.
Statement of Changes in Retained Earnings
For the Year Ended December 31, 1999

Retained earnings, 1/1/99	$ 55,000
Add: Net income for the year	13,000
Less: Dividends for the year	(5,000)
Retained earnings balance 12/31/99	$ 63,000

CHAPTER 10. *Explanatory Notes and Other Financial Information*

10-1. Class discussion can focus on the importance of these items to a reader's full understanding of the company's financial statements (financial position, results of operations, and cash flows).

10-3.

ROI	=	MARGIN	x	TURNOVER

$$\frac{\text{OPERATING INCOME}}{\text{AVERAGE IDENTIFIABLE ASSETS}} = \frac{\text{OPERATING INCOME}}{\text{NET REVENUES}} \times \frac{\text{NET REVENUES}}{\text{AVERAGE IDENTIFIABLE ASSETS}}$$

INTEL CORPORATION
1996 ROI by Geographic Area

	United States	*Europe*	*Japan*	*Asia-Pacific*
Net revenues	$18,514	$6,793	$2,479	$5,848
Operating income	5,255	1,118	340	509
Identifiable assets, June 30, 1996	12,892	2,405	659	1,361
Identifiable assets, June 30, 1995	12,603	2,517	665	893
Average identifiable assets	12,748	2,461	662	1,127
Margin	28.4%	16.5%	13.7%	8.7%
Turnover	1.5	2.8	3.7	5.2
ROI	41.2%	45.4%	51.4%	45.2%

Analysis of results: These results suggest that Intel does what it needs to do, where it needs to do it, to enhance its overall ROI. In the Unites States, margin is highest, but total asset turnover is lowest. In the Asia-Pacific area, the opposite is true: margin is lowest and turnover is highest. Yet, ROI is remarkably consistent across geographic areas.

Intel's transfer pricing policy of "generally above cost and consistent with rules and regulations of governing tax authorities" is not very descriptive; this may very well play an important role in determining *where* its profits ultimately reside. Since most of Intel's production occurs in the U.S., most of the "Transfers between geographic areas" are also reflected in the U.S. net revenues figure—of the $13,652 of inter-company sales shown in the "Eliminations" column, $9,846 were transfers from the U.S. to other geographic areas. Thus, the 28.4% margin earned in the U.S. segment may be more of a reflection of Intel's transfer pricing policy than anything else. In essence, the "above cost" transfer price is a necessary payment in compensation to the U.S. segment for making the additional required investment in identifiable assets necessary to meet the production needs of other segments.

10-5. a. Original earnings per share is $3.12. To reflect a 3 for 1 stock split, divide by 3. Adjusted EPS = **$1.04**

b. For 1999, 1997 earnings per share as adjusted in 1998 will have to be adjusted again by dividing by 2. Adjusted EPS for 1997, to be reported in 1999 = $1.04 / 2 = **$0.52**

c. To reflect a 10% stock dividend, divide unadjusted earnings per share by 1.10. Adjusted EPS = $3.12 / 1.10 = **$2.84**

10-7.
Earnings per share, as restated..........	$0.60
Multiply by 2 to reflect 2 for 1 stock split.......	$1.20
Multiply by 1.05 to reflect 5% stock dividend.	**$1.26**
Proof: Original earnings per share.....	$1.26
Adjust for stock split (divide by 2)......	$0.63
Adjust for 5% stock dividend (divide by 1.05)	$0.60

10-9. The auditors' opinion is that the identified financial statements *present fairly*, *in all material respects* (emphasis added), the financial position, results of operations, and cash flows in conformity with generally accepted accounting principles. Thus, the auditor does guarantee that the statements are free from *immaterial* errors or irregularities, nor that the statements are presented with absolute accuracy.

10-11. a. Net revenues in 1989 = **$3,127 million**

b. Gross profit in 1992 = $5,844 – $2,557 = **$3,287 mil.**

c. Difference between operating income and net income in 1994 = $3,387 – $2,288 = **$1,099 mil.**

d. Year(s) in which net income decreased as compared to the previous year = **1989, 1993**

e. Potential obligation under put warrants = **$275 mil.** *(table, p.23)*

10-11. f. Amount of short-term debt = **$389 mil.** *(table, p.23)*
Amount of long-term debt = **$728 mil.** *(table, p.24)*

g. Total assets invested in operations outside of the Unites States =
$4,784 mil. *(table, p.30)*

h. Amount committed for the construction of property, plant, and equipment =
Approximately $1.6 billion *(p.30)*

i. Amount of available-for-sale securities classified as cash equivalents =
$3,932 mil. *(table, p.24)*

j. Gross profit for the third quarter of 1996 = $5,142 – $2,201 =
$2,941 mil. *(table, p.37—use September 28 column)*

k. Amount of interest income earned = **$364 mil.** *(table, p.26)*

10-13. a.-e. Answers vary depending on the company analyzed.

CHAPTER 11. *Financial Statement Analysis*

11-1. Key data would be the recent (3-5 year) trend in earnings per share, cash dividends per share, market price, and P/E ratio. These data would be in tabular and graphic format.

Market price would be noted weekly. Quarterly and annual data to note are earnings and dividend trends.

The sell/hold/buy decision is based on stock price performance relative to the price objective established from analysis of the above data.

11-3.

INTEL CORPORATION
Common Size Balance Sheet
December 30, 1995

Total current assets	46.3%
Property, plant and equipment, (net)	42.7
Long-term investments and other noncurrent assets	11.1
Total assets	100.0%

Total current liabilities. 20.7%
Total noncurrent liabilities * 10.0
Total shareholders' equity .... <u>69.3</u>
Total liabilities and shareholders' equity .... <u>100.0%</u>

* Includes: long-term debt, deferred tax liabilities, and put warrants.

11-5. a. Working capital = (current assets − current liabilities) = CA − CL = $300,000
Current ratio = (current assets / current liabilities) = CA / CL = 2.0

Solution approach:
1) In the current ratio equation, multiply both sides by CL, giving:
   CA = 2CL
2) In the working capital equation, substitute 2CL for CA, giving:
   2CL − CL = $300,000
   Current liabilities = $300,000
3) Current assets can be determined as: CA = 2CL = (2 * $300,000) = $600,000

b. Current assets = (Cash + Accounts Receivable + Merchandise Inventory) = $600,000
Current liabilities = $300,000
Current ratio = 2.0
Acid-test ratio = 1.5

Solution approach:
1) The difference between the current ratio and the acid-test ratio is that Merchandise Inventory is excluded from the numerator of the acid-test ratio.
2) The numerator of the acid test ratio = (CL * 1.5) = ($300,000 * 1.5) = $450,000, which represents Cash + Accounts Receivable.
3) $600,000 − $450,000 = **$150,000 Merchandise Inventory.**

c. **Solution approach:**
The journal entry for collecting an account receivable involves a debit to one current asset (Cash) and a credit to another current asset (Accounts Receivable). Thus, current assets do not change in total, and there is no effect on working capital or the current ratio. **Current ratio = 2.0 Working capital = $300,000**

d. **Solution approach:**
The journal entry for the payment of an account payable involves a debit to a current liability (Accounts Payable) and a credit to a current asset (Cash). Thus, current assets and current liabilities decrease by an equal amount, and there is no effect on working capital. However, the current ratio increases because current assets become proportionately higher than current liabilities.

11-5. d.

	Before	*After*
Current assets (A)	$600,000	$500,000
Current liabilities (B)	300,000	200,000
Working capital (A − B)	300,000	**300,000**
Current ratio (A / B)	2.0	**2.5**

e. ***Solution approach:***

The journal entries for the sale of inventory would be:

Dr. Cash (included in acid-test numerator)	$60,000	
Cr. Sales		$60,000
Dr. Cost of Goods Sold	50,000	
Cr. Merchandise Inventory (excluded from acid-test numerator)		50,000

By selling inventory for cash, Arch Company will improve its **acid-test ratio** to **1.7** because a current asset that is included in the acid-test numerator (Cash of $60,000) will replace a current asset that was previously excluded from the acid-test numerator (Merchandise Inventory of $50,000).

$$\text{Acid-test ratio} = \frac{\text{Cash (including temporary cash investments)} + \text{Accounts receivable}}{\text{current liabilities}}$$

Before transaction: ***After transaction:***
$450,000 / $300,000 = 1.5   ($450,000 + $60,000) / $300,000 = **1.7**

11-7.

Transaction/event	*Financial ratio*	*Effect*	*Explanation*
a. Split the common stock 2 for 1.	Book value per share of common stock.	−	The denominator doubles so the BV/share will be ½ of original.
b. Collected accounts receivable.	Number of days' sales in accounts receivable.	−	Decrease in accounts receivable with no effect on average days' sales.
c. Issued common stock for cash.	Total asset turnover	−	Increase in average total assets with no effect on sales.
d. Sold treasury stock.	Return on equity	−	Increase in average owners' equity with no effect on net income.
e. Accrued interest on a note receivable.	Current ratio	+	Increase in current assets for interest receivable.
f. Sold inventory on account.	Acid-test ratio	+	Numerator increases (inventory turns into accounts receivable).

11-7. *Transaction/event*	*Financial ratio*		*Effect*	*Explanation*
g. Wrote off an uncollectible account.	Accounts receivable turnover	NE		Net realizable value of accounts receivable is not affected by the write-off entry.
h. Declared a cash dividend.	Dividend yield	+		Dividends per share increase with no determinable effect on market price per share.
i. Incurred operating expenses.	Margin	–		Expenses reduce net income.
j. Sold equipment at a loss.	Earnings per share	+		Losses reduce net income.

11-9. a. *Solution approach:*

Base your evaluation on a quick "eyeballing" of the data.

Working capital:
1. La-Z-Boy Incorporated — Slow but steady growth.
2. The Sherwin-Williams Company — Steady growth until 1996, when something unusual appears to have happened (see part *e* below).
3. The Quaker Oats Company — For some reason, the company appears committed to operating with negative working capital.
4. Microsoft Corporation — Tremendously high rate of growth (mostly in cash and cash equivalents).

Current ratio:
1. La-Z-Boy Incorporated — Very stable, with slight downward trend since 1994.
2. The Sherwin-Williams Company — Stable until 1995, with dramatic drop-off in 1996.
3. The Quaker Oats Company — Noticeable downward trend with a low-point in 1995.
4. Microsoft Corporation — Noticeable downward trend despite the dramatic increase in working capital each year (see part *b* below).

b. Microsoft's working capital is growing very quickly, but its current ratio continues to fall each year. Clearly, the company is becoming more liquid each year. Essentially, what has happened is that both current assets and current liabilities have grown each year — while current assets have grown more in terms of dollar amount, current liabilities have grown more in terms of proportion. The growth in current liabilities relates mostly to accrued expense items and has more to do with the *timing* of payment than the *ability* to make payment when due.

c. As a large-scale manufacturer of food products, Quaker Oats probably maintains extremely low inventory quantities by utilizing just-in-time purchasing techniques (see Chapter 12) and by maintaining a back-log of sales orders so that virtually all finished goods are sold immediately to a limited number of large wholesalers. By offering these

11-9. c. *(continued)*

wholesale customers cash discounts to encourage prompt payment, the company's "investment in accounts receivable" is thereby minimized. Finally, because of its size and credit worthiness, Quaker Oats may be able to negotiate favorable credit terms with its major suppliers, allowing an extended deferral of payments on accounts.

As a furniture manufacturer/retailer, La-Z-Boy must maintain high levels of inventory to provide its customers with a wide variety of choices (e.g. color, fabric, style, price). Accounts receivable also tend be high in the furniture industry due to a variety of manufacturer financing arrangements (i.e., floor planning with authorized dealers).

d. Yes. Quaker Oats has obviously made a commitment to operating with negative working capital by minimizing its investment in inventories and accounts receivable and by extending the average payment period for accounts payable and accrued expenses. To survive in the long-run, an extremely effective cash management program (including cash equivalents) must be implemented to ensure that all liabilities can be paid when due. In this regard, it should be remembered that current liabilities include all liabilities that fall due within one year of the balance sheet date — and that cash only needs to be available on the date payment is due.

e. Notice in particular the dramatic changes in the "Cash and cash equivalents" and "Short- term borrowings" captions from 1995 to 1996. Notice also that each of the other current asset and current liability captions increased significantly from 1995 to 1996. What caused these dramatic changes in 1996? During the year, Sherwin-Williams invested more than $670.7 million in the acquisition of Pratt & Lambert United, Inc. and many smaller domestic and foreign acquisitions. These acquisitions were financed through the use of $267.6 million of cash and cash equivalents, plus short-term borrowings, long-term debt and excess operating cash flow generated during the year.

Points for Discussion: This question provides an opportunity to reinforce the parent-subsidiary relationship introduced in Chapter 2, and to discuss the consolidation process in general. With this example, students can easily understand why accounts receivable, inventories, accounts payable, and other balance sheet accounts increase dramatically when a major purchase transaction occurs.

Another point to emphasize is that ratio analysis often provides important clues as to what is happening within a company. In this case, the 1996 changes in working capital and the current ratio were too large to be accounted for by day to day operating activities. A closer look at the financial statements, explanatory notes, and management's discussion and analysis will normally reveal the source of any unusual changes in the trend of data.

11-11. a.

ROI	=	MARGIN	x	TURNOVER
NET INCOME		NET INCOME		SALES
AVERAGE TOTAL ASSETS	=	SALES	x	AVERAGE TOTAL ASSETS

1999 ROI = ($192 / $3,050) * [$3,050 / (($3,090 + $2,811) / 2)]
  = **6.3%** margin * **1.034** turnover = **6.5%**
1998 ROI = ($187 / $2,913) * [$2,913 / (($2,455 + $2,811) / 2)]
  = **6.4%** margin * **1.106** turnover = **7.1%**

b. ROE = Net income / Average owners' equity
  1999 ROE = $192 / (($1,007 + $1,026) / 2) = **18.9%**
  1998 ROE = $187 / (($918 + $1,026) / 2) = **19.2%**

c.

	1999	1998	1997
Current assets	$677	$891	$736
Current liabilities	(562)	(803)	(710)
Working capital	**$115**	**$ 88**	**$ 26**
Current ratio (current asset / current liabilities)	**1.2**	**1.1**	**1.0**

d. Earnings per share = Net income / Weighted average number of shares outstanding

  1999 EPS = $192 / 41.3 = **$4.65**
  1998 EPS = $187 / 46.7 = **$4.00**

e. Price/Earnings ratio = Market price / Earnings per share

  13 = $??? / $4.65
  Market price = **$60.45**

f. Cash dividends per share = ($50 million total cash dividend / 41.3 million weighted
  average number of shares outstanding) = **$1.21**

  Dividend yield = ($1.21 cash dividend per share / $60.45 market price per share) = **2%**

g. Dividend payout ratio = ($1.21 dividend per share / $4.65 earnings per share) = **26%**

h. Average days' sales = ($3,050 sales / 365 days) = $8.356 million

  Number of days' sales in accounts receivable = ($309 accounts receivable /
  $8.356 average day's sales) = **37.0 days**

11-11. i. Debt ratio = Total liabilities / (Total liabilities + Total owners' equity)

12/31/99 Debt ratio = ($562 + $1,521) / $3,090 = **67.4%**
12/31/98 Debt ratio = ($803 + $982) / $2,811 = **63.5%**

Debt/equity ratio = Total liabilities / Total owners' equity

12/31/99 Debt/equity ratio = ($562 + $1,521) / $1,007 = **207%**
12/31/98 Debt/equity ratio = ($803 + $982) / $1,026 = **174%**

j. Times interest earned = Operating income / Interest expense

For 1999: = $296 / $84 = **3.5 times**
For 1998: = $310 / $65 = **4.8 times**

k. A young, single professional would probably be more interested in potential growth of capital rather than current dividend income, and would probably be willing to invest in a stock that represented a relatively risky investment. Based on these criteria, the significant growth in earnings per share and the relatively high financial leverage could make this stock an attractive, though risky, potential investment.

The liquidity of the company is relatively low, based on an "average" current ratio of 2.0. Without further information about the composition of the current asset and current liability accounts, it is difficult to assess the firm's liquidity. The number of days' sales in accounts receivable indicates that the accounts receivable are relatively current, assuming that the credit terms are net 30.

The company's ROI is relatively low, and the two-year trend is down. This would be a major concern, and the reasons for this situation would be sought. The price/earnings ratio of 13 is typical for a firm with a falling ROI; the fact that the P/E ratio has remained within the "normal" range may indicate that future earnings prospects for this firm are fairly strong.

11-13. a. 1. Margin = ($5,157 net income / $20,847 net revenues) = **24.7%**
   Turnover = Net revenues / Average total assets = $20,847 / (($17,504 + 23,735) / 2)
      = **1.01**
   ROI = (24.7% margin * 1.01 turnover) = **25.0%**

2. ROE = Net income / Average stockholders' equity
   = $5,157 / (($12,140 + 16,872) / 2) = **35.6%**
3. Price/earnings ratio = ($131.00 market value per common share / $5.81 earnings
   per common and common equivalent share outstanding) = **22.5**

4. Dividend yield = ($0.19 dividends declared per share / $131.00 market value per common share) = **0.1%**

5. Dividend payout ratio = ($0.19 dividends per common share / $5.81 earnings per common and common equivalent share outstanding) = **3.3%**

b. 1. Working capital = ($13,864 current assets – $4,863 current liabilities) = **$9,001 mil.**

2. Current ratio = ($13,864 current assets / $4,863 current liabilities) = **2.85**

3. Acid-test ratio = (($4,165 cash and cash equivalent + $3,742 short-term investments + $87 trading assets + $3,723 accounts receivable) / $4,863 current liabilities) = $11,717 / $4,863 = **2.41**

c. 1. Average day's sales = ($20,847 annual net revenues / 365 days) = $57.115 million
Number of days' sales in accounts receivable = ($3,723 accounts receivable / $57.115 average day's sales) = **65.2 days**

(Note: This result may be overstated to some extent because it is based on the assumption that all of $20,847 net revenues resulted from credit sales.)

2. Average day's cost of goods sold = ($9,164 annual cost of sales / 365 days) = $25.107 million
Number of days' sales in inventory = ($1,293 inventories / $25.107 average day's cost of goods sold) = **51.5 days**

3. Accounts receivable turnover = Net revenues / Average accounts receivable = $20,847 / (($3,116 + $3,723) / 2) = **6.1 times**

4. Inventory turnover = Cost of sales / Average inventories = ($9,164 / (($2,004 + $1,293) /2) = **5.6 times**

5. Net property, plant and equipment turnover = Net revenues / Average property, plant and equipment = $20,847 / (($7,471 + $8,487) / 2) = **2.6 times**

d. 1. Debt ratio = (Total liabilities / Total liabilities and stockholders' equity) = (($4,863 total current liabilities + $728 long-term debt + $997 deferred tax liabilities + $275 put warrants) / $23,735 total liabilities and stockholders' equity) = $6,863 / $23,735 = **28.9%**

11-13. d. 2. Debt/equity ratio = (Total liabilities / Total stockholders' equity)
  = (($4,863 total current liabilities + $728 long-term debt + $997 deferred tax liabilities + $275 put warrants) / $16,872 total stockholders' equity)
  = $6,863 / $16,872 = **40.7%**

3. Times interest earned = (Earnings before interest and taxes / Interest expense)
  = ($7,553 operating income / $25) = **302 times**

(*Note:* An alternative calculation for the numerator would be: ($5,157 net income + $25 interest expense + $2,777 provision for taxes) = $7,959. This is higher than the reported operating income of $7,553 by an amount equal to interest income of $406. As a result, times interest earned would be: $7,959 / $25 = **318 times**

e. 1. Net revenues per employee = Net revenues / Average number of employees for the year = $20,847 / ((41,600 + 48,500) /2) =**$462,752 per employee**

2. Operating income per employee = Operating income / Average number of employees for the year = $7,553 / ((41,600 + 48,500) /2) =**$167,658 per employee**

11-15. a.1. Income statement (or statement of operations).
  2. Net income (or net earnings).
  3. Earnings per share of common stock.
  4. Statement of changes in owners' (or stockholders') equity.
  5. Retained earnings.
  6. Owners' (or stockholders') equity.
  7. Working capital.
  8. Owners' (or stockholders') equity.

b. 1.

ROI	=	**MARGIN**	x	**TURNOVER**
OPERATING INCOME **AVERAGE TOTAL ASSETS**	=	**OPERATING INCOME** **SALES**	x	**SALES** **AVERAGE TOTAL ASSETS**

Margin = ($498 operating profit / $8,251 sales) = **6.0%**
Turnover = Sales / ((Total assets less current liabilities + Current liabilities) / 2)
  = $8,251 / [(($4,873 + $2,758) + ($4,289 + $2,472)) / 2] = **1.15**
ROI = (6.0% Margin * 1.15 Turnover) = **6.9%**

2. ROE = (Net income / Average owners' equity) = (Profit / Average ownership)
  = $350 / (($3,565 + $3,149) / 2) = **10.4%**

11-15. c. 1. Average day's sales = ($8,251 annual sales / 365 days) = $22.6 million

Number of days' sales in accounts receivable = ($2,174 accounts receivable / $22.6 average day's sales) = **96.2 days**

2. Inventory turnover = Cost of goods sold / Average inventory
= $6,523 / (($1,323 + $1,211) / 2) = **5.1 times**

3. Plant and equipment turnover = Sales / Average plant and equipment
= Sales / ((Buildings, machinery, and equipment + Land) / 2)
= $8,251 / [(($2,467 + $96) + ($2,431 + $97)) / 2] = **3.2 times**

d. 1. Debt/equity ratio = ($1,287 long-term debt / $3,565 ownership) = **36.1%**

2. Debt ratio = ($1,287 long-term debt / ($1,287 long-term debt + $3,565 ownership)) = **26.5%**

3. Times interest earned = (Earnings before interest and taxes / Interest expense)
= ($498 operating profit / $209) = **2.4 times**

e. 1. Price/earning ratio = (Market price per share / Earning per share)
= ($42.00 / $3.51 profit per share of common stock after extraordinary tax benefit) = **12.0**

2. Dividend payout ratio = (Dividends per share / Earning per share)
= ($0.50 dividends paid per share of common stock / $3.51 profit per share of common stock after extraordinary tax benefit) = **14.2%**

3. Dividend yield = (Dividends per share / Market price per share)
= ($0.50 dividends paid per share of common stock / $42.00) = **1.2%**

CHAPTER 12. *Managerial/Cost Accounting and Cost Classifications*

12-1.

	Product				
	Direct	*Indirect*	*Period*	*Variable*	*Fixed*
Wages of assembly-line workers	X			X	
Depreciation—plant equipment		X			X
Glue and thread		X		X	
Shipping costs			X	X	
Raw materials handling costs		X		X	

12-1.

	Direct	Indirect	Period	Variable	Fixed
			Product		
Salary of public relations manager			X		X
Production run setup costs		X		X	
Plant utilities		X		X	X
Electricity cost of retail stores			X	X	X
Research and development expenses.......			X	X	X

Note: The last three items are each likely to have a mixed cost behavior pattern.

12-3. a. *Raw material:* cotton/ wool/ rayon used for jersey, or material used for team emblems.
   b. *Direct labor:* wages of production-line machine operator.
   c. *Variable manufacturing overhead:* plant utilities costs, or indirect materials (i.e., thread).
   d. *Fixed manufacturing overhead:* depreciation of machinery, or property taxes on plant.
   e. *Fixed administrative expense:* salaries of administrative officers.
   f. *Fixed indirect selling expense:* advertising costs.
   g. *Variable, direct selling expense:* shipping costs.

12-5. a. *Differential cost:* What costs will differ if a friend comes along?
   b. *Allocated cost:* How to allocate? Based on number of people, weight, number of suitcases, or what?
   c. *Sunk cost:* What costs have already been incurred and cannot be recovered, even if you don't make the trip?
   d. *Opportunity cost:* What are other opportunities for you to earn revenue? What is the cost of alternative travel for your classmate?

12-7. a. Predetermined overhead application rate = ($408,750 estimated total overhead cost / 54,500 estimated direct labor hours) = **$7.50 per direct labor hour.**

   b. **Total cost for 750 coffee mugs produced:**
Raw materials.........	$ 810
Direct labor (90 direct labor hours * $9.50 per hour).........	855
Overhead (90 direct labor hours * $7.50 predetermined rate).......	675
Total manufacturing cost..............	$2,340

   Cost per coffee mug produced = ($2,340 total cost / 750 mugs) = **$3.12 per coffee mug.**

   c. Cost of coffee mugs sold = (530 mugs * $3.12 per mug) = **$1,653.60**
   Cost of coffee mugs in inventory = (220 mugs * $3.12 per mug) = **$686.40**

12-9. a. 9,000 machine hours * $12.70 per machine hour = **$114,300 budgeted overhead.**

   b. Actual overhead incurred... $121,650
   Applied overhead (9,100 machine hours* $12.70 per machine hour)......... (115,570)
   Underapplied overhead... **$ 6,080**

   c. The overapplied or underapplied overhead for the year is normally transferred to cost of goods sold in the income statement. Since most products made during the year are sold during the same year, manufacturing overhead costs are assumed to relate primarily to the products sold. However, if the over- or underapplied overhead is material in dollar amount, then it may be allocated between work-in-process, finished goods, and cost of goods sold, based on respective year-end balances.

12-11. **Total cost for 530 ties produced:**
   Raw materials... $1,950
   Direct labor (75 direct labor hours) 840
   Overhead applied based on raw materials ($1,950 * 140%) 2,730
   Overhead applied based on direct labor hours (75 hours * $7.20) 540
   Total manufacturing cost... $6,060

   Cost per tie produced = $6,060 / 530 units = **$11.43 per unit** (rounded)

12-13. a. Total manufacturing cost = (Direct materials + Direct labor + Manufacturing overhead)

   Direct materials... $3,500,000
   Direct labor (160,000 hours * $20 per hour).................................. 3,200,000
   Manufacturing overhead:
   Materials handling ($1.50 per part * 275,000 parts used)........... $ 412,500
   Milling and grinding ($11.00 per machine hour * 95,000 hours). 1,045,000
   Assembly and inspection ($5.00 per labor hour * 160,000 hours)......... 800,000
   Testing ($3.00 per unit * 50,000 units tested)......................... 150,000 2,407,500
   Total manufacturing cost... $9,107,500

   Cost per unit produced and tested = $9,107,500 / 50,000 units = **$182.15 per unit.**

   b. The activity based costing approach is likely to provide better information for manufacturing managers because overhead costs are applied based on the activities that *cause* the incurrance of cost (i.e., cost drivers). Thus, management attention will be directed to the critical activities that can be controlled to improve the firm's operating performance. ABC systems also produce more accurate product costing information, which can lead to better decision making.

12-15. a. Total cost = ($320 fixed cost + ($0.14 variable cost per mile * 1,529 miles)) = **$534.06**

b. No, it would not be meaningful to calculate an average cost per mile, because that would involve unitizing the fixed expenses, and they do not behave on a per mile basis. Whatever average cost per mile were calculated would be valid only for the number of miles used in the calculation. An average cost for any other number of miles driven would be different, because the fixed expenses per mile would decrease for each additional mile driven.

12-17. a. Absorption cost per sweater $11.60
Less: Fixed manufacturing overhead per sweater ($22,500 / 9,000)........... (2.50)
Variable cost per sweater... **$ 9.10**

b. 1,600 sweaters * $2.50 = $4,000 more cost released to the income statement this month under absorption costing than under variable costing. Thus, cost of goods sold under variable costing will be $4,000 lower than under absorption.

c. Total cost = Fixed cost + (variable rate * activity)
= $22,500 + ($9.10 * number of sweaters)

12-19. a. Variable manufacturing costs:
Raw materials... $ 62,100
Direct labor... 16,500
Variable manufacturing overhead....................................... 11,250
Total variable costs.. $ 89,850
Fixed manufacturing overhead.. 18,000
Total manufacturing costs... $107,850

Variable cost per rod = $89,850 / 15,000 = **$5.99 each**
Absorption cost per rod = $107,850 / 15,000 = **$7.19 each**

b. The fixed cost per rod is $7.19 − $5.99 = $1.20. This can also be computed as: $18,000 / 15,000 = $1.20. The total fixed cost associated with the 300 fishing rods in inventory is: 300 * $1.20 = $360. This amount would be included in ending inventory under absorption costing, but would be included in cost of goods sold under variable costing. Thus, under variable costing, operating income would be $360 less than under absorption costing.

c. Total cost = $18,000 + $5.99 per fishing rod produced.
The cost of making 200 more units = 200 * $5.99 = **$1,198**

12-21. a.

Raw materials..	$ 33,100
Direct labor..	65,200
Manufacturing overhead...	44,800
Cost of goods manufactured..	**$143,100**

Cost per unit = $143,100 / 5,300 = **$27**

b. Cost of goods sold = $27 * 4,800 = **$129,600**

c. The difference between cost of goods manufactured and cost of goods sold is in the finished goods inventory account on the balance sheet. Since more units were produced (5,300) than sold (4,800), the finished goods account will increase by $13,500 ($27 per unit * 500 units), and cost of goods sold will be $13,500 less than cost of goods manufactured.

d.

Kimane, Ltd.
Income Statement
For the month of November

Sales	$244,800
Cost of goods sold..	(129,600)
Gross profit	$115,200
Selling and administrative expenses....................................	(46,100)
Operating income..	$ 69,100
Interest expense	(9,100)
Income before taxes	$ 60,000
Income tax expense	(18,000)
Net income	$ 42,000

12-23. a. *Note:* This problem does not require a formal statement of cost of goods manufactured; the requirements can be solved using a "T" account approach.

Raw materials:

Inventory, Sept. 30..	$ 33,500	
Purchases during October.................................	123,900	
Raw materials available for use.	157,400	
Less: Inventory, Oct. 31....................................	(27,600)	
Cost of raw materials used.................................		$129,800
Direct labor cost incurred		312,200
Manufacturing overhead applied		192,300
Total manufacturing costs, October		$634,300
Add: Work-in-process, Sept. 30...........................		71,300
Less: Work-in-process, Oct. 31		(64,800)
Cost of goods manufactured, October.		**$640,800**

12-23. b. Finished goods, Sept. 30 .... $ 47,200
        Cost of goods manufactured 640,800
        Cost of goods available for sale $688,000
        Less: Finished goods, Oct. 31. .... (41,900)
        Cost of goods sold **$646,100**

12-25. a. Predetermined fixed manufacturing overhead application rate = $312,000 / 96,000
        machine hours = **$3.25 per machine hour.**

   b. Raw materials, beginning balance .. .. $ 39,000
       Add: Purchases during the year 240,000
       Less: Raw materials used during the year... .... ?
       Ending balance....... .... $ 27,000

       Solving for the missing amount, raw materials used = **$252,000**

   c. Direct labor hours worked during the year = ($420,000 direct labor costs incurred /
       $16.00 per hour direct labor rate) = 26,250 direct labor hours
       Variable manufacturing overhead applied to work in process = (26,250 direct labor
       hours * $6 per hour) = **$157,500**

   d. Fixed manufacturing overhead applied to work in process = (88,000 machine hours
       * $3.25 per hour) = **$286,000**

   e. ***Analysis of the Work in Process Inventory account:***
       Beginning balance .. .. $ 33,000
       Add: Raw materials used 252,000
       Direct labor 420,000
       Fixed manufacturing overhead applied....... 286,000
       Variable manufacturing overhead applied 157,500
       Total manufacturing costs 1,148,500
       Less: Cost of goods manufactured. .... (?   )
       Ending balance .... $ 51,500
       Solving for the missing amount, cost of goods manufactured = **$1,097,000**

   f. ***Analysis of the Finished Goods Inventory account:***
       Beginning balance .. .. $ 104,000
       Add: Cost of goods manufactured 1,097,000
       Less: Cost of goods sold .... ?
       Ending balance .... $ 122,000
       Solving for the missing amount, cost of goods sold = **$1,079,000**

CHAPTER 13. *Cost-Volume-Profit Analysis*

13-1. a. *Solution approach:* First, calculate variable cost per unit in February and use the same per unit cost for April. Second, fixed cost will be the same for each month. Third, with knowledge of total costs for April, and variable and fixed costs for April, solve for mixed costs for April.

	February	*April*
Activity	5,000 units	8,000 units

Costs:

Variable ($10,000 / 5,000 units = $2 per unit)	$10,000	$16,000
Fixed (same total amount each month)	30,000	30,000
Mixed (Total costs − (Variable + Fixed))	20,000	**24,500**
Total	$60,000	$70,500

b. Variable rate = (High $ − Low $) / (High units − Low units)

$\quad$ = ($24,500 − $20,000) / (8,000 − 5,000)

$\quad$ = $4,500 / 3,000 = **$1.50 per unit**

Total mixed cost = Fixed cost + Variable cost

$\quad$ $24,500 = ? + ($1.50 * 8,000 units)

$\quad\quad$ **? = $12,500**

Cost formula = Fixed cost + (Variable rate * Volume) = **$12,500 + $1.50 per unit**

Proof at 5,000 units: Mixed cost = $12,500 + ($1.50 * 5,000 units) = $20,000

13-3. *Note to Student:* The purpose of this assignment is to help you to build an understanding cost-volume-profit relationships by solving for the 'missing pieces of the puzzles.' In this regard, it may be helpful to insert a *Contribution Margin* column, or to rearrange the data using the expanded contribution margin model.

Answer:	*Sales*	*Variable Costs*	*Contribution Margin Ratio*	*Fixed Costs*	*Operating Income (Loss)*
Firm A	$320,000	**$217,600**	32%	**$64,100**	$38,300
Firm B	**655,000**	465,050	**29%**	118,000	71,950
Firm C	134,000	**99,160**	26%	36,700	**(1,860)**
Firm D	**73,750**	59,000	20%	**19,670**	(4,920)

13-3. *Calculations:*

> **Firm A**   VC = Sales * (1 − CM%) = $320,000 * 68% = **$217,600**
>   CM = Sales − VC = $320,000 − $217,600 = $102,400
>   or CM = Sales * CM% = $320,000 * 32% = $102,400
>   FC = CM − Oper.Inc. = $102,400 − $38,300 = **$64,100**
>   or FC = (Sales * CM%) − Oper.Inc. = ($320,000 * 32%) − $38,300 = **$64,100**

> **Firm B**   CM = FC + Oper.Inc. = $118,000 + $71,950 = $189,950
>   Sales = CM + VC = $189,950 + $465,050 = **$655,000**
>   CM% = CM / Sales = $189,950 / $655,000 = **29%**

> **Firm C**   VC = Sales * (1 − CM%) = $134,000 * 74% = **$99,160**
>   CM = Sales − VC = $134,000 − $99,160 = $34,840
>   or CM = Sales * CM% = $134,000 * 26% = $34,840
>   Oper.Loss = CM − FC = $34,840 − $36,700 = **$(1,860)**

> **Firm D**   Sales = VC / (1 − CM%) = $59,000 / 80% = **$73,750**
>   CM = Sales − VC = $73,750 − $59,000 = $14,750
>   or CM = Sales * CM% = $73,750 * 20% = $14,750
>   FC = CM + Oper.(Loss) = $14,750 + $4,920 = **$19,670**

13-5. a. Revenues (8,000 units * $4 per unit) $32,000
   Variable expenses:
   Cost of goods sold (8,000 units * $ 2.10 per unit) $16,800
   Selling expenses (8,000 unit * $0.10 per unit).........   800
   Administrative expenses (8,000 units * $0.20 per unit)   1,600
   Total variable expenses...............   19,200
   Contribution margin $12,800
   Fixed expenses:
   Cost of goods sold $6,000
   Selling expenses   1,200
   Administrative expenses   4,000
   Total fixed expenses..   11,200
   Operating income...... .... $ 1,600

   b. Contribution margin per unit = Total CM / Volume = $12,800 / 8,000 units = **$1.60**
      Alternative approach: CM per unit = Selling price per unit − Variable expense per unit
         = $4.00 − $2.40 = **$1.60 per unit**
      Contribution margin ratio = CM / Revenues
         = $12,800 / $32,000 = **40%**

b. *Alternative approach:* CM ratio = CM per unit / Selling price per unit
   = $1.60 / $4.00 = **40%**

c. 1. *Volume of 12,000 units:*

	Per Unit	*	Volume	=	Total	%
Revenue	$4.00					100%
Variable Expense	2.40					60
Contribution Margin	$1.60	*	12,000	=	$19,200	40%
Fixed Expense					(11,200)	
Operating Income					**$ 8,000**	

Alternative approach: 4,000 more units sold @ $1.60 CM per unit = $6,400 increase in contribution margin and operating income. Present operating income is $1,600, so new operating income will be $8,000.

2. *Volume of 4,000 units:*

	Per Unit	*	Volume	=	Total	%
Revenue	$4.00					100%
Variable Expense	2.40					60
Contribution Margin	$1.60	*	4,000	=	$ 6,400	40%
Fixed Expense (no change)					(11,200)	
Operating Loss					**$(4,800)**	

Alternative approach: Operating income decreases by $6,400 (4,000 units * $1.60 per unit) from present operating income of $1,600, causing an operating loss of $4,800.

d. 1. Use the contribution margin ratio of 40%. Revenue increase of $12,000 causes a $4,800 increase (40% * $12,000) in contribution margin and operating income. Operating income = $1,600 + $4,800 = **$6,400**

2. Revenue decrease of $7,000 causes a $2,800 decrease (40% * $7,000) in contribution margin and operating income. Operating income changes to a loss = $1,600 − $2,800 = **$(1,200)**

13-7. a. Sales $65,000
Variable expenses (80% * $65,000). .... (52,000)
Contribution margin (20% $65,000) $13,000
Fixed expenses .... (18,000)
Operating loss .... $(5,000)

13-7. a. *Note:* Operating loss remains the same, so Fixed expenses = ($13,000 Contribution margin + $5,000 Operating loss).

    b. Increase in sales (30% * $65,000).. $19,500
       Contribution margin ratio 20%
       Increase in contribution margin........ .... $ 3,900
       Previous operating loss.................. ....   (5,000)
       Adjusted operating loss .... **$(1,100)**

       Operating loss = $(5,000) + $3,900 = **$(1,100).** The increase in contribution margin is also a decrease in the operating loss, because fixed expenses do not change.

    c. At break-even, contribution margin = fixed expenses = $18,000
      Contribution margin = (20% contribution margin ratio * ??? sales) = $18,000
      Sales = ($18,000 fixed expenses / 20% CM ratio) = **$90,000 at break-even.**

13-9. a.

	Per Unit	*	*Volume*	=	*Total*
Revenue	$15				
Variable Expense	9				
Contribution Margin	$ 6	*	?	=	$ 27,000
Fixed Expense					(27,000)
Operating Income					$ 0

    At the break-even point, total contribution margin must equal total fixed expenses.
    Break-even volume = ($6 contribution margin per unit * ??? volume) = $27,000
    Thus, break-even volume = **4,500 units**
    Total revenue = (4,500 units * $15 per unit) = **$67,500**

    b.

	Per Unit	*	*Volume*	=	*Total*
Revenue	$15				
Variable Expense	9				
Contribution Margin	$ 6	*	5,400	=	$32,400
Fixed Expense					(27,000)
Operating Income					**$ 5,400**

    c.

	Per Unit	*	*Volume*	=	*Total*
Revenue	$13				
Variable Expense	9				
Contribution Margin	$ 4	*	8,400	=	$33,600
Fixed Expense					(27,000)
Operating Income					**$ 6,600**

d. Does the increase in volume move fixed expenses into a new relevant range? Are variable expenses really linear?

e.

	Per Unit	*	Volume	=	Total
Revenue	$16				
Variable Expense	9				
Contribution Margin	$ 7	*	5,400	=	$37,800
Fixed Expense					(33,000)
Operating Income					**$ 4,800**

f. 1. *Volume of 5,400 units per month:*

	Per Unit	*	Volume	=	Total
Revenue	$15.00				
Variable Expense	9.80				
Contribution Margin	$ 5.20	*	5,400	=	$28,080
Fixed Expense #					(22,800)
Operating Income					**$ 5,280**

Current fixed expenses $27,000
    Decrease in fixed expenses (2 salespersons @ $2,500). .... (5,000)
    Increase in fixed expenses (2 salespersons @ $400) 800
    Adjusted fixed expenses $22,800

2. *Volume of 6,000 units per month:*

	Per Unit	*	Volume	=	Total
Revenue	$15.00				
Variable Expense	9.80				
Contribution Margin	$ 5.20	*	6,000	=	$31,200
Fixed Expense					(22,800)
Operating Income					**$ 8,400**

g.

	Per Unit	*	Volume	=	Total
Revenue	$15				
Variable Expense	9				
Contribution Margin	$ 6	*	6,000	=	$36,000
Fixed Expense					(28,000)
Operating Income					**$ 8,000**

The sales force compensation plan change results in $400 more operating income than does the plan to increase advertising.

13-11. a. b. ***Current Operation:***

	Luxury	Economy	Total
Revenue	$20 * 10,000 = $200,000	$12 * 20,000 = $240,000	$440,000
Variable Expense	8	7	
Contribution Margin	$12 * 10,000 = $120,000	$ 5 * 20,000 = $100,000	**$220,000**
Fixed Expense			(70,000)
Operating Income			**$150,000**

Total contribution margin = $120,000 + $100,000 = **$220,000**

Average contribution margin ratio = $220,000 / $440,000 = **50%**

Operating income = $220,000 − $70,000 = **$150,000**

c. Break-even point in sales dollars = Fixed expenses / Contribution margin ratio

= $70,000 / 50% = **$140,000**

d. Because sales mix might change. For example, if the company sold *only* the economy model, total contribution margin would equal the economy model contribution margin ratio ($5 / $12 = 41.666%) multiplied by the current break-even point in sales dollars of $140,000, which equals $58,333. Note that this amount is less than the $70,000 of fixed expenses, so the firm would have to generate a higher sales volume to break even. The opposite would be true if the company sold *only* the luxury model—with a contribution margin ratio of 60% ($12 / $20), total contribution margin would be $84,000 ($140,000 * 60%), and the break-even point in sales dollars would fall from $140,000 to $116,667 ($70,000 fixed expenses / 60% contribution margin ratio).

e. ***Proposed Expansion:***

	Luxury	Economy	Value	Total
Rev.	$20 * 6,000 = $140,000	$12 * 17,000 = $204,000	$15 * 8,000 = $120,000	$464,000
V. E.	8	7	8	
C. M.	$12 * 6,000 = $ 72,000	$ 5 * 17,000 = $ 85,000	$ 7 * 8,000 = $ 56,000	$213,000
Fixed Expenses				(84,000)
Operating Income				**$129,000**

f. No. Based on this data analysis, adding the Value model would result in lower total operating income by $21,000 ($150,000 current operation versus $129,000 proposed).

g. No. Although 2,000 more units of the Value model would increase total contribution margin and operating income by $14,000 (2,000 units @ $ 7 CM per unit), operating income would rise only to $143,000, which is still less than under the current operation.

13-13. a. Use the model, enter the known data, and solve for the unknown.

	Per Unit	*	*Volume*	=	*Total*	*%*
Revenue	$?					100%
Variable Expense	7.80					65%
Contribution Margin	$?	*		=	$	35%

Variable expenses = 65% of selling price. Selling price = $7.80 / 65% = **$12.00**

b.

	Per Unit	*	*Volume*	=	*Total*	*%*
Revenue	$12.00					100%
Variable Expense	7.80					65%
Contribution Margin	$ 4.20	*	?	=	$?	35%
Fixed Expense					(15,000)	
Operating Income					$ 6,000	

Total contribution margin = ($15,000 + $6,000) = $21,000. Total contribution margin divided by the contribution margin per unit of $4.20 gives **5,000 units** of the new product that would have to be sold to increase operating income by $6,000.

13-15. a.

	Per Unit	*	*Volume*	=	*Total*	*%*
Revenue	$1.25					100%
Variable Expense	0.35					28%
Contribution Margin	$0.90	*	400	=	$ 360	72%
Fixed Expense					(120)	
Operating income from increased volume					$ 240	
Variable expenses of 600 cones given away, @ $0.35					(210)	
Net increase in operating income					$ 30	

b. Yes. Not only does the promotion itself result in increased operating income, but it is also likely that customers will purchase some other products (e.g., food and/or beverages) on which additional contribution margin will be earned.

13-17. a.

	Per Unit	*	*Volume*	=	*Total*	*%*
Revenue	$32					100.0%
Variable Expense	20					62.5%
Contribution Margin	$12	*	4,100	=	$49,200	37.5%
Fixed Expense					(43,200)	
Operating Income					$ 6,000	

13-17. b.

	Per Unit	*	*Volume*	=	*Total*	*%*
Revenue	$32					100.0%
Variable Expense	20					62.5%
Contribution Margin	$12	*	?	=	$43,200	37.5%
Fixed Expense					(43,200)	
Operating Income					$ 0	

Break-even volume = $43,200 / $12 per unit = **3,600 units**
Break-even revenues = 3,600 units * $32 per unit = **$115,200**

c. 1.

	Per Unit	*	*Volume*	=	*Total*	*%*
Revenue	$32					100.00%
Variable Expense	14					43.75%
Contribution Margin	$18	*	4,100	=	$73,800	56.25%
Fixed Expense					(67,800)	
Operating Income					**$ 6,000**	

2.

	Per Unit	*	*Volume*	=	*Total*	*%*
Revenue	$32					100.00%
Variable Expense	14					43.75%
Contribution Margin	$18	*	?	=	$67,800	56.25%
Fixed Expense					(67,800)	
Operating Income					$ 0	

Break-even volume = $67,800 / $18 = **3,767 units** (rounded)
Break-even revenues = 3,767 units * $32 = **$120,533** (rounded)

3. As sales volume moves above the break-even point, contribution margin and operating
   income will increase by a greater amount per unit sold than under the old cost structure.

4. The new cost structure has much more risk, because if sales volume declines, the
   impact on contribution margin and operating income will be greater than under the
   old cost structure.

13-19. a. Raw materials per unit $1.50
   Direct labor per unit 1.50
   Variable overhead per unit 2.00
   Fixed overhead per unit .... 2.00 #
   Total cost per unit $7.00

   # The fixed overhead per unit is based on the total fixed overhead for the year of
      $100,000 divided by the current output of 50,000 units per year.

b. The above calculation includes an inappropriate unitization of fixed expenses. Unless the additional production of 30,000 units results in a movement to a new relevant range, total fixed expenses will not change.

c. The offer should be accepted because it would generate a contribution margin of $1 per unit (revenue of $6 per unit less variable cost of $5 per unit).

13-21. *Pros:*

1. The sale will still generate a positive contribution margin ratio of 23% (rounded). To illustrate, assume that the normal selling price is $1.00—which would mean that the normal contribution margin is $0.50. If the discount is given, the selling price will fall to $0.65—which would mean that the contribution margin will fall to $0.15, and the contribution margin ratio will fall to 23% ($0.15 / $0.65).
2. Saturn Candy Company will achieve "goodwill" with these customers and others concerned with corporate "social responsibility" issues.
3. The candy given to the children will increase brand awareness and could lead to greater sales volume in the future.
4. The Substance Abuse Awareness Club is a positive moral force in the community.

Cons:

1. Saturn Candy Company incurs an opportunity cost equal to the lost contribution margin if the candy could have been sold at the regular price in the ordinary course of business.
2. When other customers learn of the discounted sale, they may ask for the same special price for other "worthy causes." Unless Saturn Candy Company develops a policy with some limits for this sort of special pricing, the company could easily lose control of its production cost per unit.
3. Special pricing transactions that are not based on quantity discounts may be in violation of federal price discrimination laws. Legal counsel should be consulted before agreeing to the special price.

Recommendation: An appropriate corporate policy and other safeguards concerning special order pricing arrangements should be developed, and the candy should be sold at the special price.

13-23. a. As a firm increases operating leverage by adding more fixed expenses to its cost structure, the break-even point in terms of units and sales dollars also increases. Thus, a principal risk associated with operating leverage is that a decrease in sales—which leads to decreases in contribution margin, operating income, and cash flows—may result in an inability to cover fixed expenses. Why? Because a small percentage decline in sales will cause a very large percentage decline in operating income for a firm with high operating

13-23. a. *(continued)*

leverage. Another risk associated with operating leverage relates to the loss of flexibility that occurs when fixed costs (e.g., robotics) are substituted for variable costs (e.g., labor). Machines cannot be laid off during the slow season.

b. 1. Financial leverage relates to an firm's use of long-term debt in its *capital structure*, and operating leverage relates to a firm's use of fixed costs in its *cost structure*.

2. Financial leverage reflects a *financing* decision on the part of management—how much money to borrow, and how much interest expense to take on. Operating leverage reflects an *operating* decision on the part of management—how much machinery and equipment to invest in, and how much fixed expense to take on.

3. *Financial leverage magnifies ROE relative to ROI.* This adds risk: ROI must exceed the cost of debt (i.e., the interest rate on borrowed funds) in order for financial leverage "pay off" for the firm. *Operating leverage magnifies operating income relative to sales.* This adds risk: The firm must generate enough additional sales (and contribution margin) to cover any additional fixed expenses it takes on in order for operating leverage to "pay off".

4. With financial leverage, the magnification on ROE works both ways; the more leveraged the firm is, the more its stockholders lose as a percentage of their investment in a loss year. With operating leverage, the magnification on operating income also works both ways; the more leveraged the firm is, the greater its operating loss in a year when sales volume falls short of the break-even point.

CHAPTER 14. *Budgeting and Performance Reporting*

14-1. a. Use the cost of goods sold model, and work from the bottom up and the top down to calculate production:

Beginning inventory	1,000 medallions
Production	?
Goods available for sale.................	?
Less: Ending inventory	(800)
Quantity sold	2,000

Goods available for sale = 2,000 + 800 = 2,800 medallions
Production = 2,800 − 1,000 = **1,800 medallions**

b. Use the same approach, but notice that quantity used is a function of quantity produced from the production budget. Each medallion requires 2/3 of a yard of ribbon.

Beginning inventory	50 yards
Purchases	?
Raw materials available for use	?
Less: Ending inventory	(20)
Raw materials used in production (2/3 * 1,800 medallions)	1,200

Raw materials available for use = 1,200 + 20 = 1,220 yards
Purchases = 1,220 − 50 = **1,170 yards**

14-3. a. Use the raw material inventory/usage model:

	Quarter I	*Quarter II*
Beginning inventory	5,000	9,000
Add: Purchases	?	?
Raw materials available for use	?	?
Less: Ending inventory (25% of next quarter's usage)...	(9,000)	(5,500)
Usage (2 ounces * number of gallons of product to be produced).....	20,000	36,000

	Quarter I	*Quarter II*
Working backwards (up the model):		
Raw materials available for use.......	29,000	41,500
Purchases (subtract beginning inventory)....	**24,000**	**32,500**

b. Inventory provides a "cushion" for delivery delays or production needs in excess of the production forecast.

14-5.

	July	*August*	*September*
Sales forecast	$250,000	$220,000	$310,000
Cost of sales @ 54%	135,000	118,800	167,400

Purchases budget:		
Beginning inventory	$410,000	$356,400
Purchases	?	?
Cost of merchandise available for sale..........	?	?
Less: Ending inventory (300% * next month's cost of goods sold)	(356,400)	(502,200)
Cost of goods sold	$135,000	$118,800

Cost of merchandise available for sale = (Cost of goods sold + Ending inventory) .	$491,400	$621,000
Purchases = (Cost of merchandise available for sale − Beginning inventory).....	**$ 81,400**	**$264,600**

14-7.

	May	*June*	*July*	*August*
Sales forecast..	$240,000	$280,000	$300,000	$350,000
Cash collections:				
30% of current month's sales			$ 90,000	$105,000
50% of prior month's sales			140,000	150,000
18% of second prior month's sales			43,200	50,400
Total cash collections budget			**$273,200**	**$305,400**

14-9. a.

	September	*October*
Sales forecast	$42,000	$54,000
Purchases budget	37,800	44,000
Operating expense budget	10,500	12,800
Beginning cash	**$40,000**	
Cash receipts:		
August 31 accounts receivable	20,000	
September sales	0	
Total cash receipts..	**$20,000**	
Cash disbursements:		
August 31 accounts payable and accrued expenses	$24,000	
September purchases (75% * $37,800)	28,350	
September operating expenses (75% * $10,500)	7,875	
Total cash disbursements	**$60,225**	
Ending cash	**$ (225)**	

b. QB Sportswear's management should try to accelerate the collection of accounts receivable, slow down the payment of accounts payable and accrued expenses, and/or negotiate a bank loan. If sales growth continues at a very high rate, they probably will need to secure some permanent financing through sale of bonds or stock.

14-11. *Answer (and one possible numbered sequence of solving the problem):*

	July	*August*	*September*	*Total*
Cash balance, beginning	$ 26	9. $ 20	10. $ 20	$ 26
Add collections from customers	1. **68**	107	11. **136**	17. **311**
Total cash available	94	8. **127**	156	337

Less disbursements:

Purchase of inventory	3. **50**	60	48	18. **158**
Operating expenses	30	7. **39**	16. **24**	19. **93**
Capital additions	34	8	15. **2**	44
Payment of dividends	-	-	14. **9**	9
Total disbursements	2. **114**	107	83	304
Excess (deficiency) of cash available over disbursements	(20)	6. **20**	73	20. **33**
Borrowings	5. **40**	-	-	21. **40**
Repayments (including interest)	-	-	13. **41**	22. **41**
Cash balance, ending	4. **$ 20**	$ 20	12. **$ 32**	$ 32

Solution approach: 1. $94 − $26 = **$68**, 2. $94 + 20 (deficiency of cash available) = **$114**, 3. $114 − $30 − $34 = **$50**, 4. Minimum month-end balance, 5. $20 + 20 (deficiency of cash available) = **$40**, 6. Equal to ending cash balance for August because there were no borrowings or repayments during the month. 7. $107 − $60 − $8 = **$39**, 8. $107 + $20 (excess of cash available) = **$127**, 9. $127 − $107 = **$20** (or **$20** ending balance from July carried forward), 10. Ending cash balance from August is carried forward to beginning cash balance of September = **$20**, 11. $156 − $20 = **$136**, 12. Ending cash balance for the third quarter is the ending cash balance for September = **$32**, 13. $73 − $32 = **$41**, 14. Total dividends = **$9**, and no dividends were paid in July and August, 15. $44 total capital additions − $34 − $8 = **$2**, 16. $83 − $48 − $2 − $9 = **$24**, 17. $337 − $26 = **$311**, 18. Total purchases (across) = $50 + $60 + $48 = **$158**, 19. Total operating, expenses (across) = $30 + $39 + $24 = **$93**, or $304 − $158 − $44 − $9 = **$93**, 20. $337 − $304 = **$33**, 21. Borrowings from July, 22. Repayments in September.

14-13. a.

	April	May	June	Total
Expected sales in units	7,000	10,000	8,000	25,000
Selling price per unit	$40	$40	$40	$40
Total sales	**$280,000**	**$400,000**	**$320,000**	**$1,000,000**

b. ***Cash collections from:***

	April	May	June	Total
March sales	$132,000 #			$132,000
April sales	112,000	$154,000		266,000
May sales		160,000	$220,000	380,000
June sales			128,000	128,000
Total cash collections	**$244,000**	**$314,000**	**$348,000**	**$906,000**

\# Sales from February would have been fully collected (or written off) by the end of March. Thus, the $132,000 net realizable value of accounts receivable represents the 55% of March sales that will be collected in April (6,000 units sold in March * $40 * 55% = $132,000).

14-13. c.

	April	May	June	Total
Beginning inventory of finished goods....	3,500	5,000	4,000	3,500
Units to be produced	**8,500**	**9,000**	**8,500**	**26,000**
Goods available for sale................	12,000	14,000	12,500	29,500
Desired ending inventory of finished goods (50% of next month's budgeted sales)............	(5,000)	(4,000)	(4,500)	(4,500)
Quantity of goods sold.................	7,000	10,000	8,000	25,000

Note: In the total column, the beginning and ending inventory figures represent the number of units on hand at April 1, 1999 and June 30, 1999, respectively. Thus, the "goods available for sale" line does not add across.

d.

	April	May	June	Total
Beginning inventory of raw materials	10,200	10,800	10,200	10,200
Purchases of raw materials.............	**26,100**	**26,400**	**24,300**	**76,800**
Raw materials available for use	36,300	37,200	34,500	87,000
Desired ending inventory of raw materials (40% of next month's estimated usage) #........	(10,800)	(10,200)	(9,000) ##	(9,000)
Quantity of raw materials to be used in production ###	25,500	27,000	25,500	78,000

\# Next month's "units to be produced" (see answer to part c) is multiplied by three pounds to determine raw material requirements, which is then multiplied by 40%.

\#\# To determine the desired ending inventory of raw materials for June, the "units to be produced" in July must be determined. This is done in the same manner as shown in the answer to part c for April, May, and June:

	July
Beginning inventory of finished goods (carried over from June).....	4,500
Units to be produced	**7,500**
Goods available for sale............	12,000
Desired ending inventory of finished goods (50% of August's budgeted sales)........	(3,000)
Quantity of goods sold............	9,000

7,500 * 3 pounds * 40% = **9,000**

\#\#\# "Units to be produced" each month (see answer to part c) * 3 pounds per unit.

Note: In the total column, the beginning and ending inventory figures represent the number of pounds on hand at April 1, 1999 and June 30, 1999, respectively. Thus, the "raw materials available for use" line does not add across.

e. Cash payments for:	April	May	June	Total
March purchases........	$ 26,280 #			$ 26,280
April purchases.........	125,280	$ 31,320		156,600
May purchases.........		126,720	$ 31,680	158,400
June purchases.........			116,640	116,640
Total cash payments	$151,560	$158,040	$148,320	$457,920

\# Purchases from February and all prior months would have been fully paid by the end of March. Thus, the $26,280 of expected accounts payable at March 31, 1999, represents the 20% of March purchases that will be paid for in April.

Note: Each month's "purchases of raw materials" in pounds (see answer to part *d*) is multiplied by $6.00 to determine the dollar amount of raw material purchases, which is then multiplied by 80% in the month of purchase and 20% in the following month to determine cash payments.

14-15. a. The president's remark ignores the misleading result of arbitrarily allocated fixed expenses.

b.
Current net income of company.....		$10,000
Less: Lost contribution margin of Division B.......		(10,000)
Add: Division B direct fixed expenses that would be eliminated:		
Total Division B fixed expenses per report	$11,000	
Less: Allocated corporate ($21,000 / 3 divisions)	(7,000)	4,000
Company net income without Division B..		$ 4,000

c. Never arbitrarily allocate fixed expenses!

14-17. a. Supplies are a variable expense. The supplies budget should be flexed (i.e., it should be increased to provide funds for the additional 12 students above the number anticipated when the original budget was established).

b. No. The budget should still be flexed, but in this case it would be reduced.

14-19. a. Cost formula = $19,400 + $7.70 per machine hour
   Budget = $19,400 + ($7.70 * 6,700 machine hours) = **$70,990**

14-19. b.

	Original Budget (6,700 MH)	Flexed Budget (7,060 MH)	Actual Cost	Variance
Total maintenance cost......	$70,990	$73,762 #	$68,940	**$4,822** F

Flexed budget = $19,400 + ($7.70 * 7,060 machine hours) = $73,762

CHAPTER 15. *Standard Costs and Variance Analysis*

15-1. a. Worktype 1 (0.15 hours @ $12.30 per hour) .... $ 1.845
Worktype 1 (0.30 hours @ $10.90 per hour) 3.270
Worktype 3 (0.60 hours @ $19.50 per hour) 11.700
Total direct labor cost per pedestal.. .... **$16.815**

b. No, because the engineer developed ideal standards. It is unlikely that the standards would be met in practice, and they would not provide positive motivation or result in accurate costing.

15-3. a. Raw material cost..... .... $2.83 per bushel
Direct labor and variable overhead... .... 0.42 per bushel
Fixed overhead .... 0.35 per bushel
Total absorption cost .... **$3.60 per bushel**

Each bushel yields 15 pounds of product. Cost per pound = $3.60 / 15
= **$0.24 per pound.**

b. This cost per pound is not very useful for management planning and control because it includes unitized fixed expenses, which do not behave on a per unit basis.

15-5. a. *Raw material purchase price variance:*
(Standard price − Actual price) * Actual quantity purchased
($5.00 − $4.95) * 7,400 pounds = **$370 F**

b. *Raw material usage variance:*
(Standard usage − Actual usage) * Standard price
((2,000 cases * 4 pounds) − 8,300 pounds) * $5.00 per pound = **$1,500 U**

c. *Direct labor rate variance:*
(Standard rate − Actual rate) * Actual hours
($13.00 − $13.50 #) * 5,800 hours = **$2,900 U**
Actual rate: $78,300 / 5,800 hours = $13.50

d. **Direct labor efficiency variance:**
   (Standard hours − Actual hours) * Standard rate
   ((2,000 cases * 3 hours) − 5,800) * $13.00 = **$2,600 F**

e. **Variable overhead spending variance:**
   (Standard rate − Actual rate) * Actual hours
   ($6.00 − $6.15 #) * 5,800 hours = **$870 U**
   # Actual rate: $35,670 / 5,800 hours = $6.15

f. **Variable overhead efficiency variance:**
   (Standard hours − Actual hours) * Standard rate
   ((2,000 cases * 3 hours) − 5,800) * $6.00 = **$1,200 F**

Explanation of results: In order to create a favorable purchase price variance, the purchasing manager may have purchased lower-than-standard *quality* raw material inputs. This may have caused an excess amount of waste and spoilage, resulting in an unfavorable raw materials usage variance that *by far* exceeded the cost savings of $0.05 per pound. The unfavorable labor rate variance of $0.50 per hour may have been caused by using a more skilled and/or experienced workforce than was anticipated. However, this cost was largely offset by increased labor efficiency (i.e., less down-time, re-work). The favorable labor efficiency variance caused a favorable variable overhead efficiency variance because variable overhead is applied on the basis of direct labor hours.

15-7. a. Standard hours allowed = 3.5 hours * 24 tune-ups = 84 hours
   Efficiency variance was 6 hours unfavorable, therefore actual hours = 84 + 6 = **90 hours.**

Standard labor cost allowed for actual hours ($15 per hour * 90 hours)	$1,350
Less: Favorable labor rate variance	(81)
Actual total labor cost	**$1,269**

   Actual labor rate per hour = $1,269 / 90 hours = **$14.10 per hour**

   b. Direct labor efficiency variance:
      (Standard hours − Actual hours) * Standard rate
      (84 − 90) * $15 = **$90 U**

   c. Less skilled, lower paid workers took longer than standard to get the work done. Net variance is $9 U ($90 U − $81 F). This was not a good trade-off based on the variance. From a qualitative viewpoint, less skilled workers may not do as good of a job.

15-9. a. Purchase price variance = (Standard price − Actual price) * Actual quantity purchased
= ($8.00 per board foot − **???** actual price) * 19,000 board feet purchased = $2,850 U.
Thus, the purchase price per board foot was $0.15 U ($2,850 U / 19,000), or **$8.15.**

b. 1,500 units produced * 12 board feet per unit = **18,000 standard board feet allowed.**

c. Direct material usage variance = (Standard usage − Actual usage) * Standard price =
(18,000 board feet allowed − 17,200 issued into production) * $8.00 per board foot =
$6,400 F

d. The purchasing manager may have purchased higher-than-standard *quality* raw material
inputs. This may have allowed Dutko, Inc., to reduce waste and spoilage, resulting in a
favorable raw materials usage variance that more than offset the $0.15 per board foot
unfavorable price variance.   Based on the variances during November, this is a good
trade-off for the management of Dutko, Inc., to make.

15-11. a.

	Original Budget	Flexed Budget	Actual	Variance
Direct labor	$1,800	$1,716 #	$1,888	$172 U

2,860 books / 20 books per hour = 143 standard hours allowed * $ 12 per hour = $1,716 flexed budget.

b. Direct labor efficiency variance = (143 standard hours − 160 actual hours) = **17 hours U.**

c. Direct labor rate variance = (Standard rate − Actual rate) * Actual hours
= ($12 − ($1,888 / 160 hours)) * 160 hours = ($12 − $11.80) * 160 = **$32 F**

15-13. No. For example, management might be able to control results better if the labor efficiency
variance is reported daily, in hours. The labor rate variance might be reported only weekly
or monthly because labor rates are likely to be governed by contractual provisions that are
not subject to short-term control. The reason for calculating variances is to encourage
action to eliminate unfavorable variances and to capture favorable variances—not simply
to assess blame. Thus, performance reporting systems should be designed to provide the
most timely information (i.e., hourly, daily, weekly, or monthly) in the most appropriate
manner (i.e., dollar amounts, quantities used, or hours worked) to the individuals within
the organization who are in the best position to achieve the organization's objectives.

15-15. a. Raw material usage, and direct labor and variable overhead efficiency variances are in the
aggregate about 15% of the total standard cost of goods produced. This indicates that
the standards are not a very effective tool for controlling raw material, direct labor, and
variable overhead costs.

15-15. b. The variances were favorable, so the standards are higher than actual costs incurred. Therefore, ending inventory values at standard costs will be higher than actual cost.

c. Use the 15% difference between standard and actual. Ending inventory should be reduced to 85% of standard cost to adjust it to actual cost. 85% * $158,780 = $134,963. The adjustment would be a $23,817 (15% * $158,780) reduction in ending inventory.

15-17. a.

	Simple	*Complex*
Work hours per day	7.5	7.5
Divided by: Standard processing time per claim (in hours)	0.75	2.5
Standard number of claims processed (per day per worker)	10.0	3.0
Multiplied by: Number of days in the month	20.0	20.0
Standard claims processed (per month per worker)	200.0	60.0
Claims processed	3,000	600
Standard number of workers required for the month	**15**	**10**

Thus, a total of **25** workers should have been available to process the April claims.

b.

Actual number of workers	27
Standard number of workers required for the month	25
Efficiency variance, in number of workers	**2 U**
Efficiency variance, in dollars (2 workers * $ 90 per day * 20 days)	**$3,600 U**

15-19. a. Predetermined overhead application rate $= \dfrac{\text{Estimated overhead \$}}{\text{Estimated activity}} = \dfrac{\$36,000}{(40,000 \text{ units} * 0.5 \text{ hours})}$

= **$1.80 per machine hour**

b. 39,000 units produced * 0.5 machine hours per unit = **19,500 machine hours allowed.**

c. Applied overhead = $1.80 * 19,500 hours = **$35,100**

d. ($37,000 actual overhead incurred − $35,100 overhead applied) = **$1,900 underapplied.**

e. ($36,000 budgeted overhead − $37,000 actual overhead) = **$1,000 U budget variance.**

((20,000 budgeted hours − 19,500 standard hours allowed for units produced) * $1.80 predetermined overhead application rate) = **$900 U volume variance.**

CHAPTER 16. *Capital Budgeting*

16-1. a.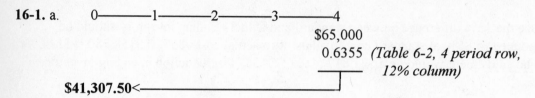

b. This is a future value problem, the opposite of present value. As shown in the diagram, $41,307.50 invested today at 12% interest compounded annually would grow to $65,000 in four years.

c. Less could be invested today because at a higher interest rate, more interest would be earned. This can be seen by calculating the present value of $65,000 in four years at an interest rate greater than 12%. As can be seen in Table 6-2, the present value factors are smaller as interest rates get higher.

16-3. a. If the investment is too high, the net present value will be too low.

b. If the cost of capital is too low, the net present value will be too high.

c. If the cash flows from the project are too high, the net present value will be too high.

d. If the number of years over which the project will generate cash flows is too low, the net present value will be too low.

16-5. a.

```
                                    0—1—2—3—4—5—6—7—8
Investment ... ...........    $(85,000)
Annual cash flow...... .....................$14,000 per year
Salvage value ........... ...................... ........... ......... ...........  $9,000
                              |           5.3349  (Table 6-3        0.4665  (Table 6-2
    $(85,000) <───────────|        ─── 8 period row, ─── 8 period row,
       74,689 <───────────────────────┘      10% column)      10% column)
        4,198 <─────────────────────────────────────┘
  $ (6,113) net present value
```

b. Because the net present value is negative, the internal rate of return on this project will be lower than the cost of capital of 10%.

16-7. a.

0——1——2——3——4——5——6——7——8

Investment .. .. $(120,000)

Annual cash flow..... .... $21,000 per year

Salvage value $15,000

                           4.9676 *(Table 6-3*   0.4039 *(Table 6-2*

$(120,000) <——————————   —— *8 periods,*   —— *8 periods,*

  104,320 <—————————————————   *12%)*   *12%)*

    6,058 <——————————————————————

$ (9,622) net present value

b. Profitability index = ($110,378 present value of inflows / $120,000 investment) = **0.92**

c. Internal rate of return (actual rate of return) is considerably less than the cost of capital of 12% because the net present value is negative and the profitability index is quite low.

d. Payback period = **5.7 years**.

Investment .. .. $(120,000)

Total return in years 1-5 ($21,000 annual cash flow * 5 years)...... 105,000

Return required in year 6 ($15,000 / $21,000 = 0.7 years)   15,000

Total return in 5.7 years .... $ 120,000

16-9. a. The net present value is positive $2,220 (present value of inflows of $26,220 less the investment of $24,000). Therefore, the return on investment is greater than 20%.

b. The payback period should not carry much weight at all, because it does not recognize the time value of money.

16-11.

Proposal	Investment	Net PV	PV of Inflows (Investment + Net PV)	Profitability Index (PV of Inflows / Outflows)
1	$50,000	$30,000	$80,000	$80,000 / $50,000 = **1.6**
2	60,000	24,000	84,000	84,000 / 60,000 = **1.4**
3	30,000	15,000	45,000	45,000 / 30,000 = **1.5**
4	45,000	9,000	54,000	54,000 / 45,000 = **1.2**

Proposal 1 is most desirable because its profitability index is the highest.

16-13. a. *Notes:* All amounts are rounded to the nearest US$1.00   psf = per square foot, sf = square feet, 1.25 = conversion factor, PV = present value factor (10 years, 12%), PVa = present value of an annuity factor (10 years, 12%).

16-13. a.

	US$	US$
Initial investment:		
Real estate (CI$150 psf * 1,000 sf * 1.25).....	(187,500)	
Equipment for health spa...........	(35,000)	
Inventory of cosmetics and skin care products..	(8,000)	(230,500)
Annual operating costs:		
Cleaning (CI$0.10 psf * 1,000 sf * 12 months * 1.25 * 5.6502 PVa)......	(8,475)	
Utilities (CI$0.40 psf * 1,000 sf * 12 months * 1.25 * 5.6502 PVa)	(33,901)	
Health spa assistant (US$25,000 * 5.6502 PVa).....	(141,255)	
Advertising (US$3,000 * 5.6502 PVa)	(16,951)	
Maintenance and insurance (US$4,500 * 5.6502 PVa)........	(25,426)	(226,008)
Annual cash inflows (CI$8,000 * 12 months * 1.25 * 5.6502 PVa).........		678,024
Future sale of real estate (CI$300 psf * 1,000 sf * 1.25 * 0.3220 PV).....		120,750
Net present value		**$342,266**

b.

	US$	US$
Initial investment:		
Real estate (CI$150 psf * 2,500 sf * 1.25).....	(468,750)	
Equipment for fitness center......	(50,000)	
Equipment for health spa...........	(35,000)	
Inventory of cosmetics and skin care products..	(8,000)	(561,750)
Annual operating costs:		
Cleaning (CI$0.10 psf * 2,500 sf * 12 months * 1.25 * 5.6502 PVa)......	(21,188)	
Utilities (CI$0.60 psf * 2,500 sf * 12 months * 1.25 * 5.6502 PVa)	(127,130)	
Health spa assistant (US$25,000 * 5.6502 PVa).....	(141,255)	
Aerobics instructors (2 * US$20,000 * 5.6502 PVa)	(226,008)	
Physical trainer (US$30,000 * 5.6502 PVa).	(169,506)	
Advertising (US$3,000 * 5.6502 PVa)	(16,951)	
Maintenance and insurance (US$4,500 * 5.6502 PVa)........	(25,426)	(727,464)
Annual cash inflows:		
Fitness center (US$300 * 500 members * 1.25 * 5.6502 PVa).	1,059,413	
Health spa (CI$8,000 * 12 months * 1.25 * 5.6502 PVa)........	678,024	1,737,037
Future sale of real estate (CI$300 psf * 2,500 sf * 1.25 * 0.3220 PV).....		301,875
Net present value		**$ 749,698**

c. *Note:* Changes from the solution to part *b* are shown in **bold**.

	US$	US$
Initial investment:		
Real estate (CI$150 psf * 2,500 sf * 1.25).....	(468,750)	
Equipment for fitness center......	(50,000)	
Equipment for health spa...........	(35,000)	
Inventory of cosmetics and skin care products..	(8,000)	(561,750)

Annual operating costs:
 Cleaning (CI$0.10 psf * 2,500 sf * 12 months * 1.25 * 5.6502 PVa)....... (21,188)
 Utilities (CI$0.60 psf * 2,500 sf * 12 months * 1.25 * 5.6502 PVa)....... (127,130)
 Health spa assistant (US$25,000 * 5.6502 PVa)...... .... (141,255)
 Aerobics instructors (2 * US$20,000 * 5.6502 PVa) .... (226,008)
 Physical trainer (US$30,000 * 5.6502 PVa). .... (169,506)
 Advertising (US$3,000 * 5.6502 PVa) .... (16,951)
 Maintenance and insurance (US$4,500 * 5.6502 PVa)........ .... <u>(25,426)</u> (727,464)

Annual cash inflows:
 Fitness center (US$300 * **300 members** * 1.25 * 5.6502 PVa). **635,648**
 Health spa (**CI$6,000** * 12 months * 1.25 * 5.6502 PVa)........ .... <u>**508,518**</u> 1,144,166

Future sale of real estate (**CI$200** psf * 2,500 sf * 1.25 * 0.3220 PV)..... <u>201,250</u>

Net present value ... . <u>**$ 56,202**</u>

d. If Lorna initially decides to open the health spa *only*, she should consider leasing (rather than purchasing) the 1,000 square foot unit for the following reasons:

• By leasing, her initial investment cost would be reduced to only US$43,000 because the real estate cost of CI$150,000 would be eliminated. This would allow her to get started with less business risk and she would maintain flexibility in terms of her desire to open the fitness center / health spa in one location in the future.

• Leasing would eliminate the hassle and possible business interruption of having to sell the 1,000 square foot unit before she could afford to purchase the 2,500 square foot unit. By leasing on an annual basis, she will have plenty of time to search for the most suitable location for the combined business, and will not face the possibility of having to run her business out of two locations (or to make two mortgage payments).

• Although the *nominal value* of real estate in Grand Cayman is likely to double over the next 10 years (from CI$150 to CI$300 per square foot), the *present value* of the future selling price of Lorna's unit (US$120,750) is less than the cost of purchasing it today (US$187,500). Because the present value of $1 to be received in 10 years at 12% is only 0.3220, real estate values would have to triple (rather than double) for the investment to yield a positive payoff.

• One possible drawback to leasing is the loss of collateral for borrowing purposes.

e. *Analysis:*
 1. Without considering the cost of Lorna's salary, the net present value calculations in parts *a* and *b* adequately support either alternative. The profitability index for each of these alternatives would be extremely high, calculated as follows:

16-13. e. 1. *(continued)*

	1,000 sf unit (see part *a*)	2,500 sf unit (see part *b*)
PV of annual cash inflows	$678,024	$1,737,037
+ PV of future sale of real estate	120,750	301,875
– PV of annual operating costs.....	(226,008)	(727,464)
= PV of net cash inflows.............	$572,766	$1,311,448
/ PV of net cash outflows (i.e., initial investment)....	230,500	561,750
= Profitability index......................	**2.48**	**2.33**

2. One additional line should now be added to the solutions presented for parts *a* and *b*. Without adjusting Lorna's "reasonably comfortable salary" of CI$4,000 for inflation over the next 10 years, the following results would occur (changes in **bold**):

	1,000 sf unit (see part *a*)	2,500 sf unit (see part *b*)
PV of annual cash inflows	$678,024	$1,737,037
+ PV of future sale of real estate	120,750	301,875
– PV of annual operating costs.....	(226,008)	(727,464)
– PV of Lorna's salary (CI$4,000 * 12 months *** 1.25 * 5.6502 PVa)**.............	**(339,012)**	**(339,012)**
= PV of net cash inflows.............	$ 233,754	$ 972,436
/ PV of net cash outflows (i.e., initial investment)....	230,500	561,750
= Profitability index......................	**1.01**	**1.73**

3. It now becomes clear that the real money to be made is in the full-scale operation. The combined fitness center / health spa allows Lorna to pay herself a reasonably comfortable salary *and still earn an excess return!* This makes intuitive sense— by operating a small personal service business (i.e., health spa only) with the help of one personal assistant, Lorna would be taking a low risk, low return strategy. The combined business has more risk, but it also offers higher potential returns.

4. The analysis above represents only *quantitative* factors. Lorna should also take a number of *qualitative* factors into account, such as: 1) the possibility of estimation errors with respect to her projections, 2) an assessment of non-financial risks involved with each aspect of her business, 3) any possible synergistic effects of operating the combined business in terms of attracting fitness center members by offering them discounts to health spa services, and 4) whether Lorna's 12% cost of capital represents a conservative estimate of her long-run cost of acquiring funds. If not, what is her incremental cost of borrowing? Would the net present value of either alternative change significantly if the discount rate were changed?

Recommendation:
After consulting with Lorna in terms of how she perceives the various risks involved, I would recommend that she either: 1) consider purchasing the 2,500 square foot unit immediately and begin pre-selling the fitness center memberships to ensure its success, or 2) lease the 1,000 square foot unit for one year and begin to build her business reputation by operating the health spa—with a target of opening the combined operation at the end of the initial one-year lease term.

16-15. a.

$$\text{Accounting rate of return} = \frac{\text{Net income}}{\text{Average investment}} = \frac{\$29,000 - \$10,000 \,\#}{(\$100,000 + \$90,000 \,\#\#) / 2} = \mathbf{20\%}$$

Depreciation expense = (Cost − Salvage) / Life
= ($80,000 -- $50,000) / 3 = $10,000

Investment at end of the year = Investment at beginning of the year, less Accumulated depreciation
= $100,000 − $10,000 = $90,000

b. *Investment:*		*Year 1*	*Year 2*	*Year 3*	*Year 4*
Machine	$(80,000)				
Working Capital	(20,000)				
Cash returns:					
Operations		$14,000	$24,000	$29,000	$20,000
Salvage					50,000
Working Capital					20,000
Totals	$(100,000)	$14,000	$24,000	$29,000	$90,000
PV Factor for 18%		0.8475	0.7182	0.6086	0.5158
Present value		$11,865	$17,237	$17,649	$46,422
Sum of present values	93,173 <───				
Net present value	**$ (6,827)**				

Based on this analysis, the investment would *not* be made because the net present value is negative, indicating that the ROI on the project is less than the discount rate of 18%.

c. The net present value analytical approach is the best technique to use because it recognizes the time value of money.

READY NOTES

for use with

ACCOUNTING: WHAT
THE NUMBERS MEAN

by

David H. Marshall and Wayne W. McManus

Your life just got easier! This booklet includes *Ready Notes* to accompany *Accounting: What the Numbers Mean*. *Ready Notes* was designed as a classroom supplement to accompany *Ready Shows*.   More importantly, *Ready Notes* was developed for you, the student.

Somewhere in your educational experience you have undoubtedly encountered a common dilemma facing many students--the feeling of helplessness that comes from trying to write down everything your instructor says and at the same time actually paying attention to what is being taught. *Ready Notes* address this problem by providing pre-prepared lecture outlines to accompany the *Ready Shows* your instructor will be using in class. Rather than spending time copying material that is already in the book, you will be able to focus on the most important aspects of what your instructor is saying. You still will be expected to take notes, but the nature of those notes will change.

Ready Notes includes reproductions of actual projected screens that you will be seeing in class. While not all of the slides are included, in most chapters at least one representative slide for each concept is included in *Ready Notes*.   To assist you in following the instructor, the slide number appears in the upper left-hand corner of each slide. The *Task Force Clip Art* used in this booklet and with *Ready Shows* is used with the permission of New Visions Technology, Inc.

As with any learning aid, few students succeed without attending class and preparing properly. Used properly, *Ready Notes* will help you achieve your goals for this course. Good luck!

Table of Contents

LEARNING OBJECTIVES

After studying this chapter you should understand:

❶ A definition of accounting.
❷ Who the users of information are, and why they find accounting information useful.
❸ Several of the categories of accounting, and the kinds of work that professional accountants in each company perform.
❹ The development of accounting, from a broad historical perspective.
❺ That the Financial Accounting Standards Board (FASB) is the current standard setting body for generally accepted accounting principles.

Irwin/McGraw-Hill   *© The McGraw-Hill Companies, Inc., 1999*

LEARNING OBJECTIVES

After studying this chapter you should understand:

❻ That financial statements do not result from following a codified set of hard and fast rules; that there are, in fact, alternative methods of accounting for and reporting similar economic activities.
❼ The key elements of ethical behavior for a professional accountant.
❽ The reasons for the FASB's Conceptual Framework project.
❾ The objectives of financial reporting for business enterprises.
❿ The plan of the book.

Irwin/McGraw-Hill   *© The McGraw-Hill Companies, Inc., 1999*

What is accounting?

Irwin/McGraw-Hill   *© The McGraw-Hill Companies, Inc., 1999*

1-10

Accounting is the process of:

- **Identifying**
- **Measuring**
- **Communicating**

} Economic information about an entity > For decisions and informed judgments

Irwin/McGraw-Hill © *The McGraw-Hill Companies, Inc., 1999*

1-11

Users and Uses of Accounting Information

- MANAGEMENT
- INVESTORS
- CREDITORS
- EMPLOYEES
- GOVERNMENTAL AGENCIES

Irwin/McGraw-Hill © *The McGraw-Hill Companies, Inc., 1999*

1-12

CLASSIFICATIONS OF ACCOUNTING

✓ Financial Accounting
✓ Managerial Accounting/Cost Accounting
✓ Auditing--Public/Internal
✓ Governmental and Not-for-Profit Accounting
✓ Income Tax Accounting

Irwin/McGraw-Hill © *The McGraw-Hill Companies, Inc., 1999*

1-13

Professional Degrees

- **CERTIFIED PUBLIC ACCOUNTANT (CPA)**
- **CERTIFIED MANAGEMENT ACCOUNTANT (CMA)**
- **CERTIFIED INTERNAL AUDITOR (CIA)**

Irwin/McGraw-Hill   © The McGraw-Hill Companies, Inc., 1999

1-14

FINANCIAL ACCOUNTING STANDARD SETTING

✓ *Statements of Financial Accounting Standards*--Over 100 issued. Deal with specific accounting/reporting issues.

✓ *Statements of Financial Accounting Concepts*--6 issued. An attempt to provide a common foundation to support financial accounting standards.

Irwin/McGraw-Hill   © The McGraw-Hill Companies, Inc., 1999

1-15

Key Objectives of Financial Reporting (SFAC #1)

- Relate to external financial reporting.
- Support business and economic decisions.
- Provide information about cash flows.
- Primary focus on earnings based on accrual accounting.
- <u>Not</u> to measure directly the value of a business enterprise.
- Information reported subject to evaluation by individual financial statement users.
- Accounting standards are still evolving.

Irwin/McGraw-Hill   © The McGraw-Hill Companies, Inc., 1999

1-16

International Accounting Standards

- ➤ (IASC) International Accounting Standards Committee
- ➤ Standards differ significantly among countries
- ➤ Individual country standards reflect local market needs and country regulation and taxation practices

Irwin/McGraw-Hill © The McGraw-Hill Companies, Inc., 1998

1-18

ETHICS AND THE ACCOUNTING PROFESSION

- AICPA Code of Professional Conduct
- IMA Standard of Ethical Conduct for Management Accountants

- OBJECTIVITY
- INTEGRITY
- INDEPENDENCE
- COMPETENCE

Irwin/McGraw-Hill © The McGraw-Hill Companies, Inc., 1998

2-2

LEARNING OBJECTIVES

After studying this chapter you should understand:

- ❶ The kind of information reported on each financial statement and the way financial statements are related to each other.
- ❷ What transactions are and the meaning and usefulness of the accounting equation.
- ❸ The meaning of each of the captions on the financial statements illustrated in this chapter.
- ❹ The broad, generally accepted concepts and principles that apply to the accounting profession.

Irwin/McGraw-Hill   © The McGraw-Hill Companies, Inc., 1998

2-4

LEARNING OBJECTIVES

After studying this chapter you should understand:

- ● Several limitations of financial statements.
- ● What a corporation's annual report is, and why it is issued.
- ● Business practices related to organizing a business, fiscal year, par value, and parent-subsidiary corporations.

Irwin/McGraw-Hill   © The McGraw-Hill Companies, Inc., 1998

2-7

FROM TRANSACTIONS TO FINANCIAL STATEMENTS

Financial
Transaction

An economic interchange between entities.

Irwin/McGraw-Hill   © The McGraw-Hill Companies, Inc., 1998

2-10

FROM TRANSACTIONS TO FINANCIAL STATEMENTS

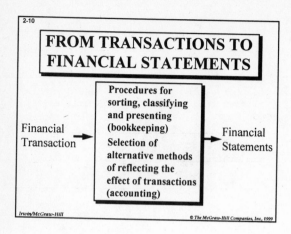

Financial Transaction → Procedures for sorting, classifying and presenting (bookkeeping) / Selection of alternative methods of reflecting the effect of transactions (accounting) → Financial Statements

Irwin/McGraw-Hill

© The McGraw-Hill Companies, Inc, 1999

2-11

FINANCIAL STATEMENTS

- **Balance Sheet**--Financial position <u>at a point in time</u>.
- **Income Statement**--Earnings for <u>a period of time</u>.
- **Statement of Cash Flows**--Summary of cash flows for <u>a period of time</u>.
- **Statement of Changes in Owners' Equity**-- Investments by owners, earnings of the firm, and distributions to owners.

Irwin/McGraw-Hill

© The McGraw-Hill Companies, Inc, 1999

2-12

MAIN STREET STORE, INC.
Balance Sheet
August 31, 1999

Assets		Liabilities and Owners' Equity	
Current assets:		**Current liabilities:**	
Cash	$ 34,000	Short-term debt	$ 20,000
Accounts receivable	80,000	Accounts payable	35,000
Merchandise inv.	170,000	Other acc. liabilities	12,000
Total current assets	$284,000	Total current liabilities	$ 67,000
Plant and equipment:		Long-term debt	50,000
Equipment	40,000	Total liabilities	$117,000
Less: Accum. depr.	4,000	Owners' equity	203,000
		Total liabilities and	
Total assets	$320,000	owners' equity	$320,000

Irwin/McGraw-Hill

© The McGraw-Hill Companies, Inc, 1999

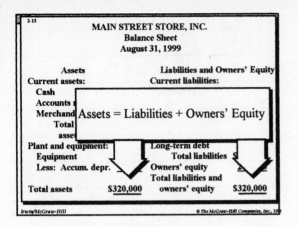

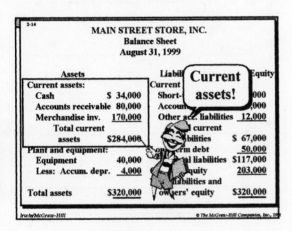

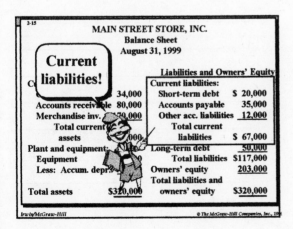

2-16

MAIN STREET STORE, INC.
Income Statement
For the Year Ended August 31, 1999

Net sales	$1,200,000
Cost of goods sold	850,000
Gross profit	$ 350,000
Selling, general, and administrative exp.	311,000
Income from operations	$ 39,000
Interest expense	9,000
Income before taxes	$ 30,000
Income taxes	12,000
Net income	$ 18,000
Net income per share of common stock outstanding	$ 1.80

Irwin/McGraw-Hill © The McGraw-Hill Companies, Inc, 1999

2-20

MAIN STREET STORE, INC.
Statement of Changes in Owners' Equity
For the Year Ended August 31, 1999

Paid in capital:

Beginning balances	$ - 0 -
Common stock, par value, $10, 50,000 shares authorized, 10,000 shares issued and outstanding	100,000
Additional paid-in capital	90,000
Balance, August 31, 1999	$190,000

Retained earnings:

Beginning balance	$ -0-
Net income for the year	18,000
Less: Cash dividends of $.50 per share	(5,000)
Balance, August 31, 1999	$ 13,000
Total owners' equity	$203,000

Irwin/McGraw-Hill © The McGraw-Hill Companies, Inc, 1999

2-22

KEY RELATIONSHIP

Retained Earnings beginning balance
+ Net income for the period
- Dividends paid to stockholders
= Retained Earnings ending balance

Irwin/McGraw-Hill © The McGraw-Hill Companies, Inc, 1999

2-23

MAIN STREET STORE, INC.
Statement of Cash Flows
For the Year Ended August 31, 1999

Cash flows from operating activities:

Net income...	$ 18,000
Add (deduct) items not affecting cash:	
Depreciation expense...	4,000
Increase in accounts receivable..........................	(80,000)
Increase in merchandise inventory.....................	(170,000)
Increase in current liabilities.............................	67,000
Net cash used by operating activities...............	$(161,000)
Cash flows from investing activities:	
Cash paid for equipment..	$ (40,000)

(continued on next slide)

Irwin/McGraw-Hill   © The McGraw-Hill Companies, Inc., 1999

2-24

MAIN STREET STORE, INC.
Statement of Cash Flows
For the Year Ended August 31, 1999

Cash paid for equipment....................................	$ (40,000)
Cash flows from financing activities:	
Cash received from issue of long-term debt..........	$ 50,000
Cash received from sale of common stock.............	190,000
Payment of cash dividend on common stock........	(5,000)
Net cash provided by financing activities..........	$235,000
Net increase in cash for the year..................................	$ 34,000

Irwin/McGraw-Hill   © The McGraw-Hill Companies, Inc., 1999

2-25

KEY TERMINOLOGY

> Cash flows from operating activities

> Cash flows from financing activities

> Cash flows from investing activities

> Change in cash for the year

Irwin/McGraw-Hill   © The McGraw-Hill Companies, Inc., 1999

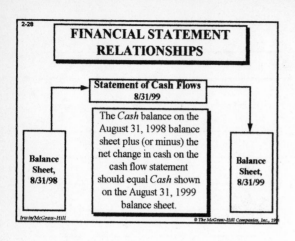

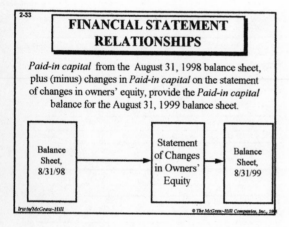

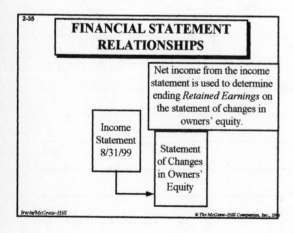

2-37

FINANCIAL STATEMENT RELATIONSHIPS

The ending *Retained Earnings* balance on the statement of changes in owners' equity is carried forward to the August 31, 1999 balance sheet.

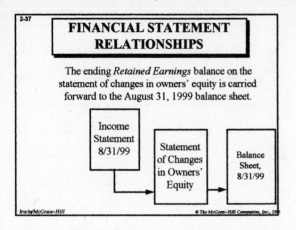

Irwin/McGraw-Hill © The McGraw-Hill Companies, Inc., 1999

2-39

FINANCIAL STATEMENT RELATIONSHIPS

The amount shown as total owners' equity on the August 31, 1999 balance sheet should match total owners' equity on the statement of changes in owners' equity

| Statement of Changes in Owners' Equity | Balance Sheet, 8/31/99 |

Irwin/McGraw-Hill © The McGraw-Hill Companies, Inc., 1999

2-40

FINANCIAL STATEMENT RELATIONSHIPS

KEY IDEAS

- Transactions affecting the income statement also affect the balance sheet.
- For the balance sheet to balance, income statement transactions must be reflected in the Retained Earnings part of owners' equity.
- The statement of cash flows explains why the cash amount changed during the period.

Irwin/McGraw-Hill © The McGraw-Hill Companies, Inc., 1999

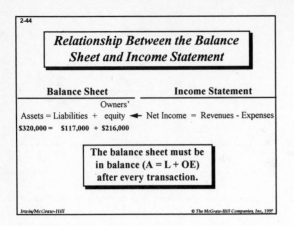

2-44

Relationship Between the Balance Sheet and Income Statement

Balance Sheet			Income Statement

Assets = Liabilities + Owners' equity ◄— Net Income = Revenues - Expenses

$320,000 = $117,000   + $216,000

The balance sheet must be in balance (A = L + OE) after every transaction.

Irwin/McGraw-Hill © The McGraw-Hill Companies, Inc., 1999

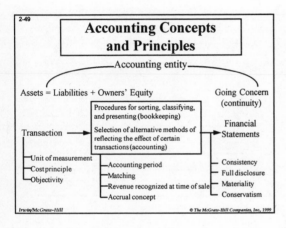

2-49

Accounting Concepts and Principles

Accounting entity

Assets = Liabilities + Owners' Equity   Going Concern (continuity)

Transaction → Procedures for sorting, classifying, and presenting (bookkeeping)

Selection of alternative methods of reflecting the effect of certain transactions (accounting)

Financial Statements

- Unit of measurement
- Cost principle
- Objectivity

- Accounting period
- Matching
- Revenue recognized at time of sale
- Accrual concept

- Consistency
- Full disclosure
- Materiality
- Conservatism

Irwin/McGraw-Hill © The McGraw-Hill Companies, Inc., 1999

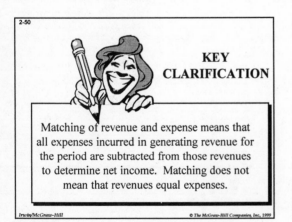

2-50

KEY CLARIFICATION

Matching of revenue and expense means that all expenses incurred in generating revenue for the period are subtracted from those revenues to determine net income. Matching does not mean that revenues equal expenses.

Irwin/McGraw-Hill © The McGraw-Hill Companies, Inc., 1999

3-2

LEARNING OBJECTIVES

After studying this chapter you should understand:

❶ Why financial statement ratios are important.

❷ The significance and calculation of return on investment.

❸ The DuPont model, an expansion of the basic return on investment calculation, and the terms *margin* and *turnover*.

❹ The significance and calculation of return on equity.

Irwin/McGraw-Hill   © *The McGraw-Hill Companies, Inc, 1999*

3-4

LEARNING OBJECTIVES

After studying this chapter you should understand:

❺ The meaning of liquidity, and why it is important.

❻ The significance and calculation of three measures of liquidity: working capital, the current ratio, and the acid-test ratio.

❼ How ratio trends can be used most effectively.

Irwin/McGraw-Hill   © *The McGraw-Hill Companies, Inc, 1999*

3-5

Measurements and Trend Analysis

GPA for all students for the last four semesters--

      2.85, 2.76, 2.70, 2.65

JUDGMENT: Pat's performance has improved while performance of all students has declined.

Irwin/McGraw-Hill   © *The McGraw-Hill Companies, Inc, 1999*

3-6

Measurements and Trend Analysis

Pat's GPA is 2.8 on a 4.0 scale.

Pat's GPA for the last four semesters--
1.9, 2.3, 2.6, 2.8

JUDGMENT: Pat's performance has been improving.

Irwin/McGraw-Hill   © The McGraw-Hill Companies, Inc, 1999

3-7

KEY POINTS

◎The trend of data is frequently more significant than the data itself.

◎Comparison of individual and group trends is important when making judgments.

Irwin/McGraw-Hill   © The McGraw-Hill Companies, Inc, 1999

3-8

RETURN ON INVESTMENT (ROI)

$$\text{RATE OF RETURN} = \frac{\text{AMOUNT OF RETURN}}{\text{AMOUNT INVESTED}}$$

Irwin/McGraw-Hill   © The McGraw-Hill Companies, Inc, 1999

3-11

KEY POINTS

* Rate of return is an annual percentage rate unless otherwise specified, therefore...
* The amount of return is the amount received during the year and...
* The amount invested is the average amount invested during the year.
* ROI is a significant measure of economic performance because it describes the results obtained by management's use of the assets made available during the year.

Irwin/McGraw-Hill © The McGraw-Hill Companies, Inc, 1999

3-13

The DuPont Model for Calculating Return on Investment

$$\text{Return on Investment} = \frac{\text{Net income}}{\text{Sales}} \times \frac{\text{Sales}}{\text{Average total assets}}$$

MARGIN   TURNOVER

Irwin/McGraw-Hill © The McGraw-Hill Companies, Inc, 1999

3-17

The DuPont Model for Calculating Return on Investment

$$\text{Return on Investment} = \frac{\$34,910}{\$611,873} \times \frac{\$611,873}{\$383,687}$$

$$\frac{\$364,720 + \$402,654}{2}$$

Irwin/McGraw-Hill © The McGraw-Hill Companies, Inc, 1999

3-19

KEY IDEAS

✓ Margin describes the profitability from sales.

✓ Turnover describes the efficiency with which assets have been used to generate sales.

✓ Overall profitability - return on investment is a function of both profitability of sales and the efficient use of assets.

Irwin/McGraw-Hill   © The McGraw-Hill Companies, Inc, 1999

3-20

KEY POINTS

✎ Net income and sales are <u>for the year</u>. For consistency, total assets is the average of total assets from the balance sheet at the beginning and end of the year.

✎ Operating income may be used in the margin calculation instead of net income, and average operating assets may be used in the turnover calculation. As long as the data used are consistently calculated, the <u>trend</u> of ROI will be useful for judgments.

Irwin/McGraw-Hill   © The McGraw-Hill Companies, Inc, 1999

3-21

RETURN ON EQUITY (ROE)

$$\text{Return on Equity} = \frac{\text{Net income}}{\text{Average owners' equity}}$$

Irwin/McGraw-Hill   © The McGraw-Hill Companies, Inc, 1999

3-24

KEY POINT

As in ROI, net income is <u>for the year</u>, therefore it is related to the average of the owners' equity at the beginning and end of the year.

Irwin/McGraw-Hill © The McGraw-Hill Companies, Inc., 1999

3-25

KEY IDEAS

✓ ROI relates net income to average total assets, and expresses a rate of return on the assets used by the firm.

✓ ROE relates net income to average owners' equity, and expresses a rate of return on that portion of the assets provided by the owners of the firm.

Irwin/McGraw-Hill © The McGraw-Hill Companies, Inc., 1999

3-26

WORKING CAPITAL

Working capital = Current assets − Current liabilities

Irwin/McGraw-Hill © The McGraw-Hill Companies, Inc., 1999

3-29

WORKING CAPITAL

KEY DEFINITIONS

◇**Current assets**: Cash and assets likely to be converted to cash within a year.

◇**Current liabilities**: Obligations that must be paid within a year.

Irwin/McGraw-Hill   © The McGraw-Hill Companies, Inc, 1999

3-30

WORKING CAPITAL

KEY IDEA

A measure of the firm's ability to pay its current obligations.

Irwin/McGraw-Hill   © The McGraw-Hill Companies, Inc, 1999

3-31

CURRENT RATIO

$$\text{Current ratio} = \frac{\text{Current assets}}{\text{Current liabilities}}$$

Irwin/McGraw-Hill   © The McGraw-Hill Companies, Inc, 1999

3-34

CURRENT RATIO

KEY IDEA

The current ratio is usually a more useful measurement than the amount of working capital because it is a ratio measurement.

Irwin/McGraw-Hill   © The McGraw-Hill Companies, Inc., 1999

3-35

ACID-TEST RATIO

$$\text{Acid-test ratio} = \frac{\text{Cash (including temporary cash investments)} + \text{Accounts receivable}}{\text{Current liabilities}}$$

Irwin/McGraw-Hill   © The McGraw-Hill Companies, Inc., 1999

3-38

ACID-TEST RATIO

KEY IDEA

Focusing on cash and accounts receivable provides a more short-term measure of liquidity than the current ratio.

Irwin/McGraw-Hill   © The McGraw-Hill Companies, Inc., 1999

3-39

VERTICAL GRAPH SCALES

Arithmetic Scale

KEY FEATURE

Vertical scale distances are equal.

KEY IDEA

A constant rate of growth plots as an increasingly steep line over time.

Irwin/McGraw-Hill · © The McGraw-Hill Companies, Inc, 1999

3-40

VERTICAL GRAPH SCALES

Logarithmic Scale

KEY FEATURE

Vertical scale distances are increasingly narrow and compressed.

KEY IDEA

A constant rate of growth plots as a straight line.

Irwin/McGraw-Hill · © The McGraw-Hill Companies, Inc, 1999

3-41

VERTICAL GRAPH SCALES

KEY OBSERVATIONS

✓ The horizontal scale will almost always be an arithmetic scale, with equal distance between the dates of data observations.

✓ Semi-logarithmic format means that only the vertical scale is logarithmic; the horizontal scale is arithmetic.

Irwin/McGraw-Hill · © The McGraw-Hill Companies, Inc, 1999

LEARNING OBJECTIVES

4-2

After studying this chapter you should understand:

❶ The expansion of the basic accounting equation to include revenues and expenses.

❷ How the expanded accounting equation stays in balance after every transaction.

❸ How the income statement is linked to the balance sheet through owners' equity.

❹ The meaning of the bookkeeping terms *journal, ledger, T-account, account balance, debit, credit* and *closing the books.*

Irwin/McGraw-Hill   © The McGraw-Hill Companies, Inc., 199

LEARNING OBJECTIVES

4-4

After studying this chapter you should understand:

❺ That the bookkeeping system is a mechanical adaptation of the expanded accounting equation.

❻ How to analyze a transaction, prepare a journal entry, and determine the effect of a transaction on working capital.

❼ The five questions of transaction analysis.

Irwin/McGraw-Hill   © The McGraw-Hill Companies, Inc., 199

TRANSACTIONS AND THE FINANCIAL STATEMENTS

4-5

☞ Transactions affect the balance sheet and/or the income statement.

☞ The balance sheet must be in balance after every transaction.

☞ The *Retained Earnings* account on the balance sheet includes net income from the income statement.

☞ Balance sheet accounts may have amount balances at the end of a fiscal period, and before transactions of the subsequent period are recorded.

Irwin/McGraw-Hill   © The McGraw-Hill Companies, Inc., 199

4-7

KEY TERMINOLOGY

Each individual asset, liability, owners' equity, revenue, or expense "account" may additionally be described with its category title.

- **"Cash Asset Account"**
- **"Accounts Payable Liability Account"**
- **"Common Stock Owners' Equity Account"**
- **"Sales Revenue Account"**
- **"Wages Expense Account"**

Irwin/McGraw-Hill   © The McGraw-Hill Companies, Inc, 1999

4-8

KEY RELATIONSHIP

> Transactions during a fiscal period cause the balance of the affected account(s) to increase or decrease.

> *Bookkeeping* is the process of keeping track of these changes.

Irwin/McGraw-Hill   © The McGraw-Hill Companies, Inc, 1999

4-9

BOOKKEEPING JARGON

> **Journal**--a chronological record of each transaction.

> **Ledger**--a book of all of the accounts; accounts are usually arranged in the sequence found on the balance sheet and income statement, respectively.

Irwin/McGraw-Hill   © The McGraw-Hill Companies, Inc, 1999

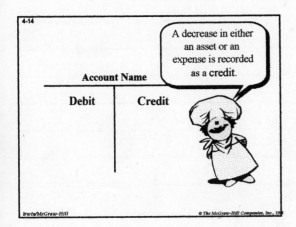

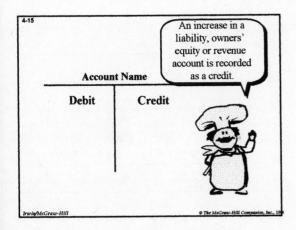

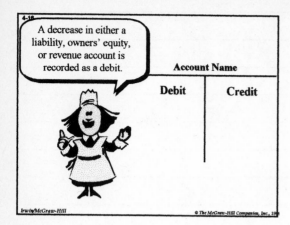

4-18

A decrease in either a liability, owners' equity, or revenue account is recorded as a debit.

Account Name	
Debit	Credit

Irwin/McGraw-Hill   © The McGraw-Hill Companies, Inc., 1998

4-17

ADJUSTING ENTRIES

Two categories of adjusting entries.

- **Accruals**--Transactions for which cash has not been received or paid, but the effect of which must be recorded in the accounts to accomplish matching.

- **Reclassification**--The bookkeeping for the original transaction was appropriate when it was recorded, but the passage of time requires a reclassification of the original bookkeeping to reflect correct account balances as of the date of the financial statements.

Irwin/McGraw-Hill   © The McGraw-Hill Companies, Inc., 1998

4-18

KEY IDEAS

✓ Accrual accounting means that revenues are recognized when <u>earned</u> (not when cash is received) and that expenses are reflected in the period in which they are <u>incurred</u> (not when cash is paid).

✓ Adjusting entries result in matching revenues and expenses, which is the objective of accrual accounting.

Irwin/McGraw-Hill   © The McGraw-Hill Companies, Inc., 1998

4-19

TRANSACTION ANALYSIS

To understand either the bookkeeping procedure for a transaction, or the effect of a transaction on the financial statements, the following questions must be answered.

❶ What's going on?

❷ What accounts are affected?

❸ How is each account affected?

❹ Does the balance sheet balance?

❺ Does my analysis make sense?

Irwin/McGraw-Hill   © The McGraw-Hill Companies, Inc., 1998

4-22

The firm borrowed $2,500 by issuing a 12% note payable.

Balance Sheet	Income Statement
Assets = Liabilities + Owners' equity	Net income = Revenues - Expenses
Cash Note Payable	
+2,500 +2,500	

The journal entry would be:

Dr. Cash   2,500
     Cr. Notes Payable   2,500

Irwin/McGraw-Hill   © The McGraw-Hill Companies, Inc., 1998

4-24

Accrued interest of $25 is recorded at the end of each month for ten months.

Balance Sheet	Income Statement
Assets = Liabilities + Owners' equity	Net income = Revenues - Expenses
Interest	Interest
Payable	Expense
+25	+25

$2,500 x .12 x 1/12 = $25

Irwin/McGraw-Hill   © The McGraw-Hill Companies, Inc., 1998

4-25

Accrued interest of $25 is recorded at the end of each month for ten months.

Balance Sheet	Income Statement
Assets = Liabilities + Owners' equity	Net income = Revenues - Expenses
Interest Payable +25	Interest Expense +25

The journal entry would be:

Dr.	Interest Expense	25	
	Cr. Interest Payable		25

Irwin/McGraw-Hill © The McGraw-Hill Companies, Inc., 1998

4-27

At the end of ten months, the loan and accrued interest are paid.

Balance Sheet	Income Statement
Assets = Liabilities + Owners' equity	Net income = Revenues - Expenses
Cash -2,750	Note Payable -2,500
	Interest Payable -250

$2,500 x .12 x 10/12 = $250

Irwin/McGraw-Hill © The McGraw-Hill Companies, Inc., 1998

4-28

At the end of ten months, the loan and accrued interest are paid.

Balance Sheet	Income Statement
Assets = Liabilities + Owners' equity	Net income = Revenues - Expenses
Cash -2,750	Note Payable -2,500
	Interest Payable -250

The journal entry would be:

Dr.	Note Payable	2,500	
Dr.	Interest Payable	250	
	Cr. Cash		2,570

Irwin/McGraw-Hill © The McGraw-Hill Companies, Inc., 1998

5-2

LEARNING OBJECTIVES

After studying this chapter you should understand:

❶ What is included in the *Cash* account reported on the balance sheet.

❷ The bank reconciliation procedure.

❸ The features of a system of internal control, and why internal controls are important.

❹ How short-term marketable securities are reported on the balance sheet.

❺ How accounts receivable are reported on the balance sheet.

Irwin/McGraw-Hill   © The McGraw-Hill Companies, Inc., 199

5-4

LEARNING OBJECTIVES

After studying this chapter you should understand:

❼ How notes receivable and related accrued interest are reported on the balance sheet.

❽ How inventories are reported on the balance sheet.

❾ The alternative inventory cost-flow assumptions, and their respective effects on the statements when price levels are changing.

❿ The impact of inventory errors on the balance sheet and income statement.

⓫ What prepaid expenses are, and how they are reported on the balance sheet.

Irwin/McGraw-Hill   © The McGraw-Hill Companies, Inc., 199

5-6

CURRENT ASSETS

Current assets are cash and those assets expected to be converted to cash or used up in the operating activities of the entity within one year.

ACCOUNTS THAT COMPRISE CURRENT ASSETS

- Cash
- Marketable (or Short-Term) Securities
- Accounts and Notes Receivable
- Inventories
- Prepaid Expenses

Irwin/McGraw-Hill   © The McGraw-Hill Companies, Inc., 199

5-7

KEY IDEA

Every entity has an <u>operating cycle</u> in which products and services are purchased, services are performed on account (usually), payment is made to employees and suppliers, and finally cash is received from customers. If the entity is a manufacturer, the product is made and held as inventory before it is sold. Current assets reflect the investment required to support this cycle.

Irwin/McGraw-Hill   © The McGraw-Hill Companies, Inc, 1999

5-8

Internal Control Structures

KEY IDEA

1) Operating effectiveness and efficiency

2) Financial reporting reliability

3) Compliance with applicable laws and regulaions

ACCOUNTING CONTROLS

Assure accuracy of bookkeeping records and financial statements.

Protect assets from unauthorized use or loss.

Irwin/McGraw-Hill   © The McGraw-Hill Companies, Inc, 1999

5-9

Internal Control Structures

ADMINISTRATIVE CONTROLS

Encourage adherence to management's policies.

Provide for efficient operations.

KEY OBSERVATION

Internal controls are positive; they support achievement of organizational objectives.

Irwin/McGraw-Hill   © The McGraw-Hill Companies, Inc, 1999

5-10

CASH

✓ The cash amount on the balance sheet is the amount of cash owned by the entity on the balance sheet date.

✓ Thus the ledger account balance of cash must be reconciled with the bank statement's ending balance, and the ledger account balance must be adjusted as necessary.

✓ The adjustment will reflect bank timing differences and book errors.

Irwin/McGraw-Hill   © The McGraw-Hill Companies, Inc., 199

5-11

BANK RECONCILIATION

Timing Differences

① Deposits in transit
② Outstanding checks
③ Bank service charges
④ NSF (not sufficient funds) checks
⑤ Errors

Irwin/McGraw-Hill   © The McGraw-Hill Companies, Inc., 19

5-12

MARKETABLE SECURITIES

➔ Short-term marketable securities that will be held until maturity are shown on the balance sheet at cost, which is usually about the same as market value.

➔ Securities expected to be held for several months after the balance sheet date are shown at their market value.

➔ Interest income from marketable securities that has not been received must be accrued.

Irwin/McGraw-Hill   © The McGraw-Hill Companies, Inc., 19

5-13

ACCOUNTS RECEIVABLE

KEY ISSUES

☑ Accounts receivable are reported on the balance sheet at their "net realizable value," which is the amount of cash expected to be collected from the accounts receivable.

Irwin/McGraw-Hill © The McGraw-Hill Companies, Inc., 199

5-14

ACCOUNTS RECEIVABLE

KEY ISSUES

☑ When sales are made on account, there is a very high probability that some accounts receivable will not be collected.

Irwin/McGraw-Hill © The McGraw-Hill Companies, Inc., 199

5-15

ACCOUNTS RECEIVABLE

KEY ISSUES

☑ The matching of revenues and expenses concept requires that the "cost" of uncollectible accounts receivable be reported in the same period as the revenue that was recognized when the account receivable was created.

Irwin/McGraw-Hill © The McGraw-Hill Companies, Inc., 19

5-16

ACCOUNTS RECEIVABLE

KEY POINTS

☑ The "cost" of uncollectible accounts (*Bad Debts Expense*) must be estimated. This leads to valuation adjustments.

☑ The amount of accounts receivable not expected to be collected is recorded and reported in an *Allowance for Bad Debts* account.

☑ The *Allowance for Bad Debts* account is a "contra asset" reported on the balance sheet as a subtraction from *Accounts Receivable*.

Irwin/McGraw-Hill   © The McGraw-Hill Companies, Inc., 199

5-17

ACCOUNTS RECEIVABLE

Accounts receivable	$10,000
Less: Allowance for bad debts	(500)
Net accounts receivable	$ 9,500

or

Accounts receivable, less allowance for bad debts of $500	$ 9,500

Irwin/McGraw-Hill   © The McGraw-Hill Companies, Inc., 199

5-18

INVENTORIES

The inventory asset account contains the cost of items that are being held for sale. When an item of inventory is sold, it's cost is transferred from the inventory asset account (in the balance sheet) to the cost of goods sold expense account (in the income statement).

Irwin/McGraw-Hill   © The McGraw-Hill Companies, Inc., 199

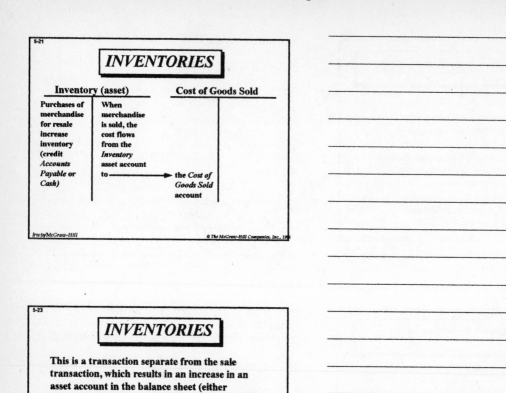

5-21

INVENTORIES

Inventory (asset) | **Cost of Goods Sold**

Purchases of merchandise for resale increase inventory (credit *Accounts Payable* or *Cash*)

When merchandise is sold, the cost flows from the *Inventory* asset account to ⟶ the *Cost of Goods Sold* account

Irwin/McGraw-Hill   © The McGraw-Hill Companies, Inc., 199

5-23

INVENTORIES

This is a transaction separate from the sale transaction, which results in an increase in an asset account in the balance sheet (either *Accounts Receivable* or *Cash*), and an increase in *Sales*, a revenue account in the income statement.

KEY ISSUE

When the inventory includes the cost of several units of the item sold, how is the cost of the item sold determined?

Irwin/McGraw-Hill   © The McGraw-Hill Companies, Inc., 199

5-24

INVENTORY COST FLOW ASSUMPTIONS

* Specific identification
* Weighted average
* First-in, first-out (FIFO)
* Last-in, first-out (LIFO)

Irwin/McGraw-Hill   © The McGraw-Hill Companies, Inc., 199

5-25

WEIGHED-AVERAGE

Date		Qty		Rate	Amount
9/1/98	Beginning inventory	5	@	$1,500	$ 7,500
11/7/98	Purchase	8	@	$1,600	12,800
3/13/99	Purchase	12	@	$1,650	19,800
5/22/99	Purchase	10	@	$1,680	16,800
7/28/99	Purchase	6	@	$1,700	10,200
8/30/99	Purchase	4	@	$1,720	6,880
Total boats available for sale		45			$73,980
Number of boats sold		37			
Number of boats in 8/31/99 inventory		8			

5-29

WEIGHED-AVERAGE

Date		Qty		Rate	Amount
9/1/98					
11/7/9	**Cost of Goods Sold**				
3/13/9	**$1,644 per boat x 37 = $60,828**				
5/22/9					
7/28/99	Purchase	6	@	$1,700	10,200
8/30/99	Purchase	4	@	$1,720	6,880
Total boats available for sale		45			$73,980
Number of boats sold		37	@	$1,644	(60,828)
Number of boats in 8/31/99 inventory		8	@	$1,644	$13,152

5-30

FIRST-IN, FIRST-OUT

Date		Qty		Rate	Amount
9/1/98	Beginning inventory	5	@	$1,500	$ 7,500
11/7/98	Purchase	8	@	$1,600	12,800
3/13/99	Purchase	12	@	$1,650	19,800
5/22/99	Purchase	10	@	$1,680	16,800
7/28/99	Purchase	6	@	$1,700	10,200
8/30/99	Purchase	4	@	$1,720	6,880

5-35

FIRST-IN, FIRST-OUT

	SOLD		
	SOLD		
	SOLD		
	SOLD		
7/28/99	Purchase	4 @ $1,700	6,800
8/30/99	Purchase	4 @ $1,720	6,880
Ending inventory		8	$13,680

Cost of goods sold: $73,980 - $13,680 = $60,300

5-36

LAST-IN, FIRST-OUT

9/1/98	Beginning inventory	5 @ $1,500	$ 7,500
11/7/98	Purchase	8 @ $1,600	12,800
3/13/99	Purchase	12 @ $1,650	19,800
5/22/99	Purchase	10 @ $1,680	16,800
7/28/99	Purchase	6 @ $1,700	10,200
8/30/99	Purchase	4 @ $1,720	6,880

5-41

LAST-IN, FIRST-OUT

9/1/98	Beginning inventory	5 @ $1,500	$ 7,500
11/7/98	Purchase	3 @ $1,600	4,800
	SOLD		
	SOLD		
	SOLD		
	SOLD		
Ending inventory		8	$12,300

Cost of goods sold: $73,980 - $12,300 = $61,680

5-42

KEY ISSUES

> How do changes in the <u>cost</u> of inventory items over time affect cost of goods sold under each of the cost flow assumptions?
> How do changes in the <u>quantity</u> of inventory items affect cost of goods sold under each of the cost flow assumptions?

5-43

KEY POINT

ROI, ROE, and measures of liquidity will be affected by the inventory cost flow assumption used when the cost of inventory items changes over time.

5-44

PREPAID EXPENSES

WHAT'S GOING ON?

Prepaid expenses result from the application of accrual accounting. Some expenditures made in one period are not properly recognized as expenses until a subsequent period.

In these situations, expense recognition is <u>deferred</u> until the period in which the expense applies.

PREPAID EXPENSES FREQUENTLY INCLUDE:

Insurance premiums
Rent

6-2

LEARNING OBJECTIVES

After studying this chapter you should understand:

❶ How the cost of land, buildings, and equipment is reported on the balance sheet.

❷ How the terms *capitalize* and *expense* are used with respect to property, plant, and equipment.

❸ Alternative methods of calculating depreciation for financial accounting purposes, and the relative effect of each on the income statement (*Depreciation Expense*) and the balance sheet (*Accumulated Depreciation*).

Irwin/McGraw-Hill   © The McGraw-Hill Companies, Inc, 1999

6-4

LEARNING OBJECTIVES

After studying this chapter you should understand:

❹ Why depreciation for income tax purposes is an important concern of taxpayers, and how tax depreciation differs from financial accounting depreciation.

❺ The accounting treatment of maintenance and repair expenditures.

❻ The effect on the financial statements of the disposition of noncurrent assets, either by abandonment, sale, or trade-in.

Irwin/McGraw-Hill   © The McGraw-Hill Companies, Inc, 1999

6-6

LEARNING OBJECTIVES

After studying this chapter you should understand:

❼ The similarities in the financial statements effects of buying an asset and using a capital lease.

❽ The role of present value concepts in financial reporting and their usefulness in decision making.

❾ The meaning of various intangible assets, how their values are measured, and how their cost is reflected in the income statement.

Irwin/McGraw-Hill   © The McGraw-Hill Companies, Inc, 1999

6-7

LONG-LIVED ASSETS

KEY TERMINOLOGY

Depreciation Expense refers to that portion of
the cost of a long-lived asset recorded as an
expense in an accounting period. Depreciation
in accounting is the spreading of the cost of a
long-lived asset over its estimated useful life to
the entity. This is an application of the
matching concept.

Irwin/McGraw-Hill   © The McGraw-Hill Companies, Inc., 1999

6-8

LONG-LIVED ASSETS

KEY TERMINOLOGY

Accumulated Depreciation is a contra asset
account. The balance in this account is the
accumulated total of all of the depreciation
expense recognized to date on the related
asset(s).

Irwin/McGraw-Hill   © The McGraw-Hill Companies, Inc., 1999

6-9

LONG-LIVED ASSETS

KEY TERMINOLOGY

⌘ To capitalize an expenditure means to record the
expenditure as an asset. A long-lived asset that
has been capitalized will be depreciated.

⌘ To expense an expenditure means to record the
expenditure as an expense.

⌘ The difference between an asset's cost and its
accumulated depreciation is its net book value.

Irwin/McGraw-Hill   © The McGraw-Hill Companies, Inc., 1999

6-10

DEPRECIATION OF LONG-LIVED ASSETS

KEY POINT

The recognition of *Depreciation Expense* does not affect cash.

DEPRECIATION EXPENSE CALCULATION ELEMENTS

Asset cost

Estimated salvage value

Estimated useful life to entity

Irwin/McGraw-Hill   © The McGraw-Hill Companies, Inc., 1999

6-11

DEPRECIATION OF LONG-LIVED ASSETS

☞Straight-line
- Based on years of life
- Based on units of production

☞Accelerated
- Sum-of-the-years'-digits
- Declining-balance

Irwin/McGraw-Hill   © The McGraw-Hill Companies, Inc., 1999

6-12

Cruisers, Inc. purchased a molding machine at the beginning of 1998 at a cost of $22,000. The machine is estimated to have a useful life of five years, and an estimated salvage value of $2,000. Management estimates that 200 boat hulls will be produced.

Straight-line depreciation:

$$\frac{\text{Cost - Estimated salvage value}}{\text{Estimated useful life}} = \begin{array}{c}\text{Annual}\\ \text{Depreciation}\end{array}$$

Irwin/McGraw-Hill   © The McGraw-Hill Companies, Inc., 1999

6-14

Cruisers, Inc. purchased a molding machine at the beginning of 1998 at a cost of $22,000. The machine is estimated to have a useful life of five years, and an estimated salvage value of $2,000. Management estimates that 200 boat hulls will be produced.

<u>Units-of-production depreciation:</u>

$$\frac{\text{Cost - Estimated salvage value}}{\text{Estimated total units to be made}} = \frac{\text{Unit}}{\text{Depreciation}}$$

Irwin/McGraw-Hill · © The McGraw-Hill Companies, Inc., 1999

6-16

Cruisers, Inc. purchased a molding machine at the beginning of 1998 at a cost of $22,000. The machine is estimated to have a useful life of five years, and an estimated salvage value of $2,000. Management estimates that 200 boat hulls will be produced.

<u>Sum-of-the-years'-digits depreciation:</u>

$$(\text{Cost - Estimated salvage value}) \times \frac{\text{Remaining life in years}}{\text{Sum-of-the-years'-digits}}$$

Irwin/McGraw-Hill · © The McGraw-Hill Companies, Inc., 1999

6-18

Cruisers, Inc. purchased a molding machine at the beginning of 1998 at a cost of $22,000. The machine is estimated to have a useful life of five years, and an estimated salvage value of $2,000. Management estimates that 200 boat hulls wi

$$5 + 4 + 3 + 2 + 1$$

<u>Sum-of-the-years'-digits depreciation:</u>

$$\frac{\text{Annual}}{\text{depreciation}} = (\$22,000 - \$2,000) \times \frac{5 \text{ years}}{15 \text{ years}}$$

Irwin/McGraw-Hill · © The McGraw-Hill Companies, Inc., 1999

6-20

Cruisers, Inc. purchased a molding machine at the beginning of 1998 at a cost of $22,000. The machine is estimated to have a useful life of five years, and an estimated salvage value of $2,000. Management estimates that 200 boat hulls will be produced.

Declining-balance depreciation:

$$\text{Annual depreciation} = \text{Double the straight-line depreciation rate} \times \text{Asset's net book value at beginning of year}$$

Irwin/McGraw-Hill   © The McGraw-Hill Companies, Inc, 1999

6-23

Cruisers, Incs. purchased a molding machine at the beginning of 1998 at a cost of $22,000. The machine is estimated to have a useful life of five years, and an estimated salvage value of $2,000. Management estimates that 200 boat hulls will be produced.

Declining-balance depreciation:

$8,800 = (20% x 2) x $22,000   YEAR 1

Irwin/McGraw-Hill   © The McGraw-Hill Companies, Inc, 1999

6-24

Cruisers, Inc. purchased a molding machine at the beginning of 1998 at a cost of $22,000. The machine is estimated to have a useful life of five years, and an estimated salvage value of $2,000. Management estimates that 200 boat hulls will be produced.

Declining-balance depreciation:

$5,280 = (20% x 2) x $13,200   YEAR 2

Irwin/McGraw-Hill   © The McGraw-Hill Companies, Inc, 1999

6-25

DEPRECIATION METHODS

KEY POINTS

> Accelerated depreciation results in greater depreciation expense during the early years of the asset's life than straight-line depreciation. Most firms use straight-line depreciation for financial reporting purposes.

> Depreciation expense does not affect cash, but because depreciation is deductible for income tax purposes, most firms use an accelerated method for calculating income tax deprecation.

Irwin/McGraw-Hill   © The McGraw-Hill Companies, Inc., 1999

6-26

DEPRECIATION METHODS

KEY POINTS

> The depreciation method selected for financial reporting purposes will have an effect on ROI and ROE. To make valid comparisons between companies, it is necessary to know whether or not comparable depreciation calculation methods have been used.

> If an expenditure has been inappropriately capitalized or expensed, both assets and net income will be affected, in the current year and in future years of the asset's life.

Irwin/McGraw-Hill   © The McGraw-Hill Companies, Inc., 1999

6-27

Present Value Analysis

KEY IDEAS

> Money has value over time.

> An amount to be received or paid in the future has a value today (present value) that is less than future value.

> Why? Because the interest that can be earned between the present and the future.

Irwin/McGraw-Hill   © The McGraw-Hill Companies, Inc., 1999

6-28

Present Value Analysis

KEY RELATIONSHIPS

A time line approach creates a visual image that makes the time value of money concept easy to work with.

> What is the present value of $4,000 to be received or paid in four year, at an interest rate of 8%?

Irwin/McGraw-Hill   © The McGraw-Hill Companies, Inc, 1999

6-31

Present Value Analysis

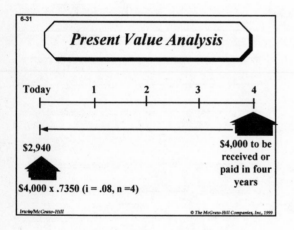

Today   1   2   3   4

$2,940

$4,000 to be received or paid in four years

$4,000 x .7350 (i = .08, n =4)

Irwin/McGraw-Hill   © The McGraw-Hill Companies, Inc, 1999

6-32

Assets Acquired by Capital Lease

KEY IDEAS

- A long-term lease is frequently a way of financing the acquisition of a long-lived asset.
- The effect of the accounting for a leased asset should not be different from the accounting for a purchased asset.

Irwin/McGraw-Hill   © The McGraw-Hill Companies, Inc, 1999

6-33

Assets Acquired by Capital Lease

ACCOUNTING FOR A LEASED ASSET

- The "cost" of a leased asset is the present value of the lease obligations.
- Depreciation expense is recorded based on this "cost."
- As annual lease payments are made, interest expense is recognized and the lease obligation is reduced.

Irwin/McGraw-Hill © The McGraw-Hill Companies, Inc., 1999

6-34

INTANGIBLE ASSETS AND NATURAL RESOURCES

KEY POINT

Although the terminology is different from that used for depreciable assets, the accounting is essentially the same; the expenditure is capitalized, and the expense is recognized periodically over the useful life of the asset to the entity.

Irwin/McGraw-Hill © The McGraw-Hill Companies, Inc., 1999

6-35

INTANGIBLE ASSETS AND NATURAL RESOURCES

TERMINOLOGY

INTANGIBLE ASSETS:
  Amortization Expense
    Usually an accumulated
    amortization account is not used.
NATURAL RESOURCES:
  Depletion Expense
  Accumulated Depletion

Irwin/McGraw-Hill © The McGraw-Hill Companies, Inc., 1999

7-2

LEARNING OBJECTIVES

After studying this chapter you should understand:

❶ The financial statement presentation of short-term debt, current maturities of long-term debt, and unearned revenues.

❷ The difference between interest calculated on a straight basis and on a discount basis.

❸ The accounting for an employer's liability for payroll and payroll taxes.

7-4

LEARNING OBJECTIVES

After studying this chapter you should understand:

❹ The importance of making estimates for certain accrued liabilities, and how these items are presented in the balance sheet.

❺ What leverage is, and how it is provided by long-term debt.

❻ The different characteristics of a bond, which is the formal document representing most long-term debt.

7-5

LEARNING OBJECTIVES

After studying this chapter you should understand:

❼ Why bond discount or premium arises, and how it is accounted for.

❽ What deferred income taxes are, and why they arise.

❾ What minority interest is, why it arises, and what it means in the balance sheet.

7-6

CURRENT LIABILITIES

DEFINITION

Current liabilities are those that must be paid within one year of the balance sheet date.

Accounts that comprise current liabilities:
> Short-term debt
> Accounts payable
> Various accrued liabilities
> Current maturities of long-term debt

Irwin/McGraw-Hill   © The McGraw-Hill Companies, Inc., 1999

7-7

CURRENT LIABILITIES

KEY IDEAS

☑ A principal concern about liabilities is that they are not understated. If liabilities are too low, expenses are probably understated also, which means that net income is overstated.

☑ The amount of current liabilities is related to the amount of current assets to measure the firm's *liquidity*, its ability to pay its bills when they come due.

Irwin/McGraw-Hill   © The McGraw-Hill Companies, Inc., 1999

7-9

INTEREST CALCULATION METHODS

Assume that $1,000 is borrowed for one year at an interest rate of 12%.

Basic Model for Calculating Interest

Interest = Principal x Rate x Time (in years)

Irwin/McGraw-Hill   © The McGraw-Hill Companies, Inc., 1999

7-10

INTEREST CALCULATION METHODS

STRAIGHT INTEREST

✧ Principal used in the interest calculation is equal to the cash received by the borrower.

✧ Interest is paid to the lender periodically during the term of the loan, or at the maturity date.

Irwin/McGraw-Hill · © The McGraw-Hill Companies, Inc., 1999

7-11

INTEREST CALCULATION METHODS

STRAIGHT INTEREST

Interest = Principal x Rate x Time (in years)
Interest = $1,000 x 0.12 x 1
Interest = $120

Irwin/McGraw-Hill · © The McGraw-Hill Companies, Inc., 1999

7-12

INTEREST CALCULATION METHODS

DISCOUNT

♦ Principal used in the interest calculation is the "amount borrowed," but then interest is subtracted from that principal to get the amount of cash made available to the borrower. This results in an effective interest rate (APR) greater than the rate used in the interest calculation.

♦ Because interest was paid in advance, only the principal amount is repaid at the loan maturity date.

Irwin/McGraw-Hill · © The McGraw-Hill Companies, Inc., 1999

7-14

INTEREST CALCULATION METHODS

> **Assume that $1,000 is borrowed for one year at an interest rate of 12%.**

$$\text{APR} = \frac{\text{Interest paid}}{\text{Money available for use x Time (in years)}}$$

Irwin/McGraw-Hill   © The McGraw-Hill Companies, Inc., 1999

7-19

LONG-TERM DEBT

KEY IDEA

Firms issue long-term debt (bonds payable) to get some of the funds needed to invest in assets. The owners do not usually provide all of the necessary funds because it is usually desirable to have some financial leverage.

Irwin/McGraw-Hill   © The McGraw-Hill Companies, Inc., 1999

7-20

FINANCIAL LEVERAGE

⊕ When money is borrowed at a fixed interest rate, the difference between ROI earned on that money and the interest rate paid affects the wealth of the borrower. This is called *financial leverage*.

⊕ Financial leverage is positive when the ROI earned on borrowed money is greater than the interest rate paid on the borrowed money. Financial leverage is negative when the opposite occurs.

Irwin/McGraw-Hill   © The McGraw-Hill Companies, Inc., 1999

7-21

FINANCIAL LEVERAGE

⊕ Financial leverage increases the risk that a firm's
ROI will fluctuate, because ROI changes as
business conditions and the firm's operating
results change, but the interest rate on borrowed
funds is usually fixed.

Irwin/McGraw-Hill © *The McGraw-Hill Companies, Inc., 1999*

7-22

LONG-TERM DEBT

BOND CHARACTERISTICS

▢ A fixed interest rate (usually) is called the <u>stated</u> rate
or <u>coupon</u> rate.
▢ Interest usually is payable quarterly or semi-annually.
▢ Individual bonds usually have a face amount (principal) of
$1,000.
▢ Bond prices are stated as a percent of the face amount.
▢ Most bonds have a stated maturity date, but most bonds are
also <u>callable</u>; they can be redeemed prior to maturity at the
option of the issuer.
▢ Frequently some collateral is provided by the issuer.

Irwin/McGraw-Hill © *The McGraw-Hill Companies, Inc., 1999*

7-23

BOND MARKET VALUE

<u>KEY POINT</u>

✱ The market value of a bond is a
function of the relationship between
market interest rates and the bond's
stated or coupon rate of interest.

Market Interest
Rates

✱ As market interest rates fall, the
market value of a bond rises.

✱ As market interest rates rise, the
market value of a bond falls.

Irwin/McGraw-Hill © *The McGraw-Hill Companies, Inc., 1999*

7-24

BOND MARKET VALUE

Cruisers, Inc. issues a 10%, $1,000 bond when market interest rates are 12%. The bond will mature in eight years. Interest is paid semiannually.

Interest: 10%/2 x $1,000 = $50
$50 x 10.1059 (6%, 16 periods) = $505.30
Principal:
$1,000 x 0.936 (6%, 16 periods) =   393.60
PROCEEDS   **$898.90**

Irwin/McGraw-Hill   © The McGraw-Hill Companies, Inc., 1999

7-25

BOND PREMIUM AND DISCOUNT

KEY IDEA

♦ When the market interest rate at the date a bond is issued is different from the stated or coupon rate of the bond, the bond will be issued at--
    -a *premium* (market interest rate < stated or coupon rate)
    -a *discount* (market interest rate > stated or coupon rate).

Irwin/McGraw-Hill   © The McGraw-Hill Companies, Inc., 1999

7-26

BOND PREMIUM AND DISCOUNT

☞ When a bond is issued at a premium, the premium is amortized to *Interest Expense* over the term of the bond, resulting in lower annual interest expense than the interest paid on the bond.
☞ When a bond is issued at a discount, the discount is amortized to *Interest Expense* over the term of the bond resulting in higher annual interest expense than the interest paid on the bond.
☞ The amortization of premium or discount results in reporting an actual interest expense from the bonds is a function of the market interest rate when the bonds were issued.

Irwin/McGraw-Hill   © The McGraw-Hill Companies, Inc., 1999

7-28

DEFERRED INCOME TAXES

WHAT'S GOING ON?

Differences between book and taxable income arise because financial accounting methods differ from accounting methods permitted for income tax purposes.

EXAMPLE: Book depreciation is usually calculated on a straight-line basis, and tax depreciation is usually based on an accelerated method.

Irwin/McGraw-Hill © The McGraw-Hill Companies, Inc., 1999

7-29

DEFERRED INCOME TAXES

KEY ISSUE

When taxable income is different from book income, income tax expense should be a function of book income before taxes, not taxable income. This is an application of the matching concept.

Irwin/McGraw-Hill © The McGraw-Hill Companies, Inc., 1999

7-30

DEFERRED INCOME TAXES

KEY IDEA

Income tax expense based on book income is usually more than the income taxes currently payable. The difference is shown a liability called *Deferred Federal Income Taxes*. This liability will become current when taxable income exceeds book income.

Irwin/McGraw-Hill © The McGraw-Hill Companies, Inc., 1999

8-2

LEARNING OBJECTIVES

After studying this chapter you should understand:

❶ The characteristics of common stock, and how common stock is presented in the balance sheet.

❷ What preferred stock is, what its advantage and disadvantage to the corporation are, and how it is presented in the balance sheet.

❸ The accounting for a cash dividend, and the dates involved in dividend transactions.

❹ What stock dividends and stock splits are, and why each is used.

Irwin/McGraw-Hill © The McGraw-Hill Companies, Inc, 1999

8-4

LEARNING OBJECTIVES

After studying this chapter you should understand:

❺ What treasury stock is, why it is acquired, and how treasury stock transactions affect owners' equity.

❻ What the cumulative foreign currency transaction adjustment is, and why it appears in owners' equity.

❼ How owners' equity transactions for the year are reported in the financial statements.

Irwin/McGraw-Hill © The McGraw-Hill Companies, Inc, 1999

8-5

| | August 31 | |
	1999	1998
Owners' equity:		
Paid-in capital:		
Preferred stock, 6%, $100 par value, cumulative, callable at $102, 5,000 shares authorized, issued, and outstanding	$ 500,000	$ 500,000
Common stock, $2 par value, 1,000,000 shares authorized, 244,800 shares issued at August 31, 1999, and 200,000 at August 31, 1998	489,600	400,000
Additional paid-in capital	3,322,400	2,820,000
Total paid-in capital	$4,312,000	$3,720,000
Retained earnings	2,828,000	2,600,000
Less: Common stock in treasury, at cost; 1,000 shares at August 31, 1999	(12,000)	--
Total owners' equity	$7,128,000	$6,320,000

Irwin/McGraw-Hill © The McGraw-Hill Companies, Inc, 1999

8-6

Owner's Equity: Paid -in Capital

ACCOUNTS INCLUDED IN PAID-IN CAPITAL

☞ *Common Stock* (sometimes called *Capital Stock*)

☞ *Preferred Stock* (if authorized by the corporation's charter)

☞ *Additional Paid-In Capital*

Irwin/McGraw-Hill   © The McGraw-Hill Companies, Inc., 1999

8-7

Owner's Equity: Paid -in Capital

KEY TERMINOLOGY FOR STOCK VALUE

Par Value--An arbitrary amount assigned to each share at incorporation.

Stated Value--No-par stock that has been assigned an assigned amount.

No-Par Value--True no-par stock without an assigned stated value.

Irwin/McGraw-Hill   © The McGraw-Hill Companies, Inc., 1999

8-10

```
Dr.  Cash (40,000 shares x $13)          520,000
        Cr.  Common Stock (40,000 x $2)          80,000
        Cr.  Additional Paid-In Capital
             (40,000 x $11)                     440,000
```

Balance Sheet	Income Statement
Assets = Liabilities + Owner' equity	Net income = Revenues - Expenses

Cash	Common Stock
+ $20,000	+ $80,000
	Additional Paid-In Capital
	+ $440,000

During the year ended August 31, 1999, Racer, Inc. sold 40,000 additional shares of its $2 par value common stock at a price of $13 per share.

Irwin/McGraw-Hill   © The McGraw-Hill Companies, Inc., 1999

8-11

Owner's Equity: Paid -in Capital

**KEY TERMINOLOGY FOR NUMBER OF
SHARES OF STOCK**

Authorized--By the corporation's charter

Issued--Sold in the past to stockholders

Outstanding--Still held by stockholders

Treasury stock--Shares of its own stock
purchased and held by the corporation

Irwin/McGraw-Hill   © The McGraw-Hill Companies, Inc, 1999

8-12

Common Stock and Preferred Stock

KEY IDEAS

> **Common stock represents the basic
ownership of a corporation.**

> **Preferred stock represents ownership, but
has some preferences relative to common
stock. These include--**

> priority claim to dividends, and

> priority claim to assets in liquidation.

**However, preferred stockholders are not
usually entitled to vote for directors.**

Irwin/McGraw-Hill   © The McGraw-Hill Companies, Inc, 1999

8-13

Common Stock and Preferred Stock

**KEY POINTS ABOUT DIVIDENDS ON
PREFERRED STOCK**

• Dividends are usually "cumulative," which means
that dividends not paid during one year (in
arrears) must be paid in future years before
dividends can be paid on common stock.

• Dividend amount is expressed as a certain amount
per share ($3.50), or a percent of par value (7% of
par value of $50).

Irwin/McGraw-Hill   © The McGraw-Hill Companies, Inc, 1999

8-15

Preferred Stock Dividend Calculations

Case 1

6%, $100 par value cumulative preferred stock, 50,000 shares authorized, issued, and outstanding. Dividends payable semiannually, no dividends in arrears. Determine the semiannual preferred dividend amount.

6% x $100 x 50,000 shares outstanding x 1/2 year

= $150,000

Irwin/McGraw-Hill   © The McGraw-Hill Companies, Inc, 1999

8-17

Preferred Stock Dividend Calculations

Case 2

$4.50, $75 par value cumulative preferred stock, 50,000 shares authorized and issued, 40,000 shares outstanding (there are 10,000 shares of treasury stock). Dividends payable quarterly, no dividends in arrears. Calculate the quarterly preferred dividend amount.

$4.50 x 40,000 shares outstanding x 1/4 year =

$45,000

Irwin/McGraw-Hill   © The McGraw-Hill Companies, Inc, 1999

8-19

Preferred Stock Dividend Calculations

Case 3

$4, $50 par value cumulative preferred stock, 100,000 shares authorized, 60,000 shares issued, 54,000 shares outstanding (there are 6,000 shares of treasury stock). Dividends payable annually . Dividends were not paid in prior two years. Calculate dividends required in current year to pay dividends in arrears and current year's preferred dividend.

$4 x 54,000 shares outstanding x 3 years = $648,000

Irwin/McGraw-Hill   © The McGraw-Hill Companies, Inc, 1999

8-20

Preferred Stock Dividend Calculations

Case 4

$2, $25 par value cumulative participating preferred stock, 30,000 shares authorized, 25,000 shares issued and outstanding. Dividends payable annually. Dividends are two years in arrears. The company has 100,000 shares of common stock outstanding (common stockholders receive a base dividend of $2 per share), and dividends for the year total $410,000.

	Preferred	Common	Balance
Total amount declared			$410,000
Preferred dividends in arrears	$100,000		310,000
Current year's preferred dividend	50,000		260,000
Common stock base dividend		$200,000	60,000
Allocated balance (1:4)	12,000	48,000	0
Total dividends paid	$162,000	$248,000	

Irwin/McGraw-Hill © The McGraw-Hill Companies, Inc, 1999

8-21

Paid-In Capital Amounts on the Balance Sheet

WHAT'S GOING ON?

* If the stock has a par value, the amounts opposite the stock captions are always par value multiplied by the number of shares issued.
* The difference between the par value and the amount received per share when the stock was issued is recorded as additional paid-in capital.
* If the stock is no-par value stock (without a stated value) the amount opposite the caption is the total amount received when the stock was issued.

Irwin/McGraw-Hill © The McGraw-Hill Companies, Inc, 1999

8-22

Retained Earnings and Dividends

KEY IDEAS

→ *Retained Earnings* increases each period by the amount of net income for that period. (Net losses decrease *Retained Earnings*.)

→ Dividends are distributions of *Retained Earnings* to the stockholders, and are a reduction in *Retained Earnings*.

→ Cash dividends are declared by the board of directors as an amount per share.

Irwin/McGraw-Hill © The McGraw-Hill Companies, Inc, 1999

8-24

Retained Earnings and Dividends

KEY IDEAS

➔ Stock dividends are declared by the board of directors as a percentage of currently issued shares. Stock dividends affect only *Retained Earnings* and *Paid-In Capital*; assets and liabilities are not affected.

➔ Cash dividends <u>are not</u> paid on treasury stock. Stock dividends <u>are</u> usually issued on treasury stock.

Irwin/McGraw-Hill   © The McGraw-Hill Companies, Inc, 1999

8-26

Cash Dividends

The board of directors declared a dividend.

Dr. Retained Earnings   xx

    Cr. Dividends Payable   xx

On the payment of the dividend.

Dr. Dividends Payable   xx

    Cr. Cash   xx

Irwin/McGraw-Hill   © The McGraw-Hill Companies, Inc, 1999

8-29

Cash Dividends

Balance Sheet	Income Statement
Assets = Liabilities + Owner' equity	Net income = Revenues - Expenses

Declaration Date
     + *Dividends* - *Retained*
       Payable   *Earnings*

Payment Date
- *Cash*   - *Dividends*
        Payable

Irwin/McGraw-Hill   © The McGraw-Hill Companies, Inc, 1999

8-30

Stock Splits

KEY IDEA

- A stock split involved issuing additional shares of stock in proportion to the number of shares currently owned by each stockholder. The relative ownership interest of each stockholder does not change.
- Because there are more shares of stock outstanding, the market price of each share will fall to reflect the split.

Irwin/McGraw-Hill   © The McGraw-Hill Companies, Inc., 1999

8-31

Stock Dividends

Racer, Inc. issued a 2% stock dividend on its $2 par value common stock when the market price was $15 per share. There were 240,000 shares outstanding at the time of the stock split.

Dr. Retained Earnings	72,000	
Cr. Common Stock		9,600
Cr. Additional Paid-In Capital		62,400

Irwin/McGraw-Hill   © The McGraw-Hill Companies, Inc., 1999

8-32

Stock Dividends

Racer, Inc. issued a 2% stock dividend on its $2 par value common stock when the market price was $15 per share. There were 240,000 shares outstanding at the time of the stock split.

Balance Sheet			Income Statement	
Assets	= Liabilities +	Owner' equity	Net income	= Revenues - Expenses
		Retained Earnings		
		- 72,000		
		Common Stock		
		+ 9,600		
		Additional Paid-In Capital		
		+ 62,400		

Irwin/McGraw-Hill   © The McGraw-Hill Companies, Inc., 1999

8-33

Stock Dividends

Note that the stock dividend affects *only* the owners' equity of the firm.

Balance Sheet			Income Statement		
Assets	= Liabilities	+ Owner' equity	Net income	= Revenues	- Expenses
		Retained Earnings			
		- 72,000			
		Common Stock			
		+ 9,600			
		Additional Paid-			
		In Capital			
		+ 62,400			

Irwin/McGraw-Hill   © The McGraw-Hill Companies, Inc., 1999

8-34

Treasury Stock

Racer, Inc. purchased 1,000 shares of its own common stock at a total cost of $12,000 during the year ended August 31, 1999.

Dr. Treasury Stock   12,000
    Cr. Cash   12,000

Irwin/McGraw-Hill   © The McGraw-Hill Companies, Inc., 1999

8-35

Treasury Stock

Racer, Inc. purchased 1,000 shares of its own common stock at a total cost of $12,000 during the year ended August 31, 1999.

Balance Sheet			Income Statement		
Assets	= Liabilities	+ Owner' equity	Net income	= Revenues	- Expenses
Cash		Treasury Stock			
- 12,000		- 12,000			

Irwin/McGraw-Hill   © The McGraw-Hill Companies, Inc., 1999

Chapter 8

8-36

Treasury Stock

Five hundred shares of this treasury stock were sold at a price of $15 per share in fiscal 2000.

Dr. Cash	7,500	
Cr. Treasury Stock		6,000
Cr. Additional Paid-In Capital		1,500

Irwin/McGraw-Hill © The McGraw-Hill Companies, Inc., 1999

8-37

Treasury Stock

Five hundred shares of this treasury stock were sold at a price of $15 per share in fiscal 2000.

Balance Sheet		Income Statement
Assets = Liabilities + Owner' equity		Net income = Revenues - Expenses
Cash	Treasury Stock	
+ 7,500	+ 6,000	
	Additional Paid-In Capital	
	+ 1,500	

Irwin/McGraw-Hill © The McGraw-Hill Companies, Inc., 1999

8-38

Statement of Changes in Retained Earnings

RACER, INC.
Statement of Changes in Retained Earnings
For the Year Ended August 31, 1999

Retained earnings balance, beginning of year	$2,600,000
Add: Net income	390,000
Less: Cash dividends	(30,000)
Preferred stock	(60,000)
2% stock dividend on common stock	(72,000)
Retained earnings balance, end of year	$2,828,000

Irwin/McGraw-Hill © The McGraw-Hill Companies, Inc., 1999

59

9-2

LEARNING OBJECTIVES

After studying this chapter you should understand:

1. What revenue is, and what the two criteria are that permits revenue recognition.

2. How cost of goods sold is determined under both perpetual and periodic inventory accounting systems.

3. The significance of gross profit (or gross margin), and how the gross profit (or gross margin) ratio is calculated and used.

4. The principal categories and components of "other operating expenses," and how these items are reported on the income statement.

Irwin/McGraw-Hill   © The McGraw-Hill Companies, Inc., 1999

9-4

LEARNING OBJECTIVES

After studying this chapter you should understand:

5. What "income from operations" includes, and why this income statement subtotal is significant to managers and financial analysts.

6. The components of the earnings per share calculation, and the reason for some of the refinements made in that calculation.

7. The alternative income statement presentation models.

8. The unusual items that may appear on the income statement.

Irwin/McGraw-Hill   © The McGraw-Hill Companies, Inc., 1999

9-5

LEARNING OBJECTIVES

After studying this chapter you should understand:

9. The purpose and general format of the statement of cash flows.

10. The difference between the direct and indirect methods of presenting cash flows from operating activities.

11. Why the statement of cash flows is significant to financial analysts and investors who rely on the financial statements for much of their evaluative data.

Irwin/McGraw-Hill   © The McGraw-Hill Companies, Inc., 1999

9-6

Cost of Goods Sold Section

Cost of beginning inventory	$ 2,004
+ Net purchases	8,453
= Cost of goods available for sale	$10,457
- Cost of ending inventory	1,293
= Cost of goods sold	$ 9,164

Irwin/McGraw-Hill   © The McGraw-Hill Companies, Inc., 1999

9-7

Income Statement

KEY OBSERVATIONS ABOUT THE
MULTIPLE-STEP MODEL

> There is a great deal of summarization.
> Captions reflect the revenue and expense categories that are most significant to understanding results of operations.
> Income from operations is sometimes more meaningful for trend comparisons than net income.

Irwin/McGraw-Hill   © The McGraw-Hill Companies, Inc., 1999

9-8

Gross Profit Ratio

INTEL CORPORATION
Gross Profit Ratio--1996
(dollars in millions)

Net sales (or net revenues)	$20,847
Cost of goods sold (or cost of sales)	9,164
Gross profit (or gross margin)	$11,683

Irwin/McGraw-Hill   © The McGraw-Hill Companies, Inc., 1999

9-10

Gross Profit Ratio

INTEL CORPORATION
Gross Profit Ratio--1996
(dollars in millions)

Net sales (or net revenues) ... $20,847
Cost of goods sold (or cost of sales) ... 9,164
Gross profit (or gross margin) ... $11,683

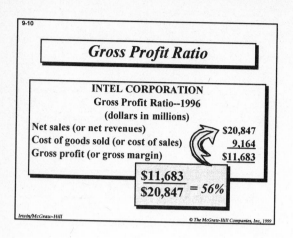

$$\frac{\$11,683}{\$20,847} = 56\%$$

Irwin/McGraw-Hill · © The McGraw-Hill Companies, Inc., 1999

9-11

Estimating Ending Inventory (Gross Profit Method)

Net sales	$100,000	100%
Cost of goods sold:		
Beginning inventory	$19,000	
Net purchases	63,000	
Cost of goods available		
for sale	$82,000	
Less: Ending inventory	?	
Cost of goods sold	?	
Gross profit	?	30%

All the known facts!

Irwin/McGraw-Hill · © The McGraw-Hill Companies, Inc., 1999

9-13

Estimating Ending Inventory (Gross Profit Method)

Net sales	$100,000	100%
Cost of goods sold:		
Beginning inventory	$19,000	
Net purchases	63,000	
Cost of goods available		
for sale	$82,000	
Less: Ending inventory	?	
Cost of goods sold	70,000	70%
Gross profit	$ 30,000	30%

All the known facts!

Irwin/McGraw-Hill · © The McGraw-Hill Companies, Inc., 1999

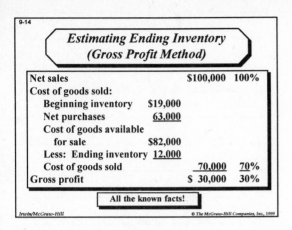

9-14

Estimating Ending Inventory
(Gross Profit Method)

Net sales	$100,000	100%
Cost of goods sold:		
Beginning inventory	$19,000	
Net purchases	63,000	
Cost of goods available		
for sale	$82,000	
Less: Ending inventory	12,000	
Cost of goods sold	70,000	70%
Gross profit	$ 30,000	30%

All the known facts!

Irwin/McGraw-Hill   © The McGraw-Hill Companies, Inc., 1999

9-15

Estimating Ending Inventory
(Gross Profit Method)

Net sales	$100,000	100%
Cost of goods sold:		
Beginning inventory	$19,000	
Net purchases	63,000	
Cost of goods available		
for sale	$82,000	
Less: Ending inventory	12,000	*Estimated Ending Inventory*
Cost of goods sold		
Gross profit	$ 30,000	30%

All the known facts!

Irwin/McGraw-Hill   © The McGraw-Hill Companies, Inc., 1999

9-16

Linkage Between Balance Sheet
and Income Statement Accounts

BALANCE SHEET	INCOME STATEMENT
Accounts Receivable-------->	Sales/Revenues
Notes Receivable and------->	Interest Income
Short-Term Investments	
Inventories-------------------->	Cost of Goods Sold
Prepaid Expenses and------->	Operating Expenses
	Accrued Liabilities

Irwin/McGraw-Hill   © The McGraw-Hill Companies, Inc., 1999

9-17

Linkage Between Balance Sheet and Income Statement Accounts

BALANCE SHEET	INCOME STATEMENT
Accumulated----------------->Depreciation Expense Depreciation	
Notes Payable and----------->Interest Expense and Bonds Payable	
Income Taxes Payable------> Income Tax Expense and Deferred Tax Liability	

Irwin/McGraw-Hill   © The McGraw-Hill Companies, Inc, 1999

9-20

Weighted-Average Shares

Periods	Number of Months	Number of Shares Outstanding	Months x Shares
9/1-1/3	4	200,000	800,000
1/3-6/25	6	240,000	1,440,000
6/25-8/31	2	225,000	450,000
Totals	12		2,690,000

$$2,690,000/12 = 224.167$$

Irwin/McGraw-Hill   © The McGraw-Hill Companies, Inc, 1999

9-22

Earnings Per Share

$$\frac{\text{Net income available for common stock}}{\text{Weighted-average number of shares of common stock outstanding}}$$

$$EPS = \frac{\$1,247,000}{224,167} = \$5.56$$

Irwin/McGraw-Hill   © The McGraw-Hill Companies, Inc, 1999

9-23

Single-Step Income Statement

CRUISERS, INC., AND SUBSIDIARIES
Consolidated Income Statement
For the Year Ended August 31, 1999, and 1998
(000 omitted)

	1999	1998
Net sales	$77,543	$62,531
Cost of goods sold	48,077	39,870
Selling expenses	13,957	10,590
General and administrative expenses	9,307	7,835
Interest expense	3,378	2,679
Other income (net)	385	193
Minority interest	432	356
Income before taxes	$ 2,777	$ 1,394
Provision for income taxes	1,250	630
Net income	$ 1,527	$ 764

Irwin/McGraw-Hill © The McGraw-Hill Companies, Inc., 1999

9-24

Multiple-Step Income Statement

CRUISERS, INC., AND SUBSIDIARIES
Consolidated Income Statement
For the Year Ended August 31, 1999, and 1998
(000 omitted)

	1999	1998
Net sales	$77,543	$62,531
Cost of goods sold	48,077	39,870
Gross profit	$29,466	$22,661
Selling, general, and administrative expenses	23,264	18,425
Income from operations	$ 6,202	$ 4,236
Other income (expense):		
Interest expense	(3,378)	(2,679)
Other income (net)	385	193
Minority interest	(432)	(356)
Income before taxes	$ 2,777	$ 1,394
Provision for income taxes	1,250	630
Net income	$ 1,527	$ 764

Irwin/McGraw-Hill © The McGraw-Hill Companies, Inc., 1999

9-25

Income Statement Presentation of Unusual Items

	1999	1998
Income from continuing operations before taxes	$2,777	$1,394
Provision for income taxes	1,250	630
Income from continuing operations	$1,527	$764
Discontinued operations, net of income taxes:		
Loss from operations	(162)	----
Loss on disposal	(79)	----
Loss from discontinued operations	$ (241)	----
Earnings before extraordinary items	$1,286	$ 764
Extraordinary item:		
Gain on termination of pension plan, net of income taxes	357	----
Net income	$1,643	$ 764

Irwin/McGraw-Hill © The McGraw-Hill Companies, Inc., 1999

9-26

Statement of Cash Flows

WHAT'S GOING ON?

☑ The income statement reports accrual basis net income. Financial statement users also want to know about the firm's cash flows.

☑ The reasons for the change in cash from the beginning of the period are summarized in three categories.
  > Cash flows from **operating** activities
  > Cash flows from **investing** activities
  > Cash flows from **financing** activities

Irwin/McGraw-Hill   © The McGraw-Hill Companies, Inc, 1999

9-27

Statement of Cash Flows

KEY QUESTIONS

➢ What happened to the cash balance during the year?

➢ What is the relationship between cash flows from operating, investing, and financing activities?

Irwin/McGraw-Hill   © The McGraw-Hill Companies, Inc, 1999

9-28

Interpreting the Statement of Cash Flows

KEY RELATIONSHIPS TO OBSERVE

✓ Did cash flows from operating activities exceed cash used for investing activities?

✓ Did financing activities cause net increase or net decrease in cash?

✓ In operating activities, what were the effects of accounts receivable, inventory, and accounts payable changes?

✓ In investing activities, what was the relationship between the investment in new assets and the sale of old assets?

✓ In financing activities, what were the net effects of long-term debt and capital stock changes? What was the effect of cash dividends paid?

Irwin/McGraw-Hill   © The McGraw-Hill Companies, Inc, 1999

9-29

Statement of Cash Flows
(Direct Method)

CRUISERS, INC., AND SUBSIDIARIES
Consolidated Statement of Cash Flows
For the Year Ended August 31, 1999, and 1998
(000 omitted)

	1999	1998
Cash flows from operating activities:		
Cash received from customers	$14,929	$13,021
Cash paid to suppliers	(6,784)	(8,218)
Payments for compensation of employees	(2,137)	(1,267)
Other operating expenses paid	(1,873)	(1,002)
Interest paid	(675)	(703)
Taxes paid	(1,037)	(532)
Net cash provided by operating activities	$ 2,423	$ 1,299

Top Part

Irwin/McGraw-Hill — © The McGraw-Hill Companies, Inc, 1999

9-30

Statement of Cash Flows
(Direct Method)

	1999	1998
Cash flows from investing activities:		
Proceeds from sale of land	$ ----	$ 200
Investment in plant and equipment	(1,622)	(1,437)
Net cash used for investing activities	$(1,622)	$(1,237)
Cash flows from financing activities:		
Additional long-term borrowing	$ 350	$ 180
Payment of long-term debt	(268)	(53)
Purchase of treasury stock	(37)	(26)
Payment of dividends on capital stock	(363)	(310)
Net cash used for financing activities	$ (318)	$ (209)
Increase (Decrease) in cash	$ 483	$ (147)
Cash balance, August 31, 1998, and 1997	276	423
Cash balance, August 31, 1999, and 1998	$ 759	$ 276

Bottom Part

Irwin/McGraw-Hill — © The McGraw-Hill Companies, Inc, 1999

9-31

Statement of Cash Flows
(Direct Method)

	1999	1998
Reconciliation of net income and net cash provided by operating activities:		
Net income	$ 1,390	$ 666
Add (Deduct) items not affecting cash:		
Depreciation expense	631	526
Minority interest	432	356
Gain on sale of land	---	(110)
Increase in accounts receivable	(30)	(44)
Increase in inventories	(21)	(168)
Increase in current liabilities	16	66
Other (net)	5	7
Net cash provided by operating activities	$ 2,423	$ 1,299

Reconciliation

Irwin/McGraw-Hill — © The McGraw-Hill Companies, Inc, 1999

9-32

Statement of Cash Flows
(Indirect Method)

Top Part

CRUISERS, INC., AND SUBSIDIARIES
Consolidated Statement of Cash Flows
For the Year Ended August 31, 1999, and 1998
(000 omitted)

	1999	1998
Cash flows from operating activities:		
Net income	$1,390	$ 777
Add (Deduct) items not affecting cash:		
Depreciation expense	631	526
Minority interest	432	356
Gain on sale of land	---	(110)
Increase in accounts receivable	(30)	(44)
Increase in inventories	(21)	(168)
Increase in current liabilities	16	66
Other (net)	5	7
Net cash provided by operating activities	$2,423	$1,299

Irwin/McGraw-Hill   © The McGraw-Hill Companies, Inc, 1999

9-33

Statement of Cash Flows
(Indirect Method)

	1999	1998
Cash flows from investing activities:		
Proceeds from sale of land	$ ----	$ 200
Investment in plant and equipment	(1,622)	(1,437)
Net cash used for investing activities	$(1,622)	$(1,237)
Cash flows from financing activities:		
Additional long-term borrowing	$ 350	$ 180
Payment of long-term debt	(268)	(53)
Purchase of treasury stock	(37)	(26)
Payment of dividends on capital stock	(363)	(310)
Net cash used for financing activities	$ (318)	$ (209)
Increase (Decrease) in cash	$ 483	$ (147)
Cash balance, August 31, 1998, and 1997	276	423
Cash balance, August 31, 1999, and 1998	$ 759	$ 276

Bottom Part

Irwin/McGraw-Hill   © The McGraw-Hill Companies, Inc, 1999

10-2

LEARNING OBJECTIVES

After studying this chapter you should understand:

❶ That the explanatory notes are an integral part of the financial statements; the notes provide detailed disclosure of information needed by users wishing to gain a full understanding of the financial statements.

❷ The kinds of significant accounting policies that are explained in the notes.

❸ The nature and content of disclosures relating to
    Accounting changes
    Business combinations
    Contingencies and commitments

Irwin/McGraw-Hill   © *The McGraw-Hill Companies, Inc., 1999*

10-4

LEARNING OBJECTIVES

After studying this chapter you should understand:

❸ Learning Objective 3 (continued)
    Contingencies and commitments
    Events subsequent to the balance sheet date
    Impact of inflation
    Segment information

❹ The role of the Securities and Exchange Commission, and some of its reporting requirements.

❺ Why a statement of management's responsibility is included with the notes.

Irwin/McGraw-Hill   © *The McGraw-Hill Companies, Inc., 1999*

10-5

Financial Statement Sequence

① Income statement
② Balance sheet
③ Statement of cash flows

Irwin/McGraw-Hill   © *The McGraw-Hill Companies, Inc., 1999*

10-6

Explanatory Notes to Financial Statements

KEY POINTS

Financial statement readers must be able to learn about the following key issues that affect their ability to understand the statements.

+ Depreciation methods

+ Inventory cost flow assumptions

+ Current and deferred income taxes

+ Employee benefit information

+ Earnings per share of common stock details
   (Stock option and stock purchase plan information)

Irwin/McGraw-Hill   © The McGraw-Hill Companies, Inc., 1999

10-8

Explanatory Notes to Financial Statements

OTHER KEY DISCLOSURES

• Management's statement of responsibility

• Management's discussion and analysis

KEY IDEA

• The explanatory notes to the financial statements must be reviewed to have a reasonably complete understanding of what the numbers mean.

Irwin/McGraw-Hill   © The McGraw-Hill Companies, Inc., 1999

10-10

Significant Accounting Policies

Depreciation method???

straight-line

units-of-production

sum-of-the-years'-digits

declining-balance

Inventory valuation method???

weighted average

FIFO

LIFO

Irwin/McGraw-Hill   © The McGraw-Hill Companies, Inc., 1999

10-11

Significant Accounting Policies

Other Policies
Basis of consolidation
Income taxes
Employee benefits
Amortization of intangibles
Earnings per share of common
stock
Stock option and stock
purchase plan

Irwin/McGraw-Hill   © The McGraw-Hill Companies, Inc., 1999

10-13

Other Disclosures

An **accounting change** is a change in an accounting principle that has a material effect on the comparability of financial statements.

The effects of a **business combination** describing the effects on the financial statements.

Irwin/McGraw-Hill   © The McGraw-Hill Companies, Inc., 1999

10-14

Other Disclosures

An **accounting change** is a change in an accounting principle that has a

It is appropriate to disclose any material **contingencies and commitments** in which the firm is involved.

The effects of a **business combination** describing the effects on the financial statements.

Irwin/McGraw-Hill   © The McGraw-Hill Companies, Inc., 1999

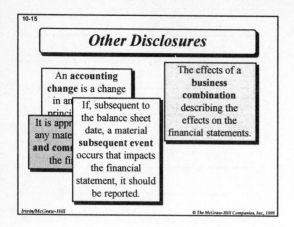

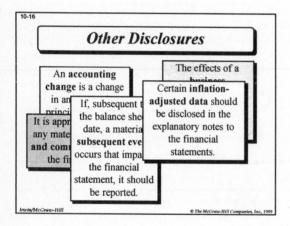

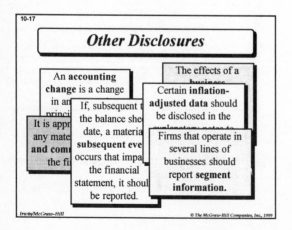

10-18

Return on investment (ROI)

$$\frac{\text{Operating Income}}{\text{Net Revenue}} \times \frac{\text{Net Revenue}}{\text{Average Identifiable Assets}}$$

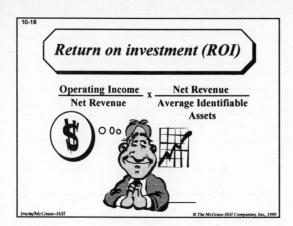

Irwin/McGraw-Hill   © The McGraw-Hill Companies, Inc., 1999

10-19

Five-Year (or Longer) Summary of Financial Data

KEY IDEAS

- Look at trend of data.
- Notice the effect of stock dividends and stock splits on per share data.
- Use the data reported for prior years to make ratio calculations for evaluative purposes.

Irwin/McGraw-Hill   © The McGraw-Hill Companies, Inc., 1999

10-21

Independent Auditors' Report

KEY IDEA

Financial statements present fairly, <u>in all material respects</u>, the financial position and results of operations.

KEY POINT

Auditors give no guarantee that financial statements are free for error or fraud.

Irwin/McGraw-Hill   © The McGraw-Hill Companies, Inc., 1999

11-2

LEARNING OBJECTIVES

After studying this chapter you should understand:

❶ How liquidity measures can be influenced by the inventory cost-flow assumption.

❷ How suppliers and creditors use a customer's payment practices to judge liquidity.

❸ The influence of alternative inventory cost-flow assumptions and depreciation methods on turnover ratios.

❹ How the number of day' sales in accounts receivable and inventory are used to evaluate the effectiveness of the management of receivables and inventory.

Irwin/McGraw-Hill   © The McGraw-Hill Companies, Inc., 1999

11-4

LEARNING OBJECTIVES

After studying this chapter you should understand:

❺ The significance of the price/earnings ratio in the evaluation of the market price of a company's common stock.

❻ How dividend yield and the dividend payout ratio are used by investors to evaluate a company's common stock.

❼ What financial leverage is, and why it is significant to management, creditors, and owners.

Irwin/McGraw-Hill   © The McGraw-Hill Companies, Inc., 1999

11-5

LEARNING OBJECTIVES

After studying this chapter you should understand:

❽ What book value per share of common stock is, how it is calculated, and why it is not a very meaningful amount for most companies.

❾ How common-size financial statements can be used to evaluate a firm's financial position and results of operations over a number of years.

❿ How operating statistics using physical, or nonfinancial, data can be used to help management evaluate the results of the firm's activities.

Irwin/McGraw-Hill   © The McGraw-Hill Companies, Inc., 1999

11-8

LIQUIDITY ANALYSIS

KEY QUESTION

> Is the firm likely to be able to pay its obligations when they come due?

LIQUIDITY MEASURES

> Working capital
> Current ratio
> Acid-test ratio

Irwin/McGraw-Hill   © The McGraw-Hill Companies, Inc., 1999

11-9

LIQUIDITY ANALYSIS

KEY ISSUE

> The inventory cost flow assumption used by the firm (FIFO, LIFO, weighted average, or specific identification) will affect these measures.

Irwin/McGraw-Hill   © The McGraw-Hill Companies, Inc., 1999

11-11

Activity Measures

KEY QUESTIONS

◇ How efficiently are the firm's assets being used?

ACTIVITY MEASURES

☑ Accounts receivable turnover (or number of day's sales in accounts receivable)
☑ Inventory turnover (or number of day's sales in inventory)
☑ Plant and equipment turnover
☑ Total asset turnover

Irwin/McGraw-Hill   © The McGraw-Hill Companies, Inc., 1999

11-13

Activity Measures

GENERAL MODEL

$$\text{Turnover} = \frac{\text{Sales for Period}}{\text{Average Asset Balance for Period}}$$

KEY IDEAS

□ Inventory activity calculations use cost of goods sold instead of sales.

□ Number of day's sales calculations use the ending balance of the asset account divided by average daily sales or average daily cost of goods sold.

Irwin/McGraw-Hill   © The McGraw-Hill Companies, Inc., 1999

11-16

Intel Corporation's Asset Turnover Calculations Illustrated

Accounts Receivable Turnover ($ millions)

Sales (net revenue) for 1996 ($ millions)	$20,847
Accounts receivable (net), 12/28/96	3,723
Accounts receivable (net), 12/30/95	3,116

$$\text{Accounts receivable turnover} = \frac{\$20,847}{(\$3,723 + \$3,116)/2}$$

= 6.1 times

Irwin/McGraw-Hill   © The McGraw-Hill Companies, Inc., 1999

11-18

Intel Corporation's Asset Turnover Calculations Illustrated

Inventory Turnover ($ millions)

Cost of goods sold for 1996	$9,164
Inventories, 12/28/96	1,293
Inventories, 12/30/95	2,004

$$\text{Inventory turnover} = \frac{\text{Cost of goods sold}}{\text{Average inventories}}$$

Irwin/McGraw-Hill   © The McGraw-Hill Companies, Inc., 1999

11-19

Intel Corporation's Asset Turnover Calculations Illustrated

Inventory Turnover ($ millions)

Cost of goods sold for 1996	$9,164
Inventories, 12/28/96	1,293
Inventories, 12/30/95	2,004

$$\text{Inventory turnover} = \frac{\$9,164}{(\$1,293 + \$2,004)/2}$$

= 5.6 times

Irwin/McGraw-Hill   © The McGraw-Hill Companies, Inc., 1999

11-21

Intel Corporation's Asset Turnover Calculations Illustrated

Plant and Equipment Turnover ($ millions)

Sales (net revenues) for 1996	$20,847
Plant and equipment, 12/28/96	8,487
Plant and equipment, 12/30/95	7,471

$$\text{Plant and equipment turnover} = \frac{\text{Sales}}{\text{Average plant and equipment}}$$

Irwin/McGraw-Hill   © The McGraw-Hill Companies, Inc., 1999

11-22

Intel Corporation's Asset Turnover Calculations Illustrated

Plant and Equipment Turnover ($ millions)

Sales (net revenues) for 1996	$20,847
Plant and equipment, 12/28/96	8,487
Plant and equipment, 12/30/95	7,471

$$\text{Plant and equipment turnover} = \frac{\$20,847}{(\$8,487 + \$7,471)/2}$$

= 2.6 times

Irwin/McGraw-Hill   © The McGraw-Hill Companies, Inc., 1999

11-23

Profitability Measures

KEY QUESTIONS

◇ What rate of return has been earned on assets or owners' equity?

◇ How expensive is the firm's common stock relative to the common stock of other companies, and what has been the dividend experience?

Irwin/McGraw-Hill © The McGraw-Hill Companies, Inc., 1999

11-24

Profitability Measures

PROFITABILITY MEASURES

> ROI--return on investment
> ROE--return on equity
> Price/earnings ratio (earnings multiple)
> Dividend yield
> Dividend payout ratio

Irwin/McGraw-Hill © The McGraw-Hill Companies, Inc., 1999

11-25

Profitability Measures

KEY IDEAS

✓ Factors in ROI calculation may differ among companies (net income or operating income in the numerator); what is important is the consistency of definition, and **trend** of ROI.

✓ ROE is based on the net income applicable to, and the equity of, **common stockholders.**

Irwin/McGraw-Hill © The McGraw-Hill Companies, Inc., 1999

11-26

Intel Corporation's Profitability Measures

Price/Earnings Ratio

Price/earnings ratio (or earnings multiple) $=$ $\dfrac{\text{Market price of common stock}}{\begin{array}{c}\text{Earnings per share of}\\\text{common stock}\end{array}}$

Irwin/McGraw-Hill   © The McGraw-Hill Companies, Inc., 1999

11-28

Cruisers, Inc.

Dividend Yield

Dividend yield: Common stock $=$ $\dfrac{\text{Annual dividend per share}}{\text{Market price per share of stock}}$

Dividend yield: Preferred stock $=$ $\dfrac{\text{Annual dividend per share}}{\text{Market price per share of stock}}$

Irwin/McGraw-Hill   © The McGraw-Hill Companies, Inc., 1999

11-30

Cruisers, Inc.

Dividend Payout Ratio

Dividend payout ratio $=$ $\dfrac{\text{Annual dividend per share}}{\text{Earnings per share}}$

Irwin/McGraw-Hill   © The McGraw-Hill Companies, Inc., 1999

11-31

Cruisers, Inc.

Dividend Payout Ratio

$$\text{Dividend payout ratio} = \frac{\$1.98}{\$5.56} = 35.6\%$$

Irwin/McGraw-Hill   © The McGraw-Hill Companies, Inc, 1999

11-32

Financial Leverage Ratios

KEY IDEAS

✧ Financial leverage refers to the use of debt (instead of owners' equity) to finance the acquisition of assets for the firm.

✧ The interest rate on debt is fixed, so if the ROI earned on the borrowed funds is greater than the interest rate owed, ROE will increase. This is referred to as "positive" financial leverage.

✧ If the ROI earned on borrowed funds is less than the interest rate owed, ROE will decrease. This is referred to as "negative" financial leverage.

Irwin/McGraw-Hill   © The McGraw-Hill Companies, Inc, 1999

11-34

Financial Leverage Ratios

KEY QUESTIONS

◈ How much financial leverage is the firm using?

◈ How much risk of financial loss to creditors and owners is there?

FINANCIAL LEVERAGE RATIOS

¤ Debt ratio

¤ Debt/equity ratio

¤ Times interest earned ratio

Irwin/McGraw-Hill   © The McGraw-Hill Companies, Inc, 1999

11-36

Other Analytical Techniques

Book Value Per Share of Common Stock

KEY IDEA

An easily calculated amount based on the balance sheet amount of owners' equity, but not very useful in most cases because balance sheet amounts do not reflect market values or replacement values.

$$\text{Book value per share of common stock} = \frac{\text{Common stockholders' equity}}{\text{Number of shares of common stock outstanding}}$$

Irwin/McGraw-Hill   © The McGraw-Hill Companies, Inc, 1999

11-37

Other Analytical Techniques

Common Size Financial Statements

KEY IDEA

Comparisons between firms (or between periods for the same firm) can be more easily understood if financial statement amounts are expressed as percentages of total assets or total revenues.

Irwin/McGraw-Hill   © The McGraw-Hill Companies, Inc, 1999

11-38

Other Analytical Techniques

Other Operating Statistics

KEY IDEA

Not all decisions and informed judgments about an entity are based on financial data. Nonfinancial statistics are frequently relevant and useful.

Irwin/McGraw-Hill   © The McGraw-Hill Companies, Inc, 1999

12-2

LEARNING OBJECTIVES

After studying this chapter you should understand:

❶ The major differences between financial accounting and managerial accounting.

❷ The difference between product costs and period costs, and the three components of product cost.

❸ The general operation of a product costing system, and how costs flow through the inventory accounts to cost of goods sold.

❹ The presentation and interpretation of a statement of cost of goods manufactured.

Irwin/McGraw-Hill   © The McGraw-Hill Companies, Inc, 1999

12-5

LEARNING OBJECTIVES

After studying this chapter you should understand:

❾ That all costs are controllable by someone at some time, but that in the short run some costs may be classified as noncontrollable.

❿ The meaning and application of the following "cost" terms: *differential, allocated, sunk,* and *opportunity.*

Irwin/McGraw-Hill   © The McGraw-Hill Companies, Inc, 1999

12-8

Cost Classifications

KEY IDEA

>There are different costs for different purposes.

COST CLASSIFICATIONS

> For cost accounting purposes:
>   Product cost
>   Period cost

> Relationship to product or activity:
>   Direct cost
>   Indirect cost

Irwin/McGraw-Hill   © The McGraw-Hill Companies, Inc, 1999

12-4

LEARNING OBJECTIVES

After studying this chapter you should understand:

❺ The difference between absorption costing and direct (or variable) costing.

❻ The difference between direct and indirect costs.

❼ The difference between variable and fixed cost behavior patterns, and the simplifying assumptions made in this classification method.

❽ Why expressing fixed costs on a per unit of activity basis is misleading and may result in faulty decisions.

Irwin/McGraw-Hill   © The McGraw-Hill Companies, Inc, 1999

12-6

Managerial Accounting Compared to Financial Accounting

KEY CHARACTERISTICS THAT DIFFER

✧ Service perspective

✧ Breadth of concern

✧ Reporting frequency and promptness

✧ Degree of precision of data used

✧ Reporting standards

Irwin/McGraw-Hill   © The McGraw-Hill Companies, Inc, 1999

12-9

Cost Classifications

COST CLASSIFICATIONS (Cont'd)

> Relationship between total cost and volume of activity:
>   Variable cost
>   Fixed cost
> Time-frame perspective
>   Controllable cost
>   Noncontrollable cost
> For other analytical purposes:
>   Differential cost
>   Allocated cost
>   Sunk cost
>   Opportunity cost

Irwin/McGraw-Hill   © The McGraw-Hill Companies, Inc, 1999

12-11

Cost Accounting Systems

KEY IDEAS

☐ Period costs (selling, general, and administrative) are accounted for as expenses in the period incurred.

☐ Product costs flow through inventory (asset) accounts, and then to the cost of goods sold account.

Raw material, direct labor, and manufacturing overhead costs are capitalized as inventory ►until the product they relate to is sold.

Irwin/McGraw-Hill   © The McGraw-Hill Companies, Inc., 1999

12-15

Flow of Cost Comparison--Manufacturer

Raw Materials Inventory		Work in Process Inventory	
The cost of raw materials *purchased* is recorded as an asset in raw material inventory	The cost of raw materials *used* in production is moved from raw materials inventory to work in process inventory	Raw materials *used*, direct labor *incurred*, and manufacturing overhead costs *applied* are recorded as an asset in work in process inventory	The cost of products *manufactured* and transferred to the warehouse is removed from work in process and added to finished goods inventory

Irwin/McGraw-Hill   © The McGraw-Hill Companies, Inc., 1999

12-17

Flow of Cost Comparison--Manufacturer

Finished Goods Inventory		Cost of Goods Sold
Cost of goods manufactured	The cost of manufactured products *sold* is removed from finished goods inventory	

Irwin/McGraw-Hill   © The McGraw-Hill Companies, Inc., 1999

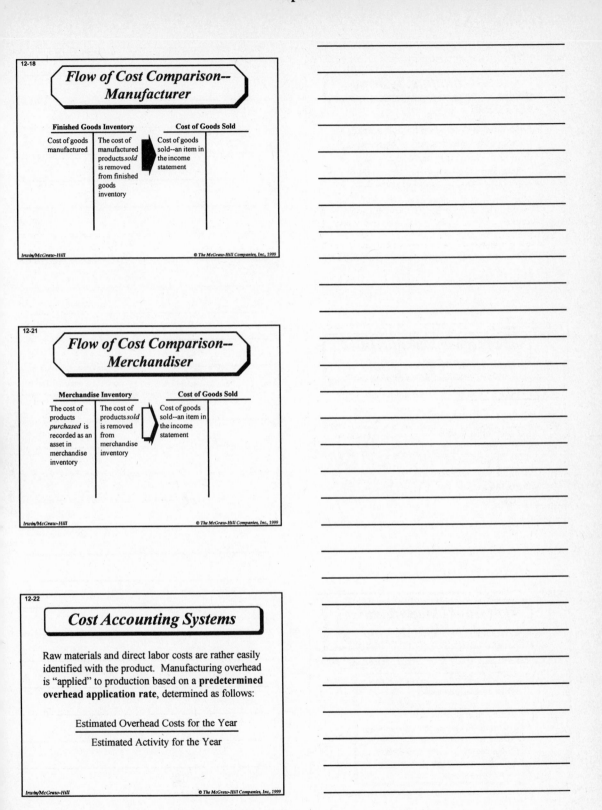

12-18

Flow of Cost Comparison-- Manufacturer

Finished Goods Inventory

Cost of goods manufactured

The cost of manufactured products *sold* is removed from finished goods inventory

Cost of Goods Sold

Cost of goods sold--an item in the income statement

Irwin/McGraw-Hill

© The McGraw-Hill Companies, Inc., 1999

12-21

Flow of Cost Comparison-- Merchandiser

Merchandise Inventory

The cost of products *purchased* is recorded as an asset in merchandise inventory

The cost of products *sold* is removed from merchandise inventory

Cost of Goods Sold

Cost of goods sold--an item in the income statement

Irwin/McGraw-Hill

© The McGraw-Hill Companies, Inc., 1999

12-22

Cost Accounting Systems

Raw materials and direct labor costs are rather easily identified with the product. Manufacturing overhead is "applied" to production based on a **predetermined overhead application rate**, determined as follows:

Estimated Overhead Costs for the Year

Estimated Activity for the Year

Irwin/McGraw-Hill

© The McGraw-Hill Companies, Inc., 1999

12-23

Cost Accounting Systems

KEY POINT

> Because the predetermined overhead application rate is based on **estimates**, there will probably be "overapplied" or "underapplied" overhead at the end of the year. This amount usually becomes part of cost of goods sold.

Irwin/McGraw-Hill   © The McGraw-Hill Companies, Inc., 1999

12-24

Cost of Goods Manufactured and Cost of Goods Sold

KEY IDEA

> Because of the inventory accounts, cost of goods manufactured and cost of goods sold are not simply the totals of costs incurred during the period.

Irwin/McGraw-Hill   © The McGraw-Hill Companies, Inc., 1999

12-25

Cost of Goods Manufactured and Cost of Goods Sold

KEY MODEL--COST OF GOODS MANUFACTURED

    Raw materials inventory, beginning
 + Raw materials purchases
 - Raw materials inventory, ending
 = Cost of raw materials used
 + Work-in-process inventory, beginning
 + Direct labor costs incurred
 + Manufacturing overhead applied
 - Work-in-process inventory, ending
 = Cost of goods manufactured

Irwin/McGraw-Hill   © The McGraw-Hill Companies, Inc., 1999

12-26

Cost of Goods Manufactured and Cost of Goods Sold

KEY MODEL--COST OF GOODS SOLD

Finished goods inventory, beginning

+ Cost of goods manufactured

- Finished goods inventory, ending

= Cost of goods sold

Irwin/McGraw-Hill   © The McGraw-Hill Companies, Inc., 1999

12-27

Income Statement

CRUISERS, INC.
Income Statement
For the Month of April

Sales	$2,012,400
Cost of goods sold	(1,103,930)
Gross profit	$ 908,470
Selling, general, and administrative expenses	(562,110)
Income from operations	$ 346,360
Interest expense	(78,420)
Income before taxes	$ 267,940
Income tax expense	(93,779)
Net income	$ 174,161

Irwin/McGraw-Hill   © The McGraw-Hill Companies, Inc., 1999

12-28

Activity Based Costing

KEY POINT

◆ An ABC system involves identifying the key activities that cause the incurrence of cost; these activities are known as **cost drivers.**

◆ Examples of cost drivers include: machine setup, quality inspection, production order preparation, and materials handling activities.

Irwin/McGraw-Hill   © The McGraw-Hill Companies, Inc., 1999

12-29

Activity Based Costing

KEY RELATIONSHIPS

∇ The number of times each activity is to be performed during the year and the total cost of each activity are estimated, and a predetermined cost per activity is calculated.

∇ "Activity based costs" are then applied to products, rather than using a traditional method of overhead application such as direct labor hours or machine hours.

Irwin/McGraw-Hill   © The McGraw-Hill Companies, Inc., 1999

12-30

Activity Based Costing

KEY IDEA

ABC systems often lead to more accurate product costing and more effective cost control, because management's attention is directed to the activities that **cause** the incurrence of cost.

Irwin/McGraw-Hill   © The McGraw-Hill Companies, Inc., 1999

12-34

Cost Flows--Absorption Costing

Manufacturing Overhead		Work in Process Inventory	
Variable and fixed overhead incurred	Variable and fixed overhead applied to work in process	Direct material used, direct labor incurred, variable and fixed overhead applied	

Selling, general, and administrative expenses are charged to operating expenses.

Irwin/McGraw-Hill   © The McGraw-Hill Companies, Inc., 1999

12-37

Cost Flows--Direct Costing

Manufacturing Overhead		Work in Process Inventory
Variable overhead incurred	Variable overhead applied to work in process	Direct material used, direct labor incurred, variable overhead applied

In addition to selling, general, and administrative expenses, fixed overhead incurred is charged to operating expenses.

Irwin/McGraw-Hill   © The McGraw-Hill Companies, Inc., 1999

12-40

Relationship of Total Cost to Volume of Activity

KEY IDEA
> **Cost behavior pattern** describes how total cost varies with changes in activity.
KEY RELATIONSHIP
> Variable cost   > Fixed cost
> (See text Exhibit 12-9)
KEY ASSUMPTIONS
> Relevant range   >Linearity

Irwin/McGraw-Hill   © The McGraw-Hill Companies, Inc., 1999

12-43

Cost Formula

KEY POINT
⇨ A **cost formula** describes the expected total cost for any volume of activity using cost behavior information.
KEY POINT
⇨ Total cost = Fixed cost + Variable cost
KEY POINT
⇨ Whenever possible, avoid utilizing fixed costs, because they do not behave that way!

Irwin/McGraw-Hill   © The McGraw-Hill Companies, Inc., 1999

13-2

LEARNING OBJECTIVES

After studying this chapter you should understand:

❶ What kinds of costs are likely to have a variable cost behavior pattern, and what kinds of costs are likely to have a fixed cost behavior pattern.

❷ How to use the high-low method to determine the cost formula for a cost that has a mixed behavior pattern.

❸ The difference between the traditional income statement format and the contribution margin income statement format.

Irwin/McGraw-Hill   © The McGraw-Hill Companies, Inc, 1999

13-4

LEARNING OBJECTIVES

After studying this chapter you should understand:

❹ The importance of using the contribution margin format to analyze the impact of cost and sales volume changes on operating income.

❺ How the contribution margin ratio is calculated, and how it can be used in CVP analysis.

❻ How changes in sales mix can affect projections made with CVP analysis.

Irwin/McGraw-Hill   © The McGraw-Hill Companies, Inc, 1999

13-5

LEARNING OBJECTIVES

After studying this chapter you should understand:

❼ The meaning and significance of break-even point, and how the break-even point is calculated.

❽ The concept of operating leverage.

Irwin/McGraw-Hill   © The McGraw-Hill Companies, Inc, 1999

13-6

Income Statement Models

TRADITIONAL MODEL

Revenues
- Cost of goods sold

Gross profit
- Operating expenses

Operating income

13-7

Income Statement Models

CONTRIBUTION MARGIN MODEL

Revenues
- Variable expenses

Contribution margin
- Fixed expenses

Operating income

13-8

Income Statement Models

KEY IDEAS

* The traditional model classifies expenses by function, and the contribution margin model classifies expenses by cost behavior pattern.

* The contribution margin model is useful for determining the effect on operating income of changes in the level of activity.

Chapter 13

13-12

High-Low Method

Month	Total Unit Cost	Total Production Volume
January	$2,500	8,000 units
February	3,500	13,000 units
March	4,000	16,000 units
April	5,500	12,000 units
May	2,000	6,000 units
June	5,000	18,000 units

$$\text{Variable rate} = \frac{\text{High cost - Low cost}}{\text{High activity - Low activity}}$$

13-15

High-Low Method

FIXED COST CALCULATION

Total cost at 18,000 units	$5,000
Less variable cost:	
18,000 units @ $.25 per unit	4,500
Fixed cost	$ 500

TOTAL COST CALCULATION

Total cost = Fixed cost + Variable rate

= $500 + $.25 per unit produced

= $500 + $4,500

13-18

Expanded Contribution Margin Model

	Per Unit	x Volume =	Total	%
Revenue	$15			
Variable expenses	9			
Contribution margin	$ 6	x 8,000 =	$48,000	40%
Fixed expenses			40,000	
Operating Income			$ 8,000	

(3)

Fixed expenses are not expressed on a per unit basis; they are subtracted from total contribution margin to get operating income

13-20

Expanded Contribution Margin Model

	Per Unit	x Volume =	Total	%
Revenue	$15			
Variable expenses	9			
Contribution margin	$ 6	x 8,000 =	$48,000	40%
Fixed expenses			40,000	
Operating Income			$ 8,000	

If a $3 per unit price cut results in an increase in sales volume to 13,000 units, what is the anticipated operating income?

Irwin/McGraw-Hill   © The McGraw-Hill Companies, Inc., 1999

13-21

Expanded Contribution Margin Model

	Per Unit	x Volume =	Total	%
Revenue	$12			
Variable expenses	9			
Contribution margin	$ 3	x 13,000 =	$39,000	25%
Fixed expenses			40,000	
Operating Income			$ (1,000)	

If a $3 per unit price cut results in an increase in sales volume to 13,000 units, what is the anticipated operating income?

Irwin/McGraw-Hill   © The McGraw-Hill Companies, Inc., 1999

13-23

Expanded Contribution Margin Model

	Per Unit	x Volume =	Total	%
Revenue	$12			
Variable expenses	9			
Contribution margin	$ 3	x 18,000 =	$54,000	25%
Fixed expenses			43,000	
Operating Income			$ 11,000	

What would be the impact on operating income if the same $3 price cut is made in conjunction with a $3,000 increase in advertising, with the expectation that volume would increase to 18,000 units?

Irwin/McGraw-Hill   © The McGraw-Hill Companies, Inc., 1999

13-25

Break-Even Point Analysis

KEY IDEA

> Managers frequently want to know the number of
units that must be sold, or the total sales dollar
required, to break-even (have zero operating
income).

VOLUME IN UNITS AT BREAK EVEN

$$\frac{\text{Fixed expenses}}{\text{Contribution margin ratio}}$$

Irwin/McGraw-Hill © *The McGraw-Hill Companies, Inc, 1999*

13-26

Break-Even Point Analysis

KEY IDEA

> Managers frequently want to know the number of
units that must be sold, or the total sales dollar
required, to break-even (have zero operating
income).

TOTAL REVENUES AT BREAK EVEN

$$\frac{\text{Fixed expenses}}{\text{Contribution margin per unit}}$$

Irwin/McGraw-Hill © *The McGraw-Hill Companies, Inc, 1999*

13-27

Break-Even Point Analysis

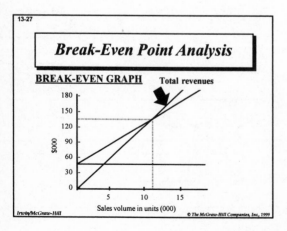

Irwin/McGraw-Hill © *The McGraw-Hill Companies, Inc, 1999*

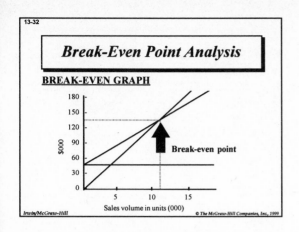

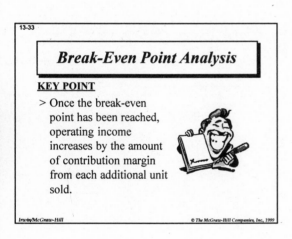

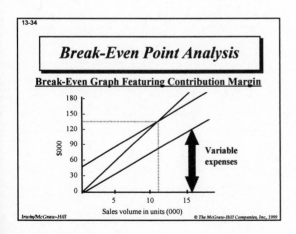

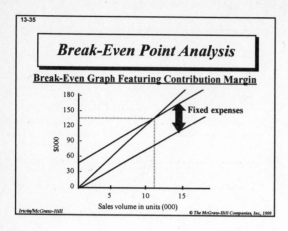

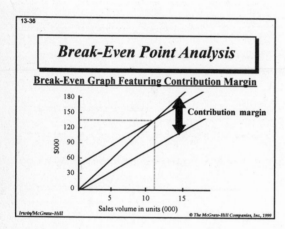

13-38

Key Assumptions to Remember When Using Contribution Margin Analysis

✓ Cost behavior patterns can be identified.

✓ Costs are linear within the relevant range.

✓ Activity remains within the relevant range.

✓ Sales mix of the firm's products with different contribution margin ratios does not change.

KEY POINT

> If these simplifying assumptions are not valid, the analysis is made more complicated but the concepts are still applicable.

Irwin/McGraw-Hill   © *The McGraw-Hill Companies, Inc, 1999*

LEARNING OBJECTIVES

14-2

After studying this chapter you should understand:

❶ Why budgets are useful, and how management philosophy can influence the budgeting process.

❷ How alternative budget time frames can be used.

❸ The significant of the sales forecast (or revenue budget) to the overall operating budget.

❹ How the purchases/production budget is developed.

❺ The importance of cost behavior pattern in developing the operating expense budget.

Irwin/McGraw-Hill © *The McGraw-Hill Companies, Inc., 1999*

LEARNING OBJECTIVES

14-4

After studying this chapter you should understand:

❻ How the cash budget is developed.

❼ Why a budgeted income statement and budgeted balance sheet are prepared.

❽ How the performance report facilitates the management-by-exception process.

❾ How the operating results of segments of an organization can be reported most meaningfully.

❿ What a flexible budget is, and how it is used.

Irwin/McGraw-Hill © *The McGraw-Hill Companies, Inc., 1999*

Budgeting

14-7

BUDGETING CATEGORIES
> Operating budget
> Capital budget

APPROACH TO BUDGETING
> Top-down
> Participative
> Zero-based

BUDGET TIME FRAMES
> Single-period budget
> Rolling (continuous) budget

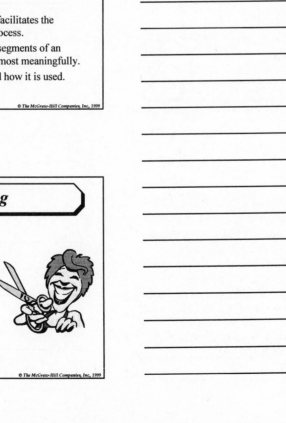

Irwin/McGraw-Hill © *The McGraw-Hill Companies, Inc., 1999*

14-9

Operating Budget Preparation Sequence

- ✓ Sales/revenue budget, or sales forecast
- ✓ Purchases/production budget
- ✓ Operating expense budget
- ✓ Budgeted income statement
- ✓ Cash budget
- ✓ Balance sheet budget

KEY POINT

> The entire budget builds on the sales/revenue budget, sometimes called the sales forecast.

14-10

Production Budget

	January	February	March
Beginning inventory	14,000	16,800	21,000
Add: Production	?	?	?
Goods available for sale	?	?	?
Less: Ending inventory	16,800	21,000	15,400
Quantity of goods sold	**10,000**	**12,000**	**15,000**

Sales forecast in units: January 10,000; February, 12,000; March, 15,000

14-12

Production Budget

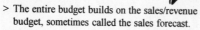

	January	February	March
Beginning inventory	14,000	16,800	21,000
Add: Production	?	?	?
Goods available for sale	26,800	33,000	30,400
Less: Ending inventory	16,800	21,000	15,400
Quantity of goods sold	10,000	12,000	15,000

Working backwards!

14-13

Production Budget

	January	February	March
Beginning inventory	14,000	16,800	21,000
Add: Production	**12,800**	**16,200**	**9,400**
Goods available for sale	26,800	33,000	30,400
Less: Ending inventory	16,800	21,000	15,400
Quantity of goods sold	10,000	12,000	15,000

Working backwards!

Irwin/McGraw-Hill © The McGraw-Hill Companies, Inc., 1999

14-15

Cash Budget

	January	February	March	April
From December 31 accounts receivable of $68,423	$38,000	$25,000	$ 3,000	$ 1,000
From January sales	10,000	24,000	4,800	---
From February sales		12,500	30,000	$ 6,000
From March sales			7,500	18,000
From April sales				10,000
Total collections	$48,000	$61,500	$45,300	$35,000

Irwin/McGraw-Hill © The McGraw-Hill Companies, Inc., 1999

14-17

Performance Reporting

KEY IDEAS

☒ If time and effort have been expended preparing a budget, it is appropriate to compare actual results with budgeted results. This is done in the performance report.

☒ If actual results approximate budgeted results, then no significant further evaluation of performance needs to be made

Management attention is given only to those activities for which actual results vary significantly from budget results. This is **management by exception.**

Irwin/McGraw-Hill © The McGraw-Hill Companies, Inc., 1999

14-18

Performance Reporting

CRUISERS, INC.
Performance Report--SeaCruiser Sailboats
April

Activity	Budget	Actual	Variance
Raw materials	$370,300	$368,510	$ 1,790 F
Direct labor	302,680	330,240	27,560 U
Manufacturing overhead:			
Variable	89,400	103,160	13,760 U
Fixed	193,200	185,800	7,400 F
Totals	$955,580	$987,710	$32,130 U

Irwin/McGraw-Hill   © The McGraw-Hill Companies, Inc., 1999

14-19

Questions Raised By The Cruisers, Inc. Report

◊ Were there significant but offsetting variances in raw materials?

◊ Which workers were not efficient?

◊ Were the new workers being paid a lower than budget wage rate until they became proficient?

◊ Is the training program for new workers effective?

◊ How does the manufacturing overhead variance affect the validity of the predetermined overhead application rate used to apply overhead to production?

Irwin/McGraw-Hill   © The McGraw-Hill Companies, Inc., 1999

14-20

Segment Reporting

KEY IDEAS

✳ When a firm has several identifiable segments (divisions, sales territories, products, etc.) management frequently wants to evaluate the operating results of each segment.

✳ Segments may be referred to as:
    Cost centers
    Profit centers
    Investment centers

Irwin/McGraw-Hill   © The McGraw-Hill Companies, Inc., 1999

14-21

Segment Reporting

KEY ISSUES

◇ Sales, variable expenses, and contribution margin for each segment can usually be easily accumulated from the accounting records.

◇ Fixed expenses include amounts associated directly with each segment, and amounts that are common to the firm as a whole. To report sensible results for each segment, **common fixed expenses should never be arbitrarily allocated to the segments** because they are not incurred directly by any of the segments.

Irwin/McGraw-Hill © The McGraw-Hill Companies, Inc., 1999

14-22

Segmented Income Statement

	Total Company	Sailboat Division	Motorboat Division	Repair Parts Division
Sales	$560,000	$320,000	$160,000	$80,000
Variable expenses	240,000	128,000	72,000	40,000
Contribution margin	$360,000	$192,000	$ 88,000	$40,000
Direct fixed expenses	170,000	100,000	40,000	30,000
Segment margin	$150,000	$ 92,000	$ 48,000	$10,000
Common fixed expenses	112,000			
Operating income	$ 38,000			

Irwin/McGraw-Hill © The McGraw-Hill Companies, Inc., 1999

14-23

Flexible Budgeting

KEY ISSUES

◆ Budget amounts are based on expected level of activity. Actual activity is unlikely to be the same as budgeted activity.

◆ Some manager is responsible for the difference between budgeted and actual activity levels, but is is usually another manager who is responsible for the costs incurred.

◆ Revenues are a function of units sold, and costs incurred are a function of cost behavior patterns.

Irwin/McGraw-Hill © The McGraw-Hill Companies, Inc., 1999

14-24

Flexible Budgeting

KEY IDEA

At the end of a period, when the actual level of activity is known, the original budget should be **flexed** so that the performance report compares actual results with budget amounts based on actual activity.

Irwin/McGraw-Hill   © The McGraw-Hill Companies, Inc., 1999

14-25

Flexible Budgeting

KEY IDEA

Only revenues and variable expenses are flexed. Fixed expenses are not a function of the level of activity (unless activity falls outside of the relevant range).

Irwin/McGraw-Hill   © The McGraw-Hill Companies, Inc., 1999

14-26

The Flexible Budget

Activity	Budget Amount	Actual Amount	Variance	Explanation
Raw materials	$ 64,056	$ 69,212	$ 5,156 U	Produced more boats than planned
Direct labor	48,720	54,992	6,272 U	Same reason
Variable overhead	10,880	12,438	1,558 U	Same reason
Fixed overhead	36,720	37,320	600 U	Immaterial
Total	$160,376	$173,962	$13,586 U	

Irwin/McGraw-Hill   © The McGraw-Hill Companies, Inc., 1999

15-2

LEARNING OBJECTIVES

After studying this chapter you should understand:

❶ Why and how standards are useful in the planning and control process.

❷ How the standard cost of a product is developed.

❸ How standard costs can be used in the cost accounting system.

❹ How and why the two components of a standard cost variance are calculated.

Irwin/McGraw-Hill © The McGraw-Hill Companies, Inc., 1999

15-4

LEARNING OBJECTIVES

After studying this chapter you should understand:

❺ The specific names assigned to variances for different product inputs.

❻ How the control and analysis of fixed overhead variances differs from that of variable cost variances.

❼ The alternative methods of accounting for variances.

Irwin/McGraw-Hill © The McGraw-Hill Companies, Inc., 1999

15-6

Standard Costs

WHAT ARE THEY?

↳ Unit budgets for materials, labor, and overhead costs components of a product or process.

↳ Standard costs are used for planning and control.

KEY IDEAS

↳ Standard costs can be based on:
  Ideal, or engineered, performance
  Attainable performance
  Past experience

↳ The standard cost of product or process components can be used to build up the total cost of a product or process.

Irwin/McGraw-Hill © The McGraw-Hill Companies, Inc., 1999

15-7

Variable Cost
Variance Analysis

KEY IDEAS

✦ It is appropriate to evaluate
performance by comparing actual
costs with standard costs, and
analyzing why any variances occurred.

✦ The reason for calculating variances is
to encourage action to eliminate
favorable variances and capture
favorable variances.

Irwin/McGraw-Hill   © The McGraw-Hill Companies, Inc, 1999

15-8

Variable Cost
Variance Analysis

KEY POINTS

>Variance terminology

Input	Quantity Variance	Cost Per Unit of Input Variance
Raw materials	Usage	Price
Direct labor	Efficiency	Rate
Variable overhead	Efficiency	Spending

Irwin/McGraw-Hill   © The McGraw-Hill Companies, Inc, 1999

15-9

Variable Cost
Variance Analysis

KEY POINTS

> Different managers are usually responsible for the
quantity and cost per unit of input variances. That
is why they are calculated and reported separately.

> The reporting of variances should lead to better
communication and coordination of activities.

Irwin/McGraw-Hill   © The McGraw-Hill Companies, Inc, 1999

15-10

Fixed Cost Variance Analysis

KEY ISSUE

For many firms, fixed manufacturing overhead has become more significant than variable manufacturing costs. Therefore, many firms are increasing efforts to control fixed overhead.

Irwin/McGraw-Hill   © The McGraw-Hill Companies, Inc., 1999

15-11

Fixed Cost Variance Analysis

KEY POINTS

* **Budget variance** is the difference between budgeted fixed overhead and actual fixed overhead costs.
* **Volume variance** is caused by the difference between the planned level of activity used in the calculation of the predetermined overhead application rate, and the actual level of activity.
* The sum of the budget variance and the volume variance equals the overapplied or underapplied fixed manufacturing overhead.

Irwin/McGraw-Hill   © The McGraw-Hill Companies, Inc., 1999

15-13

Actual	2,540 hours @ $12.95/hr.	$32,893
Standard	2,600 hours @ $12.80/hr.	33,280
Budget variance	60 F $ .15 U	$ 387 F

Labor Standards for SeaCruiser sailboat hulls are:	
Build-up labor	$12.80/hr.
Finishing labor	$19.30/hr.

Irwin/McGraw-Hill   © The McGraw-Hill Companies, Inc., 1999

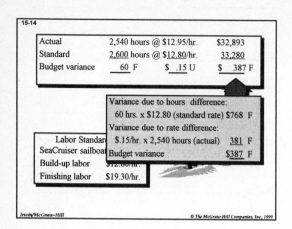

15-14

Actual	2,540 hours @ $12.95/hr.		$32,893
Standard	2,600 hours @ $12.80/hr.		33,280
Budget variance	60 F	$ .15 U	$ 387 F

Variance due to hours difference:
60 hrs. x $12.80 (standard rate) $768 F
Variance due to rate difference:
$.15/hr. x 2,540 hours (actual) 381 F
Budget variance $387 F

Labor Standard
SeaCruiser sailboat
Build-up labor $12.80/hr.
Finishing labor $19.30/hr.

Irwin/McGraw-Hill © *The McGraw-Hill Companies, Inc., 1999*

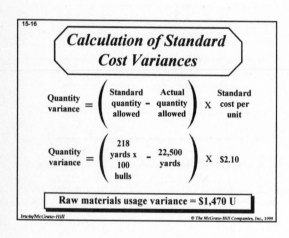

15-16

Calculation of Standard Cost Variances

$$\text{Quantity variance} = \left(\begin{array}{c} \text{Standard} \\ \text{quantity} \\ \text{allowed} \end{array} - \begin{array}{c} \text{Actual} \\ \text{quantity} \\ \text{allowed} \end{array} \right) \times \begin{array}{c} \text{Standard} \\ \text{cost per} \\ \text{unit} \end{array}$$

$$\text{Quantity variance} = \left(\begin{array}{c} 218 \\ \text{yards x} \\ 100 \\ \text{hulls} \end{array} - \begin{array}{c} 22,500 \\ \text{yards} \end{array} \right) \times \$2.10$$

Raw materials usage variance = $1,470 U

Irwin/McGraw-Hill © *The McGraw-Hill Companies, Inc., 1999*

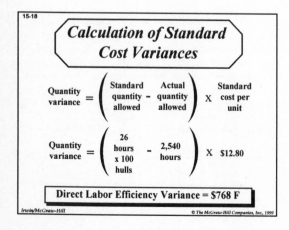

15-18

Calculation of Standard Cost Variances

$$\text{Quantity variance} = \left(\begin{array}{c} \text{Standard} \\ \text{quantity} \\ \text{allowed} \end{array} - \begin{array}{c} \text{Actual} \\ \text{quantity} \\ \text{allowed} \end{array} \right) \times \begin{array}{c} \text{Standard} \\ \text{cost per} \\ \text{unit} \end{array}$$

$$\text{Quantity variance} = \left(\begin{array}{c} 26 \\ \text{hours} \\ \text{x 100} \\ \text{hulls} \end{array} - \begin{array}{c} 2,540 \\ \text{hours} \end{array} \right) \times \$12.80$$

Direct Labor Efficiency Variance = $768 F

Irwin/McGraw-Hill © *The McGraw-Hill Companies, Inc., 1999*

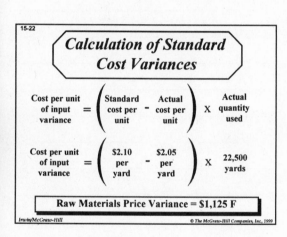

15-20

Calculation of Standard Cost Variances

Quantity variance = (Standard quantity allowed − Actual quantity allowed) X Standard cost per unit

Quantity variance = (26 hours x 100 hulls − 2,540 hours) X $3.20

Variable Overhead Efficiency Variance = $192 F

Irwin/McGraw-Hill   © The McGraw-Hill Companies, Inc., 1999

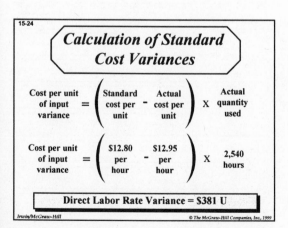

15-22

Calculation of Standard Cost Variances

Cost per unit of input variance = (Standard cost per unit − Actual cost per unit) X Actual quantity used

Cost per unit of input variance = ($2.10 per yard − $2.05 per yard) X 22,500 yards

Raw Materials Price Variance = $1,125 F

Irwin/McGraw-Hill   © The McGraw-Hill Companies, Inc., 1999

15-24

Calculation of Standard Cost Variances

Cost per unit of input variance = (Standard cost per unit − Actual cost per unit) X Actual quantity used

Cost per unit of input variance = ($12.80 per hour − $12.95 per hour) X 2,540 hours

Direct Labor Rate Variance = $381 U

Irwin/McGraw-Hill   © The McGraw-Hill Companies, Inc., 1999

16-2

LEARNING OBJECTIVES

After studying this chapter you should understand:

❶ The attributes of capital budgeting that make it a significantly different activity from operational budgeting.

❷ Why present value analysis is appropriate in capital budgeting.

❸ The concept of cost of capital, and why it is used in capital budgeting.

❹ How the net present value technique is used.

Irwin/McGraw-Hill © The McGraw-Hill Companies, Inc., 1999

16-4

LEARNING OBJECTIVES

After studying this chapter you should understand:

❺ Why the present value ratio is used to assign a profitability ranking to alternative capital expenditure projects.

❻ How the internal rate of return technique differs from the net present value approach of evaluating capital expenditure projects.

❼ How issues concerning estimates, the timing of cash flows, income taxes, and investments are treated in the capital budgeting process.

Irwin/McGraw-Hill © The McGraw-Hill Companies, Inc., 1999

16-5

LEARNING OBJECTIVES

After studying this chapter you should understand:

❽ How the payback period of a capital expenditure project is calculated.

❾ How the accounting rate of return on a project is calculated, and how it can be used most appropriately.

❿ Why not all management decisions are made strictly on the basis of quantitative analysis techniques.

Irwin/McGraw-Hill © The McGraw-Hill Companies, Inc., 1999

16-6

Capital Budgeting

WHAT'S GOING ON?

> Proposed capital expenditures usually involve returns received over extended periods of time, so it is appropriate to recognize the time value of money when evaluating whether or not the investment will generate the desired ROI.

Irwin/McGraw-Hill   © The McGraw-Hill Companies, Inc., 1999

16-8

Capital Budgeting

KEY POINT

> Present value analysis recognizes the time value of money.

KEY ISSUES

> Present value analysis uses--
     The investment amount------->
     The expected cash return------->
     And an interest rate (cost of capital)----->

Irwin/McGraw-Hill   © The McGraw-Hill Companies, Inc., 1999

16-9

Capital Budgeting

KEY ISSUES

Present value analysis is used to answer the following questions:

◊ Is the present value of the future cash flows from the investment, discounted at the cost of capital, at least equal to the amount that must be invested?

◊ If the answer is "yes," then the ROI on the capital expenditure is at least equal to the cost of capital, and the investment should be made.

Irwin/McGraw-Hill   © The McGraw-Hill Companies, Inc., 1999

16-10

Capital Budgeting Analysis Techniques

METHODS THAT USE PRESENT VALUE ANALYSIS

| Net present value (NPV) method |

✓ Given a cost of capital, compute the present value of the cash returns from the investment and then subtract the investment required.

✓ This difference is the net present value (NPV) of the project.

✓ If the NPV is positive, ROI>cost of capital, so the investment should be made.

Irwin/McGraw-Hill   © The McGraw-Hill Companies, Inc, 1999

16-11

Capital Budgeting Analysis Techniques

METHODS THAT USE PRESENT VALUE ANALYSIS

| Net present value (NPV) method |

✓ If the NPV is negative, ROI < cost of capital, so the investment should not be made.

✓ If the NPV is zero, ROI = cost of capital, the firm would be indifferent about the investment proposal.

Irwin/McGraw-Hill   © The McGraw-Hill Companies, Inc, 1999

16-12

Capital Budgeting Analysis Techniques

METHODS THAT USE PRESENT VALUE ANALYSIS

| Internal Rate of Return (IRR) Method |

☒ Solve for the interest rate at which the present value of the cash return equals the investment required. This is the proposed investment's ROI--referred to as the internal rate of return (IRR).

☒ The investment decision is made based on the relationship between the project's internal rate of return (IRR) and the firm's desired ROI (cost of capital).

Irwin/McGraw-Hill   © The McGraw-Hill Companies, Inc, 1999

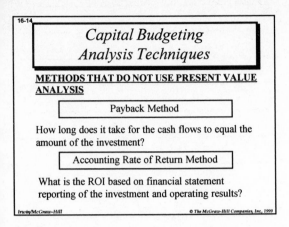

16-14

Capital Budgeting Analysis Techniques

METHODS THAT DO NOT USE PRESENT VALUE ANALYSIS

Payback Method

How long does it take for the cash flows to equal the amount of the investment?

Accounting Rate of Return Method

What is the ROI based on financial statement reporting of the investment and operating results?

Irwin/McGraw-Hill   © The McGraw-Hill Companies, Inc., 1999

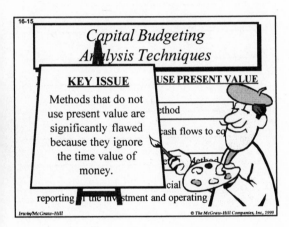

16-15

Capital Budgeting Analysis Techniques

KEY ISSUE

Methods that do not use present value are significantly flawed because they ignore the time value of money.

...USE PRESENT VALUE

...ethod

...cash flows to e...

reporting ...the investment and operating

Irwin/McGraw-Hill   © The McGraw-Hill Companies, Inc., 1999

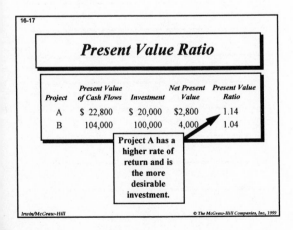

16-17

Present Value Ratio

Project	Present Value of Cash Flows	Investment	Net Present Value	Present Value Ratio
A	$ 22,800	$ 20,000	$2,800	1.14
B	104,000	100,000	4,000	1.04

Project A has a higher rate of return and is the more desirable investment.

Irwin/McGraw-Hill   © The McGraw-Hill Companies, Inc., 1999

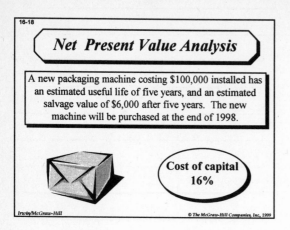

16-18

Net Present Value Analysis

A new packaging machine costing $100,000 installed has an estimated useful life of five years, and an estimated salvage value of $6,000 after five years. The new machine will be purchased at the end of 1998.

Cost of capital
16%

Irwin/McGraw-Hill   © The McGraw-Hill Companies, Inc., 1999

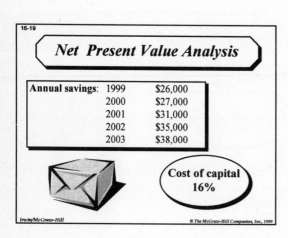

16-19

Net Present Value Analysis

Annual savings:	1999	$26,000
	2000	$27,000
	2001	$31,000
	2002	$35,000
	2003	$38,000

Cost of capital
16%

Irwin/McGraw-Hill   © The McGraw-Hill Companies, Inc., 1999

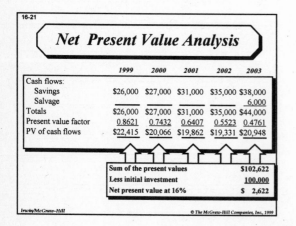

16-21

Net Present Value Analysis

	1999	2000	2001	2002	2003
Cash flows:					
Savings	$26,000	$27,000	$31,000	$35,000	$38,000
Salvage					6,000
Totals	$26,000	$27,000	$31,000	$35,000	$44,000
Present value factor	0.8621	0.7432	0.6407	0.5523	0.4761
PV of cash flows	$22,415	$20,066	$19,862	$19,331	$20,948

Sum of the present values	$102,622
Less initial investment	100,000
Net present value at 16%	$ 2,622

Irwin/McGraw-Hill   © The McGraw-Hill Companies, Inc., 1999

112

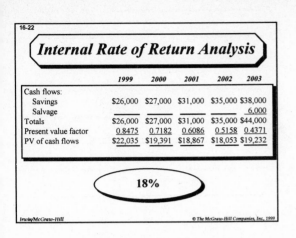

16-22

Internal Rate of Return Analysis

	1999	2000	2001	2002	2003
Cash flows:					
Savings	$26,000	$27,000	$31,000	$35,000	$38,000
Salvage					6,000
Totals	$26,000	$27,000	$31,000	$35,000	$44,000
Present value factor	0.8475	0.7182	0.6086	0.5158	0.4371
PV of cash flows	$22,035	$19,391	$18,867	$18,053	$19,232

18%

Irwin/McGraw-Hill   © The McGraw-Hill Companies, Inc., 1999

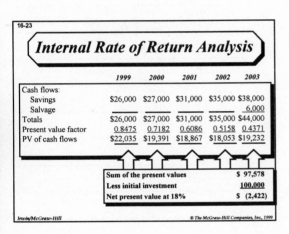

16-23

Internal Rate of Return Analysis

	1999	2000	2001	2002	2003
Cash flows:					
Savings	$26,000	$27,000	$31,000	$35,000	$38,000
Salvage					6,000
Totals	$26,000	$27,000	$31,000	$35,000	$44,000
Present value factor	0.8475	0.7182	0.6086	0.5158	0.4371
PV of cash flows	$22,035	$19,391	$18,867	$18,053	$19,232

Sum of the present values	**$ 97,578**
Less initial investment	**100,000**
Net present value at 18%	**$ (2,422)**

Irwin/McGraw-Hill   © The McGraw-Hill Companies, Inc., 1999

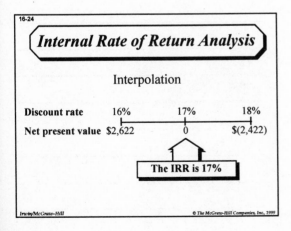

16-24

Internal Rate of Return Analysis

Interpolation

Discount rate	16%	17%	18%
Net present value	$2,622	0	$(2,422)

The IRR is 17%

Irwin/McGraw-Hill   © The McGraw-Hill Companies, Inc., 1999

16-25

Income Tax Effect

Revenues	$240,000
Variable expenses	100,000
Contribution margin	$140,000
Direct fixed expenses:	
Requiring cash disbursements	85,000
Depreciation of equipment	20,000
Operating income	$ 35,000
Income taxes @ 40%	14,000
Net income	$ 21,000

Irwin/McGraw-Hill   © The McGraw-Hill Companies, Inc., 1999

16-26

Income Tax Effect

The net income of $21,000 plus the depreciation of $20,000 provide a cash flow of $41,000.

Reven	$240,000
Variab	100,000
Contri	$140,000
Direct	
Requiring cash disbursements	85,000
Depreciation of equipment	20,000
Operating income	35,000
Income taxes @ 40%	14,000
Net income	21,000

Irwin/McGraw-Hill   © The McGraw-Hill Companies, Inc., 1999

16-28

Payback

The investment will be recovered during the fourth year.

Year	Cash Flow	Cumulative Cash Flow
1999 (1st year)	$26,000	$ 26,000
2000 (2nd year)	27,000	53,000
2001 (3rd year)	31,000	84,000
2002 (4th year)	35,000	119,000
2003 (5th year)	44,000	163,000

Irwin/McGraw-Hill   © The McGraw-Hill Companies, Inc., 1999

NOTES

NOTES

NOTES

NOTES

NOTES

NOTES

NOTES

NOTES

NOTES

NOTES

NOTES

NOTES